Divided We Stand

TEACHING ABOUT
CONFLICT IN U.S. HISTORY

JAMES A. PERCOCO

HEINEMANN
Portsmouth, NH

Heinemann
A division of Reed Elsevier Inc.
361 Hanover Street
Portsmouth, NH 03801–3912
www.heinemann.com

Offices and agents throughout the world

The author and publisher wish to thank those who have generously given permission to reprint borrowed material:

The cartoon "Deport Illegal Immigrants" by Paul Conrad is reprinted with permission of the *Los Angeles Times*. Copyright © 1997 by the *Los Angeles Times*.

The cartoon "It Is a Tribute to Their Historic Stand Against the Federal Government Way Back in the '60s—The 1960s, That Is" is reprinted by permission of Herblock Cartoons. Copyright © 2000 by Herblock in *The Washington Post*.

Excerpt from *A Rumor of War* by Philip Caputo, © 1977 by Philip Caputo. Reprinted by permission of Henry Holt & Co., LLC.

Interior Art: *Figures 1–1 and 1–2 photographed by Ellen Waylonis.*
           Figure 1–3 photographed by Brittany Zittel.
           Figure 3–3a drawn by Tony Jones.
           Figure 6–4 drawn by Allison Molan.

Library of Congress Cataloging-in-Publication Data

Percoco, James A.
    Divided we stand : teaching about conflict in US history / James A. Percoco.
      p. cm.
    Includes bibliographical references
    ISBN 0-325-00329-7
      1. United States—History—Study and teaching (Secondary).   2. United States—Social conditions—Study and teaching (Secondary).   3. Social conflict—Study and teaching (Secondary)—United States.   I. Title.

    E175.8 .P46 2001
    973'.071'273—dc21

                                                                00-047223

Editor: William Varner
Production: Elizabeth Valway
Cover design: Darci Mehall/Aureo Design
Cover photo: James A. Percoco
Manufacturing: Deanna Richardson

Printed in the United States of America on acid-free paper
05 04   VP   4 5

MAR 1 1 2005

This book is affectionately dedicated to
my 1999–2000 Applied History class.
It was hard to let you go.

Contents

Acknowledgments
vii

Foreword
xi

Preface
xv

Introduction
The Challenge of Conflict
1

One
**Of Things Revolutionary: Lexington,
Concord, and Beyond**
9

Two
**Survivors of Custer's Last Stand—
Indians, Anglos, and the West**
39

Three
The Central Dilemma: Race in American History
65

Four
**America's Second Reconstruction: 1954–1968,
Exploring the Civil Rights Movement**
105

Five
Gender and the American Past
141

Six
Remembering Vietnam
168

Epilogue
207

Appendix A
The West
211

Appendix B
**Custer/Battle of the Little
Bighorn Unit Material**
214

Appendix C
Civil Rights Movement Film Synopses
220

Appendix D
Vietnam Material
221

Appendix E
Historical Head Template
228

Appendix F
Rubric Reference Page
229

General References
237

Acknowledgments

A book, like any significant undertaking, is rarely the work of one person and *Divided We Stand* is no exception. I have enjoyed much support as I have written what I hope is a book that will make a difference. In cases such as this, I always start at the top, so I'd like first to thank God for bestowing on me the precious gift of being a teacher and for empowering me with the ability to write.

Being a member of the West Springfield High School Social Studies Department is a pure joy. All of my colleagues are exceptional at their craft, be it working with young people or mastering their subject matter. But in particular, I'd like to thank the members of the US History team, Lillie Brown, Laurie Fischer, and Ron Maggiano, who supported this project by sharing lessons plans or reviewing some of the chapters. You guys are the definition of "collegiality." In addition, thanks go to Jamie Morris for his gift of being a wordsmith in emergency cases and for pointing me in the right direction when I'm drifting. Marlene Darwin, Reading Specialist, was most helpful in aiding my planning and instruction of the reading components of The West: Myth and Reality unit.

In addition, I'd like to thank my principal, Dr. David Smith, who continues to encourage my wide range of work in this profession.

In the academy, at the college and university level, I'd like to thank James O. Horton and Phyllis Palmer at George Washington University. Jim suggested that I have Phyllis review my chapters on race and the Civil Rights movement. As a result, I learned more about myself, the complexity of racial dynamics in America, and how to better prepare my students for this world. At the University of New Mexico, Paul Andrew Hutton shared his insight on George Armstrong Custer and the Battle of the Little Bighorn and its place in our cultural memory. Brian Dippie at the University of Victoria, British Columbia, provided insight into the myth and related artwork of Custer's Last Stand. Andrew McDonald of Loyola University, New Orleans, has provided me with a better understanding of the works of novelist Howard Fast.

In the public history and museum arena, my thanks go to Paul Fees at the Buffalo Bill Historical Center, Troy Harmon and Barb Sanders at Gettysburg National Military Park, Rex Norman at Fort Laramie National Historic Site, and Marie Queener at Women's Rights National Historical

Park. The following historians also deserve recognition: Brian Pohanka for his suggestions on the Custer unit, Herman Viola for providing vital information to me and my students on the Plains Indians, Robert Utley for taking time to enlighten my students on his perspective of the Battle of the Little Bighorn, and Eric Sorg for sharing his insights on Buffalo Bill.

At the Library of Congress, I'd like to thank Lyle Minter, head of the Newspaper and Current Periodicals Room, for providing assistance to my students in their Custer project research work.

Wynell Schammel and Lee Ann Potter of the Education Staff at the National Archives always handle my requests for assistance with great enthusiasm and have helped to make me a better teacher in more ways than they will ever know. The primary-source documents relating to Rosa Parks and the Ho Chi Minh diplomatic cable were secured for this book by them.

Beth Boland, Historian for the National Park Service's Teaching with Historic Places program has also been a solid source of support for my teaching and writing.

Frank Kameny and Tom Swann were most gracious in helping me to learn more about the life and work of Leonard Matlovich. Howard Shorr also reviewed my chapter on race and lent his experience of teaching US history in Los Angeles to this project.

At the Veterans Education Project in Amherst, Massachusetts, Rob Wilson and Stephen Sossaman provided support for my chapter on Vietnam. Jan Scruggs and Holly Rotondi of the Vietnam Veterans Memorial Fund also offered their assistance with various requests related to this endeavor.

The following Vietnam Veterans provided the West Springfield High School Class of 2001 with stories of their experiences in Southeast Asia: faculty members John Deeney and Dave Harpman as well as John Dibble, Wayne Hansen, Glenn Lane, Tony Nelson, Mark Pizzo, Joe Saffron, and Karl Sakas. My colleagues on the US history team and I are most grateful for their courage and their willingness to open up and share their experiences.

At the National Council for History Education, Executive Director Elaine Reed has always encouraged my writing and professional work.

Thanks also to Jennifer Bosveld of Pudding House Writers Resource Center of Johnstown, Ohio, for allowing me to print her poem *memoralis benedicto*, found in the Epilogue.

For simply being a support, a presence, and a friend I'd like to thank high school buddy, Peter Bergh, the talented musicians Kim and Reggie Harris, computer-man Jim Frost, authors Jerry Ellis and Debi Holmes-Binney, and colleague Maggie Mey.

James Loewen provided the spirited Foreword.

I'd like to say thanks to Bill Varner for shepherding my second book with such care. You're more than an editor, you're a good friend.

The contributions of many of my students have served as a critical component of *Divided We Stand* and their contributions, be they written or artistic, are most appreciated. Some of the photographs were taken by Ellen Waylonis and Brittany Zittel. The W. E. B. DuBois historical head in Chapter 3 was drawn by Tony Jones. The political cartoon in Chapter 6 was produced by Allison Molan. Journal and paper excerpts include those of: Bridgette Bell, Mary Beth Brookshire, David Boelens, Mark Burton, Priya Chhaya, Dan Duplantier, Caitlin Dysart, Elaine Giuliani, Casey Graham, David Harris, May Kim, Kendra Kojish, Jessica Lee, Myug Lee, Brian McLain, Chris Murphy, Amber Steele, Amanda Thornburg, DeAnna Tobin, Mike Waldron, Ellen Waylonis, Elizabeth Wilcox, Lexie Wilson, and Tanisha Woodard. I am most appreciative of them, their talents, and their parents.

At home I want to embrace my family for their support—in particular my wife, Gina, and my two daughters, Stephanie and Claire, who have often looked in on me in the den to see how far I've gotten on my book!

And last, but not least, Tanks Mac!

Foreword

Across America, for the most part, high school students rank history their least liked subject. But many students at West Springfield High School in Virginia choose history as their favorite. Jim Percoco's students do extra work, attend after-school film screenings, and then compete to get into his next course. In *Divided We Stand,* he reveals why.

While the average high school course in American history spends just four *minutes* on the Vietnam War, Percoco involves his students in a rich unit where they encounter many points of view. They do not shy away from other conflicts either, such as the continuing relevance of the women's movement or popular culture's portrayal of Native Americans, including the controversy over the name of the local NFL franchise—the Washington Redskins.

There are reasons why history teachers pull their punches. Teaching about conflict can be tough. Teachers do not want to replicate the Vietnam War, the gender war of the 1970s, or any other divisive battle within their classrooms. Yet as Percoco points out, conflict is part of the human condition. If we leave it out, we present a past that never was. Such "history" only impoverishes students' understanding of our past, in turn making them less competent to participate in our national future—less competent than if they had never taken American history.

All too many courses in American history avoid real issues, as I found while doing the research that led to *Lies My Teacher Told Me: Everything Your American History Textbook Got Wrong.* The expurgated results hardly convince students that our leaders have been sturdy, our foreign policy initiatives justified, and our progress inexorable, as our history textbooks assume. Instead, students conclude that high school history classrooms are not places to discuss serious matters.

A growing cadre of teachers does better. Not content to hide behind the textbook, they encourage their classes to explore community resources, the web, the marvelous secondary literature in history, and many other resources. They challenge students not only to fill in what is missing from their textbooks but also to critique what is included. Their students develop skills in locating, marshalling, and evaluating evidence. Future politicians and newspaper columnists will not easily mislead high school graduates who have such a history course.

Divided We Stand shows teachers how to develop history courses like this. His unit on the American Revolution combines ingredients from the following extra-textbook sources:

- poetry
- propaganda broadsides from the time
- family records, diaries, and other primary sources
- paintings and sculptures
- music
- feature films
- fiction
- videos
- current events
- field trips
- monuments, memorials, and historical markers
- re-enactors
- and many secondary works of history from which he assigns excerpts.

And that only gets the class to Yorktown! Still ahead are the formation of the nation, the problems leading to the Constitutional Convention, and the writing of the U.S. Constitution.

No teacher should follow all of Jim Percoco's suggestions on how to involve students in the events and issues of the American Revolution. Indeed, given constraints of time and resources, few teachers *can*. The list of ideas and resources seems daunting. But all teachers can and should compose their own list of thirty to eighty topics that interest *them* about U.S. history. Teachers can then let their enthusiasms for each topic push them to enrich their students' lives the way Jim Percoco has enriched his. Taught chronologically, in diverse and interesting ways, these units form the core of their courses.

This list of thirty to eighty cannot be wholly arbitrary. If it does not include the Constitution, for example, or the Civil War, it's not competent. But Percoco shows that teachers need not—indeed *must* not—shun topics because they seem too hot to handle. Sprinkled throughout this book are examples of *how* to teach about tough topics. When showing an R-rated feature film, for instance, Percoco has ready a GP-rated substitute for students or parents who desire that alternative. He shows by doing when to seek advice from a colleague and when to get prior approval from a principal. As Percoco notes, where better should Americans discuss issues like the impact slavery has on our society? In

Jim's words, "a national dialogue about race rooted in classrooms of committed educators is the perfect forum to generate healing."

Much of my time these days I spend talking with teachers who have me give workshops on how to teach U.S. history better. Mostly I pass on suggestions other teachers—prior workshop attendees—taught me. Only one idea is my own invention; since it relates so closely to the theme of this book, I would be remiss if I didn't pass it on to you here. Imagine that you are introducing some troubling material—perhaps the photo of the young Vietnamese girl running naked toward the camera, fleeing a napalm attack. Your students may never have encountered an image of frontal nudity in a classroom before, to say nothing of the issues about U.S. policy that this image raises. Preface the material, whatever it is, with the phrase, "Some people tell me that ninth- (or fifth- or whatever grade your students are in) graders can't handle what I'm about to show you—that they aren't mature enough."

You can guess what will happen. They will rise to the occasion. They will even surprise you with their insights, sometimes all the more interesting because they are less encumbered by adult socialization.

So, read this book. You will find Percoco's enthusiasm contagious. The man *lives* history—he never takes a vacation without stopping to gather material for another unit! The teacher who latches on to just one idea in ten in this volume will be rewarded by enthusiasm in return, from students in the classroom. Let the adventure begin!

James Loewen

Preface

If you are like most teachers, I know you want books like this to be teacher friendly and to include the nuts and bolts of how to accomplish teaching the lesson at hand. It is my hope that *Divided We Stand* accomplishes those two goals. So before you read on, I simply want to point out a few items.

Many of the public sculptures I discuss herein can be seen and accessed on my webpage, which is part of the West Springfield High School website. In addition, I have set up interesting links for you to explore. The URL address is *www.wshs.fcps.k12.va.us*. Click on *Academics*, click on *Social Studies*, then click on my name.

At the end of each chapter, you will find a list of print, video/film, and electronic resources that will prove helpful in building your own knowledge base and curriculum. Not all the sources will have been discussed in the chapter, and in no way is the list meant to be definitive. A list of general references rounds out the text, with those books being more specifically linked to general teaching methodology, pedagogy, and United States history.

Two resources that I refer to in my book are the Center for Learning's U.S. History and AP US History Workbooks with reproducible lesson plans and Primary Source Media's *American Journey: History in Your Hands,* primary-source document CD-ROM series. Both sets of resources cover the topics discussed by chapter and Primary Source Media's CD-ROM programs can be matched to each of my chapters. You can purchase this material through Social Studies School Services in Culver City, California, at (800) 421-4246 or online at *www.socialstudies.com*.

I would like to point out that many teacher- and student-friendly lessons that dovetail nicely with the topics in this book have been developed by the National Archives Education Staff and the National Park Service's Teaching with Historic Places program. Sample lesson plans, developed by both agencies, can also be accessed on their respective websites. For further information contact:

National Archives and Records Administration
Education Staff
Washington, DC 20408
(202) 501-5210
e-mail: education@arch1.nara.gov
Digital Classroom: *www.nara.gov/education*

Teaching with Historic Places
National Register, History and Education Division
National Park Service
1849 C Street, NW, Suite 400
Washington, DC 20240
(202) 343-9536
e-mail nr_twhp@nps.gov
TWHP on Line *www.cr.nps.gov/nr/twhp/*

The Organization of American Historians' *Magazine of History* is published quarterly, with each issue reflecting a particular historical theme. These issues contain lesson plans tied to the theme of the issue. Again, many of the topics in this book can be matched with back issues of the *Magazine of History.* You can access back issues on microfilm through University Microfilms, Inc. at (800) 521-0600 or contact:

The Organization of American Historians
112 North Bryan Street
Bloomington, IN 47408-4199
(812) 855-7311

Additionally, the Organization of American Historians and the National Center for History in the Schools at the University of California, Los Angeles, also publish extensive teaching units related to a specific topic. For a listing and further information contact their website at *www.sscnet.ucla.edu/nchs/.*

To acquire the music I discuss in Chapter 4 on the Civil Rights movement you can contact:

Susan Erenrich
The Cultural Center for Social Change
3133 Connecticut Avenue, NW, Suite 432
Washington, DC 20008
(202) 462-4611

or access Kim and Reggie Harris through their website, *kimandreggie.com.*

At some places in the text I suggest that teachers make overhead transparencies of various artwork or illustrations. This is fair use and within the bounds of copyright laws so long as you are using the images for classroom purposes and as long as the source is identified.

At the end of the book, you will find six appendices that include specific worksheets discussed within the text, including a historical head template, Hollywood motion picture synopses for the films tied to Custer and the Battle of the Little Bighorn, the Western Film Festival, the Civil Rights Film Festival, and the Vietnam Film Festival. The letter the West Springfield High School US history team sends out to parents prior to the Vietnam Film Festival is also included. Finally, in Appendix F you will find assessment rubrics for all the activities discussed in the book.

Introduction

The Challenge of Conflict

Those things that hurt, instruct.

—Benjamin Franklin

I slipped the double volume cassette from its case and inserted tape one into our VCR. The movie was the 1951 Hollywood epic film of Tolstoy's *War and Peace*. A new school year was on the horizon, but I had some serious boning up to do on Russian history as I was preparing for a two-week extended teacher exchange to Russia. I had been selected along with twenty-five other teachers for a program sponsored by the United States State Department and the Council for International Education to visit schools in Russia as well as the newly independent states of the former Soviet Union. We were to meet with Russian educators and visit schools in the Russian Federation as part of this exchange program. Initiated by President Clinton, the Teaching Awards for Excellence was developed in an effort to build bridges among educators of different cultures in a spirit of cooperation, goodwill, and mutual respect and understanding. The goals of the program were to help put the fifty years of ill will and conflict generated by the Cold War behind all of the involved nations. Gathered with me to watch the film were my two daughters. I fended off as best I could their inquiries about whether the Russians were the "good guys" and the French the "bad guys." As we watched the second half of the film, particularly the sequence of Napoleon's Grand Armée retreating back to France through the brutal Russian winter, the sequence showed several freezing French soldiers dragging a cannon

1

across the frozen landscape. The futility of the moment was all too clear to my youngest daughter, Claire, who looked up to me and said. "Why are they doing that? People are so stupid." Clearly Claire recognized the futility that conflict can sometimes engender. The moment also reminded me of the time when I was finishing the classroom phase of my Applied History class. Students were responding in their journals and then discussing the various units of study we had been pursuing together. Jamie put her hand up. She said that she was disappointed in the study of history because she realized that it did not happen like she wanted it to happen or the way the "myths" of history have been passed down over time. In particular, she was reacting to the material we had studied regarding the Battle of the Little Bighorn. Jamie was honest enough to let us all know that it hurt her that history did not turn out the way it was depicted in the 1941 film classic, *They Died with Their Boots On*. My response was a tacit agreement with her sentiments and a longing on my part to return, even if ever so briefly, to when the world was divided clearly into the "good guys" and the "bad guys."

During my trip to Russia, I met with Russian educators from all levels. I also spoke and talked with students from secondary schools and colleges. Some of the questions that I was repeatedly asked in relation to America were questions related to violence—school violence, and gun violence in particular. As we spoke, the graphic images that had seared across American television in the spring of 1999 at Columbine High School in Colorado leapt to my mind. Contemporary pundits claim that American violence stems from a proliferation of social maladies, from video games to television, to problems rooted in the family. I'm not so quick to agree with their assessment. Granted human history is riddled with violence. The United States, however, was established on certain principles and out of those principles has emerged a kind of traditional belief, which is sometimes a fallacy, that this nation is always headed in a direction of positive progress. There is a history of violence in America. It is part and parcel to the American character. We only need to look at how many historic sites that dot our landscape are battlefields. I am reminded of the opening pages of Bruce Catton's single-volume Civil War history, *This Hallowed Ground* (1955) where he alludes to a dark side of the American character. Catton asserts,

> There is a rowdy strain in American life, living close to the surface but running very deep. Like an ape behind a mask, it can display itself suddenly with terrifying effect. It is slack-jawed, with leering eyes and loose wet lips, with heavy feet and ponderous cunning hands; now and then, when something tickles it, it guffaws, and when it is made angry it snarls; and it can be aroused much more easily than it can be quieted. Mike Fink and Yankee Doodle helped to father it, and Judge Lynch is one of its creations; and when it comes lumbering forth it can

make the whole country step in time to its own frantic irregular pulse-beat. (3–4)

So, it was with a heavy heart that I had to inform my Russian hosts that America does indeed have a violent streak. One need only to conjure up the images of the tragedy at Columbine High School or the other numerous school shootings in America, not to mention the 1990s phenomenon of road rage, to become a disciple of Catton's vision. For this reason alone, it is a great deal harder to be a teacher now than it was twenty years ago. In the wake of the Columbine shooting, our district superintendent sent a letter to every teacher in the division essentially reminding teachers what we already knew, that schools at some level have become places where personal safety might be compromised. He was sympathetic to the notion that most of us, "did not get into teaching to deal with the problems that schools face, but that this was now a reality that we all must face." I was away speaking at a conference when Columbine occurred. But when I returned several days later, my step had lost some of its lightness. I think most teachers across America felt some sense of violation. Ironically enough, the week that I returned to school from my trip to Russia someone called in a bomb threat to the school. The building was evacuated and students and staff members spent two hours sitting in the stadium bleachers only after school security staff and administrators had patrolled the perimeter of the school to ensure that no one was lurking with a rifle.

But it is important for you to understand that conflict and violence, while often seen as synonymous, sometimes are not. It might be trendy to talk about Columbine and other aspects of school violence, but for this work that is too narrow a focus. I think students and teachers need to understand that there is a relationship between conflict and violence, but that sometimes you can have one without the other, specifically the settling of a conflict through peaceful means and resolution. Conflict in and of itself does not necessarily lead to violence. One September, as school just got underway, I asked students to write in their journals their definition and understanding of the word *conflict*. Many students wrote that they saw conflict as being two or more forces in opposition to each other. Some students picked up on the idea of internal conflict dwelling within the spirit of the individual. We spent the school year studying American history in the standard chronological format, covering not only the wars in which America has participated but also looking at the various political and domestic conflicts that make up the American drama. At the end of the year, I asked my students to look back and read their September journal entries on conflict, to reflect on what they had written, and then to write again about conflict, this time having studied our history in depth. Some students claimed that their definition did not really change but rather the depth of their under-standing about conflict had. For example, some students who had seen conflict as being limited to physical confrontation now expressed that they saw how conflict could be generated among people with different sets of ideas as to how to accomplish a particular goal. The differing views held by Booker T. Washington and W. E. B. DuBois, among oth-ers, come to mind.

The study of history, particularly when dealing with human pas-sions and emotions, can often lead to ambiguity. Nowhere is this ambi-guity more prevalent than in the study of and the historical interpreta-tion of conflict. Even the definition of the term *conflict* can be vague or ambiguous depending on what point of view or from what context it is offered. Conflicts can also be great agents of historical change, such as the kind found in new medical techniques often advanced by war; or agents of tremendous social change, such as the kind implemented as a result of the Civil Rights movement. One could argue that some conflict can be beneficial. In the discourse of American history, it is no different. Some writers, such as Geoffrey Perret, claim as does his book title that the United States is *A Country Made by War* (1989). One need only look at all of the dimensions of American history and one will find conflict of every kind. To be certain, there is military conflict, which has played a tremendous role in the shaping of the American nation. Rob-ert E. Lee, no stranger to warfare, remarked upon seeing wave after wave of Union soldiers mowed down in front of a heavily defended Confederate position at Marye's Heights during the Battle of Freder-icksburg, "It is all well that war is so terrible, lest we grow too fond of it." But there is also social, political, economic, and cultural conflict that continues to define our national destiny. Our history is replete with all manner of struggle endured by men and women and people from all races and economic strata.

This book is written not as a piece offered to specifically solve this American problem. Rather it is a book intended to assist teachers in try-ing to help their students make sense of the dynamics involved in all manner of conflict in American history. If you are looking for conflict resolution lessons, you will not find them, per se, here. However, many of these lessons could assist those educators who work more closely with conflict resolution place conflict within an historical context. As teachers, we need to lead our students to the point within themselves where the question "So what?" has some meaning. We need to direct them to the big questions that the study of history offers all people, and certainly learning to deal with the idea of conflict, in all of its parame-ters, is one of those questions—be it tied to race, gender, or class. Our young people today live in a world filled with conflict. They need to un-derstand the roots of said conflicts in order to develop a more mature view of their world. The Virginia Center for the Teaching of International Studies puts it this way, "In a world characterized by conflict, it is necessary that American schools prepare young people to understand the conflicted world in which they will live and work." Perhaps most important is for history teachers to provide students with a view of the past that enables them to develop a kind of empathy for people who lived many years ago, with the hope that that empathy will transcend time, be transported to the present, and be acted out in ways that hearken compassion and tolerance. Although some may criticize this as "feel good" history, I counter with the lessons in this book, which are rigorous and academic in scope and focus. To me, the contemporary secondary history teacher has a dual focus, to teach authentic lessons in history rooted in serious scholarship and to provide students with an understanding that the key to implementing change in our present and future lies within the stories of the past.

As a practicing teacher, I am like one of you, on a journey that has many winds and turns. In 1998, when I published my first book, *A Passion for the Past*, I was at a different place in my teaching, and the teacher I am today is not, in my totality, the same teacher I was then. I believe to be an effective educator one must be open to continued learning experiences, modeling for students as well as other professionals the idea that learning is a life-long endeavor. It has been a struggle to put together a manuscript of this nature given the often fluctuating politically correct climate in which we now seem to be operating. My intention here was to share ideas with you that have become a part of my classroom, my professional journey, and my inquisitive nature—all of which have led to some wonderful teaching and learning experiences. My goal in writing this book was to lay out for you ideas upon which you can build or generate your own lessons that examine conflict in American history. I do not consider myself to be a self-appointed "guru," nor would I want to be one. There are areas in the history of the United States in which I am not well versed and still need to learn more about. One of the downsides to being a naturally inquisitive person/teacher is wanting to be able to know everything and teach everything. Unfortunately, that's not a realistic expectation, but it does serve as a bit of a motivator to be a life-long learner.

Given the expectations that are externally placed on secondary history and social studies teachers to not only cover the entire curriculum but also teach academic, intellectual, and life skills, it is a wonder that any of us get as far as we do. After experiencing the past twenty years of dynamic change in education, I can safely say that I do as best I can for myself, my students, and the profession at large. On a different level, this book is meant not to inflame or offend anyone; rather it is my intent to be provocative. One of the charges leveled against teachers today is that we are accused of woefully neglecting the development of critical thinking skills in our students. The lessons and learning activities that I provide and explain in these pages are meant to generate just that—critical thinking. Effective teaching and studying about conflict provide fertile ground for critical thinking. These are lessons developed so that my students can become more than just informed citizens, but also so that they can understand and appreciate just how the United States and all of its people have arrived at this particular time and place. Still, I don't want it to appear as if I've seized the moral or pedagogical high ground. A goodly part of these past twenty years has been consumed with a personal struggle and journey as a human being, who is also a teacher, trying to reconcile my inconsistencies with those of our nation. It is a painful, searing process that continues today. Any limitation that this book may possess is in part based on my unfinished journey.

There are certain goals and objectives pertaining to teaching about conflict that I think one should consider when approaching this topic. First of all, you and your students need to recognize the complex nature of teaching about and studying conflict. It is not so simple that it can be easily picked apart and analyzed. Conflict has many shades, subtleties, and nuances. Second, students need to wrestle with issues about conflict in relation to the quest for the American dream. Our nation was born out of conflict, but yet conflict did not go away when the nation was launched. In some cases, conflict actually escalated as different people and groups sought to direct the new nation. To this day, conflict remains part of our political, social, and economic landscape; we read or hear about the Democrats versus the Republicans, this or that group posturing for an expansion of rights or a bigger piece of the economic pie, and then there can be differences in what kind of history should be taught and how educators can reach that goal, should the consensus about the goal ever be reached. Students also need to understand historical paradigms and how conflict has shaped those paradigms. It is important to teach students that the "winners" often get to tell, write, and subsequently teach history—just ask any American Indian or any other person from a group that has stood outside the mainstream of American life. Another part of my agenda with students is to have them reflect on the duality of human nature. To instill this idea in students, I sometimes like to use a short segment from Michael Shaara's Pulitzer Prize–winning novel, *The Killer Angels* (1974). The scene is also acted out in the film *Gettysburg*. Joshua Lawrence Chamberlain, Colonel of the Twentieth Maine Infantry is reflecting on his attitude about human nature. "Once Chamberlain had a speech memorized from Shakespeare and gave it proudly, the old man (his father) listening but not looking, and Chamberlain remembered it still: 'What a piece of work is man . . . in action how like an angel!' And the old man, grinning, had scratched his head and then said stiffly, 'Well, boy, if he's an angel, he's sure a murderin' angel.'" Finally, one of my objectives is to demonstrate that all of us deal with conflict at some level, it's not so much the conflict itself that in the end matters, but rather how we, as individuals or as a nation, choose to resolve the conflict.

The lessons described in this book are modeled on the same "can do" approach to those lesson ideas offered in my book, *A Passion for the Past.* Additionally, the lessons are based on the age-old traditional format of teaching whereby you have clear-cut goals and ideas that you want your students to know when the lessons are complete, which in today's educational parlance we call "standards-based instruction." Once again, many of the strategies would not have been possible without the input of my colleagues, content-specific academic scholars who offered suggestions, and numerous public historians who provided insight. The activities and strategies discussed combine the time-honored paper-and-pencil/pen traditional form of student evaluation and that of alternative assessment. It is hoped that using these lessons, or lessons of a similar kind, within the context of the totality of American history, will lead to a kind of dialogue among teachers and their students, as well as among themselves, that will help to put the idea of conflict in its proper historical context, while offering a venue for discussion, much like the kind I had with my students in the wake of the 1992 Los Angeles Rodney King riot.

The chapters herein are set up by theme in a chronological fashion. Chapter content covers not only America's wars, but also the myriad ways in which conflict manifests itself in American history and life. There is a chapter on race alone that explores how Americans have struggled throughout our history with this sensitive topic that includes not only the black/white question but also examines the internment of Japanese Americans during World War II as well the issues that have faced the Latino and Hispanic communities. A chapter on gender issues fills in the gap in areas too often ignored in the mainstream teaching of United States history. You may wonder why there is no chapter on the Civil War or the two World Wars. Simply put, much of my professional writing has examined those events and how to approach crafting lessons relative to them. You will find in places, where applicable within the framework of this book, that they are explored. Those conflicts could in fact warrant their own books within the professional literature of history teaching, pedagogy, and methodology.

At the end of each chapter is a comprehensive list of resources, including videos, that can be accessed to help your particular program of instruction. The appendices provide a rubric guide to assist you in evaluating assignments that fall within the realm of "authentic alternative assessment," which I describe throughout the book; several worksheets;

and a compilation of film synopses for the chapters on the West and the Civil Rights movement. The lessons described herein have taken place in my AP United States history classes, my regular United States history classes, and my Applied History course, a kind of high school public history seminar offered as an elective to seniors. All of the lessons, strategies, and activities are matched with the National Standards for Teaching History as well as to the history standards developed by numerous state departments of education. Teachers will find that this material also reflects the age-old teaching maxim of "beginning with the end in mind," manifest more recently in standards-based pedagogies such as those offered by Jay McTighe and Grant Wiggins. The pedagogy upon which these activities rest include Bloom's taxonomy and Howard Gardner's theory of multiple intelligences. Many of the teaching tools used include political cartoons, photographs, primary-source documents, the visual arts, and music. The words you will read in some cases are the words of my students from either personal class journal entries or papers that they have written. The vignettes provided come from class discussions that we have had over the years. The stories are true and the attempts to deal effectively with difficult topics by me or in some cases by me and my colleagues reflect genuine measures of how certain situations have been handled and addressed by adults who had the best interests of the school and community in mind. My approach to teaching history is one in which students and I, their teacher, occasionally have epiphanies when the self-knowledge comes through like a blinding light within the context of a historical moment gone long ago. Those are indeed, for me, the best lessons. It doesn't hurt either to be teaching at West Springfield where a positive and respectful climate is fostered by our principal, Dr. David Smith, who sets the tone for everyone with his motto for the school being, "Take care of yourself. Take care of each other. Take care of this place."

Hopefully, you will find good food for thought in these pages. It would be heartening if what you take away from this book helps you in your teaching and work with young people. American Indians refer to the spiritual energy that flows between all living things as "medicine." By virtue of having read *Divided We Stand*, may the power of "good medicine" permeate your classroom, your hard work, and all of your relationships in an effort to open the door of mutual respect and understanding of the human community.

Chapter One

Of Things Revolutionary
Lexington, Concord, and Beyond

In the end we all kill for profit; the British, the Hessians, and us.
—Nathaniel Greene to George Washington
The Crossing by Howard Fast

The wake-up call came in at 4:15 in the morning. In the cloudy haze of my mind, I reached over and picked up the phone. Sleeping next to me was my nine-year-old daughter, Claire. She knew we were going to have to get up early and she's not a morning person, so I didn't relish the thought of having to disturb her sleep. Groggily I swung my legs over the side of the bed thinking, "I can't believe I'm doing this on the Monday of spring break." I knew that the same thoughts would be going through the minds of my Applied History students and the parent chaperones in other rooms of this hotel. My only solace was that I knew 225 years ago at around the same time, hundreds of colonial patriots from Boston to Concord, Massachusetts, were also quickly roused from a deep sleep. By the end of that April 19, 1775, their world and the future of the world was changed forever. I was hoping that by the end of our Patriot's Day my students would have a deeper appreciation for the cost and sacrifice that conflict sometimes requires when causes move to a more active and open position.

As we walked to our cars, it was still pitch black outside. Patricia turned to me and said, "Mr. Percoco, I want you to know this is against my convictions." I replied, "Just think about the conviction that those American patriots had 225 years ago to do the same thing we're doing only with a cause to propel them."

It was the exchange of gunfire at the North Bridge that would inspire the pen of Concord's Ralph Waldo Emerson to write in 1837 the immortal words of the "Concord Hymn,"

> By the rude bridge that arched the flood,
>   Their flag to April's breeze unfurled;
> Here once the embattled farmers stood,
>   And fired the shot heard round the world.

In that volley with the British, Isaac Davis, whose Acton contingent was at the head of the column of about four hundred Minutemen that marched on the bridge to force the issue with the British troops, fell dead as did another Acton Minuteman, Abner Hosmer. Davis earned the honor of being the first commissioned officer to die for the American cause of liberty. In response to the British action, the Minutemen unleashed their own volley and two British soldiers crumpled over dead.

We had gotten up early this morning to join the retracing of the march of the Acton Minutemen, an annual Patriot's Day event started in the 1960s. Beginning at 6:00 A.M., after a brief eulogy, the formation of the modern-day Acton Minutemen, a ceremonial and reenactment group, marched off to the sound of fifes and drums playing the tune "The White Cockade" in their rust-colored vests and eighteenth-century uniforms, Brown Bess muskets slung on their shoulders from the home of Captain Isaac Davis, which still stands today. The procession heads to the North Bridge, in Concord, seven miles to the east.

Anyone who wants to accompany the Minutemen may do so and each year throngs of people, including at least a thousand Boy Scouts from the area, gather in Acton to retrace the march. At the end of the day, participants receive a commemorative scroll documenting their place in this living history program. I was very familiar with the scroll because from 1966–1970 I had lived in Acton and been a youthful participant in this event. Now at forty-two, as a twenty-year veteran history teacher, I was bringing some of my students back to a place and time that had proved formidable in shaping my historical memory.

Standing with my students and my somewhat annoyed and sleepy daughter, the chill of the morning began to dissipate and the sun began to make its presence known at about 7:00 as the contingent of Acton Minutemen approached the center of town. Once at the monument, where the three Acton Minutemen who fell in 1775 are buried, the modern-day company of Minutemen fired a tribute volley before continuing the march. From here it was six miles to the bridge; a two-hour journey.

As we made our way to Concord, I tried to pace myself to the tunes of the fifes and drums. It was rather easy to fall into cadence. As a youngster living in Acton, I had always wanted to join the Acton Minutemen, and for a while tried to play the fife for them. Alas, I am not musically inclined and my dream at that time never became a reality. For most of the march, while I kept my eye on my students and Claire, I let my mind wander back to that day in 1775 and tried to envision myself as one who would tote a musket and march off to the possibility of either having my life snuffed out or snuffing out the life of someone else. I also tried to reconcile my feelings of ambiguity. Here I was, along with my students and one of my children and at least a thousand other human beings, commemorating a conflict that ended in violence. I am fascinated with war; it's the absolute test of human endurance. Yet I would never want to be in a war. Warfare and conflict produce great stories about the human condition. When you read about armed conflict, the rawness of being a human is exposed—the valor, the heroism, the cowardliness, the fear, the pain, the hunger, the greed, and the evil. Ironically, while visiting battlefields by myself or with my students, I feel a certain kind of peace that I can't explain. Maybe it's the pastoral settings in which many battles are fought; perhaps it's a peace that speaks of who we are as humans and about how we behave under extreme circumstances.

Motivation and personal principles are often part of the mixture of what gets played out in conflict. In the opening days of the War for Independence, those principles were tied up with the meaning of liberty in the 1770s—a far different notion from what it means today. I wanted my students to understand just how this was played out in a twenty-four hour period between April 18 and 19, 1775.

Related Learning and Planning

As early as the previous September, I had begun to lay the foundation for this field trip. Each spring I take my Applied History class on overnight excursions to the places where history "happens." The previous year it was to Johnstown, Pennsylvania, the site of the 1889 Johnstown flood. With the 225th anniversary of Lexington and Concord in the offing, I knew that this would be a wonderful experience for students who love history. I also had selfish reasons for taking them to Massachusetts: I wanted to return to a site of my own boyhood dreams.

I had planned some related academic activities with my class in preparation for our journey. In part this was inspired by a summer of 1999 visit to Minuteman National Historical Park, which protects and interprets the battle site at the North Bridge and the Battle Road, which follows the return route of the British Army as they retreated from Concord back to Boston. It was along this route that the colonials inflicted heavy casualties on the British column. The park has been expanded and developed more historically since the Bicentennial, and the visitors center, along the Battle Road, has been upgraded, including a new light, sound, and video program called "The Road to Revolution."

We spent two class periods examining historical interpretations of the battle from a variety of perspectives using different primary sources. (My students were seniors who had already studied American history; so they didn't need much background information. Younger students will need more support from background information.) I really wanted them to focus on the interpretation of the events of April 18–19, 1775. I wanted them to understand how the legacy of this battle had been for generations passed down to Americans principally through Henry Wadsworth Longfellow's poem, "The Midnight Ride of Paul Revere." Revere had no greater publicist than Longfellow, and generation after generation accepted Longfellow's ode as gospel truth. As poetry it is good patriotism, but plainly bad history, because it embellishes events, makes claims of things that did not happen, and leaves out other key figures. The events of the evening of April 18, 1775, were not a one-man show as Longfellow would lead us to believe. So I gave students a copy of Longfellow's poem and, while wearing a tri-cornered hat, dramatically read it aloud. Then I asked students to compare and contrast a reading selection from David Hackett Fisher's Paul Revere's Ride, published in 1995, which laid out a detailed narrative of Revere's actual ride. After they were finished, I asked them to compare and contrast the poem to the narrative history. Using the following prompts, we engaged in a discussion:

- How are the two interpretations of this historical event different?
- What might cause there to be a difference in interpretation?
- Whose rendering of history do you think is more accurate? Why?

The most glaring inconsistency is that Longfellow's poem only mentions Revere and leaves the reader with the impression that Revere completed his ride. Nothing could be further from the truth. Revere was captured by a British patrol after warning residents of Lexington. Additionally, another rider, William Dawes, had been also sent out of Boston by the Committee of Safety. Dawes met up with Revere in Lexington and shortly after, they were joined by another member of the Sons of Liberty, Dr. Samuel Prescott of Concord. Both Dawes and Prescott were stopped with Revere but succeeded in escaping. They carried the alarm farther. Students were pretty quick to pick up on this historical discrepancy. What sealed it for the students was the list of sources that

Fisher cites to complete his story. Students were provided a copy of the copious footnotes that Fisher used. I also pointed out to students that Revere and the other riders never would have yelled out, "The British are coming! The British are coming!" The colonials still believed that they were all British.

Once finished with the introductory Revere material, I distributed copies of *The Lexington-Concord Battle Road Guide* published by the Concord Chamber of Commerce. Students were to read it for homework and be prepared for discussion and assessment the following class period. The guide, which is considered by many people to be the most accurate source of the hour-to-hour activity of April 18–19, 1775, opens with a copy of the orders of General Thomas Gage, military governor of Massachusetts, to Colonel Francis Smith. By reading this letter, students were able to put the story within the proper historical context.

I make it a habit, whenever possible, to play related music as students come into my classroom. So for the several days that we took to explore this topic, students were greeted by fife and drum music. For the next class period, I used four color lithographs that were created shortly after the battle and are considered important visual primary sources of this event; one of them is shown in Figure 1–1. There is still no clarity as to who created the images. Many accounts claim that it was Connecticut militiaman Amos Doolittle, who two weeks after the battles of Lexington and Concord journeyed to Massachusetts, surveyed the land, and spoke with eyewitnesses about the affair. Then the drawings were turned into engravings for people to purchase. In some instances, it is recorded that colonial artist Ralph Earl completed the paintings and Doolittle transformed them into engravings. The Park Service credits Doolittle in their video program, and they are referred to in most sources as the Doolittle prints. In any event, they still remain significant documents of the event. I purchased some color postcards of the prints and had them enlarged and turned into color transparencies. As they looked at the images, I asked students to determine how well the images matched what they read in the *Lexington-Concord Battle Road Guide.* The Doolittle prints document four phases of the day's events: the skirmish on Lexington Green; Colonel Francis Smith and his aide, Major John Pitcarin, overlooking the town of Concord; the fight at the North Bridge; and the retreat of the British back to Boston. By looking at the images, which are considered accurate, students were able to determine how visual documents sometimes assist the writing of history, in particular this opening conflict of the American War for Independence.

Students came to see how important this event was considered at the time. Students learned that sometimes history books can be misleading. For example, when describing the early engagement of British

Figure 1–1
Teaching with the Doolittle Prints

troops with colonial militia on the Lexington Green, it is often reported, both in print and visual imagery, that the Patriots fired back on the British in unison. In fact, even though no one knows who fired the first shot that morning, we do know, and Doolittle's image of that event documents this, that eight Lexington Minutemen were killed as they tried to leave the Green under orders of their captain, John Parker. Documentation indicates that one British soldier was wounded in the event, so one would have to assume that one or two of the Minutemen did get off a shot. Of course, with this episode, there are plenty of contemporary accounts, from both sides, that the other side fired first. It is sometimes interesting to compare and contrast these accounts with students and ask them to make a determination. It's hard, as often in the midst of violent conflict, emotions take over and reality may be hazy. Then again, students have to look at when the "eyewitness" made his or her statement. Was it that day or years later?

For a wrap-up activity, I then showed a clip from the film *April Morning* (1988), a film based on Howard Fast's short novel about April 19, 1775. I asked students to compare and contrast the image of the Doolittle print about the engagement on the Lexington Green with how that incident is interpreted on film. As film goes, it's fairly accurate. The layout of the village is excellent as is the alignment of the seventy or so Minutemen and the British troops. The film deviates from real history in that it shows a disgruntled Minuteman firing the first shot from behind a stone wall and it has the main character, Adam Cooper's father, killed by the British volley. There were no Coopers on the Green in Lexington that day. It does document the death of Jonathan Harrington, who crawled to his wife and died in her arms in front of his house on the edge of the Green. This did, in fact, happen. The film does not include the presence of Prince Estabrook, a "Negro," according to period sources, who was among the wounded.

Before students left class, they examined a copy of a 1775 broadside printed shortly after the Battle of Lexington and Concord (see Figure 1–2). Forty-nine black coffins appear at the top representing forty-nine Americans who were killed; below this a banner reads, "BLOODY BUTCHERY OF THE BRITISH TROOPS." I purchased a copy of this broadside, which is a great piece of Patriot propaganda, at the Park Service gift store and had it laminated. I use it as an excellent visual for students to comprehend the significance of the event as it was perceived at the time.

The 225th Anniversary of the Battle of Lexington and Concord

To the sounds of fifes and drums coming from my stereo, my students and some of their parents filtered into my house one evening several days before our trip. We were gathered in my family room to watch *April Morning* and to reestablish the historical context of our trip. Watching the entire film allowed students the opportunity to see the retreat of the British and what they endured as they made the twelve-mile journey back to Boston. I pointed out that one of the things I would be looking for on our trip was the presence of African Americans in the story. It was as if they were left out of the public interpretation of events, even though one of the best narrative accounts of the battle, *Lexington and Concord* by Arthur B. Tourtellot, published in 1959, documents their presence.

Figure 1–2
Student Studying 1775 Broadside

The day after our long drive north from Virginia—I was affectionately calling our group the Virginia contingent of Minutemen—we set
out to step back into the past and come to terms with this conflict that
so changed the world. We actually started backward chronologically,
because the first two days of reenactment events took place two days
before we retraced the walk of the Acton Minutemen. Starting at the
Battle Road Visitor's Center, we walked three miles along the Battle Road
to the Meriam's Corner reenactment phase, stopping at the Paul Revere
capture site and periodically reading the exhibit boards along the way
that explained in detail what took place at each site. One board, located
at a bend in the Battle Road known as the Bloody Angel, described the
experience of Edmund Foster, a Minuteman from nearby Reading:

> We arrived just in time to meet the enemy. There was then, on the op-
> posite side of the road, a young growth of wood well filled with Ameri-
> cans. The enemy was now between two fires, renewed and briskly kept
> up. They ordered out a flank guard on the left to dislodge the Ameri-
> cans from their posts, behind large trees; but they only became a bet-
> ter mark to be shot at. A short but sharp contest ensued at which the

enemy received more deadly injury than at any other place from Concord to Charlestown. Eight or more of their number were killed on the spot, and no doubt, many wounded.

Even though we walked from east to west, going against the flow of what really happened, we were able to understand the story of the fight and the bloody retreat of the British as they tried to make their way back to Boston only to be constantly attacked by growing ranks of local militia and Minutemen. As we walked, we occasionally came across a marker that read, "Near here a British soldier lies buried."

We reached Meriam's Corner just in time for the 10:00 A.M. reenactment. Meriam's Corner is where the fight began with the British flight to Boston. Part of what I wanted my students to understand through the course of the weekend is that once a conflict turns violent, it often escalates and is difficult to contain. The Indians have a phrase, "It's easy to pick up the rifle, but hard to put it down." That's pretty much the story of April 19, 1775, from the moment that the first shots were fired in the dawn hours on the Lexington Green through the evening hours when the badly mauled British forces limped into Boston with their 273 casualties.

Reenactments such as this one and the one we witnessed later in the day are historically transporting—a kind of time travel—because they provide us with a strong visual to see how events unfold in a way that a book cannot. We can hear the music, look at individuals in period costume, study the formation of soldiers, and learn why it was necessary for them to fight the way they did—in massed groups, to make their firepower more effective. At its best, reenactments provide a kind of historical immediacy.

Between reenactments, we visited the large encampment of British troops and Patriots, cozily arranged side by side in a fraternity of reenacting. I gave the students time to mill around and talk with the reenactors, encouraging them to converse about their motivation both as historical figures and reenactors. Geoff, my military history enthusiast in the group, went to one of the period sutler shops (a kind of camp store set up to serve armies) and bought a colonial hat and a mock musket. He said he was ready for action for the upcoming afternoon's engagement, but he wanted to know if it was "OK" for him to have it with us. I sensed his sensitivity to school rules about students carrying weapons, even if they're toys. I followed, with curiosity, over the next several days how he and the other students kept playing around with the gun, mostly to hear how the primitive trigger sounded when it was pulled.

That afternoon we watched another portion of the retreat through part of modern Lexington, which was accurate in scope, size, and movement. As the British made their approach and as the Minutemen poured their volleys into the oncoming Redcoats, I could make out across the field a black Minuteman. He appeared, leveled his musket, fired, and then made cover back to his line under a haze of smoke and powder that wafted across the field obscuring the ranks of the colonial African American. I was glad to have made the observation and decided I would look into the black presence at Lexington and Concord in greater detail the next day when we visited the North Bridge site.

The next day, we started our activities with a visit to the Lexington Green. After the obligatory group photograph in front of the statue of Captain John Parker, we explored this little patch of land, where the day's events began to unravel for everyone. I asked my students to look around and try to recall what they had seen in *April Morning* as to the layout of the Green. Along the boundary of the Green that faces the road to Concord is a monument under which the remains of the eight Minutemen killed on the Green that morning were buried. I asked students to reflect on what Edward Linenthal (1991) calls the "politics of patriotism" as it relates to sites such as these—a kind of enshrinement of values tied to action at a given battle site. We have many such places in America, be it Lexington and Concord, the Alamo, Gettysburg, Little Bighorn, or Pearl Harbor. I always wonder why there is so much violence tied to patriotism and democracy. And I wondered if these eight men really knew what they were killed for. And I thought, would they be surprised to see what had become of their village and their actions. From the grave site, we moved over to the boulder delineating the "Line of the Minute Men" upon which are the supposed words of Captain Parker, "Stand your ground. Don't fire unless fired upon. But if they mean to have a war let it begin here." I wonder if Parker ever knew just what this war would eventually lead to?

Across the street from the Green is a tablet on which are inscribed the names of the seventy-or-so Minutemen from Lexington. Frank made sure that I saw Prince Estabrook's name, and again we all speculated about the role of blacks on April 19, 1775.

From Lexington it was over to the North Bridge battle site. We looked at the grave of two British soldiers killed at the bridge skirmish, upon which someone had placed a small Union Jack flag, and I related to my students that there actually had been a third soldier wounded at the bridge who was finished off by a hatchet blow delivered by a local Concord youth after the British had pulled back into town. My students winced at this account. The macabre story is true and it forced me to think about how something of this nature could be tied up with the grand story of our national birth of freedom. I find it hard to reconcile the two, but can intellectually dismiss my lack of reconciliation with the idea that obviously emotions were running high that day. Watching the pained expression on the faces of my students gave me pause to think what might be running through their minds.

As the afternoon wore on, we went to the Visitor's Center located at the bridge and some of our party watched the award-winning National Park film, *In the Cause of Liberty*. The film runs twenty-five minutes and lays out quite nicely the causative factors in bringing on the conflict, going back several years to the problems that developed between England and her colonies.

While students and parents watched the film, I asked one of the rangers about the presence of blacks in the day's fight. She directed me to the source, *The Black Presence in the Era of the American Revolution*, by Sidney Kaplan and Emma Nogrady Kaplan (1989). This book is a valuable tool and gets into some detail about blacks and Lexington and Concord. Upon our return to school, I purchased a copy for our library. The ranger also promised to send me a copy of their document, "The Role of Blacks in the Battle of April 19, 1775," written by park historian Douglas Sabin. It identifies several blacks, some who were slaves, who participated at the fight on the bridge and along the battle road.

Interestingly, in the summer of 2000 an African American park ranger, Bruce Harris, re-created the life of freedman Peter Salem, a participant in the action along Battle Road. His program, "A Walk with Peter Salem" brought to life a little-known story of the battle and lent a unique perspective on this event. Increasingly, the National Park Service is helping to reinterpret events at all of the battle sites they administer with a broader approach.

That evening, we attended a candlelight living history program, called "Battle Road Heroes," held at the Hartwell Tavern. Here reenactors playing period roles talked about different perspectives of the days events. Met by British light infantrymen, we were brought back again to that day in April 1775. The British soldiers told us about the costly fight along the Battle Road, while a British officer talked about the paper work he needed to complete. Inside the tavern, we met Mary, Ephraim, and Elizabeth Hartwell, owners of the tavern, and Captain William Smith, head of the Lincoln Minutemen. The women talked about how awful the day had been. They described how frightened they were and what the conflict would mean in the long run. Captain Smith spoke of his men and the reasons why they had to stand up and defend themselves and their "liberties."

The weather of Patriot's Day 2000 was not unlike that of the day in 1775, chilly and overcast. But an hour into the march we were beginning to peel off our jackets, though Geoff continued to wear his hat and carry his "musket." We arrived on the bluff overlooking the North Bridge at about 9:00 A.M. and were joined by other town Minuteman

Figure 1–3
Instructing with Daniel Chester French's *Minute Man* statue

companies who also arrived much like those from the surrounding countryside did 225 years earlier.

Classroom Follow-Up

Shortly after our return to Virginia, I collected evaluation sheets from the students and parent chaperones. These were kind of like learning logs to assess what they had derived from our experience.

Student Responses

I had written the following questions on each student sheet:

1. What did you specifically learn about the beginning of the War for Independence/American Revolution from our visit? Why is what you learned valuable to know as an American?

2. What are your thoughts about this field trip experience as it relates to the idea of conflict in American history? Why?

3. Comment on the interpretation of the beginning of the American Revolution as evidenced by the work of the National Park Service; the various reenactments you saw; the retracing of the Isaac Davis Trail; and our visits to the Lexington Green, the North Bridge, and the Battle Road. How did participation in those events, or seeing those sites, help you to understand this particular conflict in American history? Of what you saw and heard, what was most valuable to assisting you in your interpretation of those events?

4. Do you think that conflict between the colonials and the British, was inevitable or could it have been avoided? Explain.

The students offered a myriad of responses to the questions. Most said that the events were easier to understand by watching people role play history. Priya responded:

> I learned a lot about the beginning of the War for Independence. I learned about how the Lexington Green's "accidental" shot sparked a revolution. I was also able to see how the shot heard round the world at the North Bridge was so important. This is valuable to know as an American, because it was maybe in some ways a forced revolution and that as the colonies grew together in the fight they defined Americanism. I saw this as a shot that created a decision; they could continue for a path towards war, or they could beg Great Britain for forgiveness. As an American, this makes me feel pretty good, because they took the road not taken. . . . They broke away from the British Empire.

Brittany responded:

> I think the strongest part of the of the experience was the march from
> Acton to Concord. I think walking a piece of land that had once been
> a sort of battlefield makes a person realize that battlefields aren't just
> what you see in the movies. A battlefield can be anywhere, something
> that might seem like the worst place for a battle may well be the best.

Amber mused:

> I think that conflict between the colonists and the British was inevi-
> table because of the distance between the colonies and Great Britain,
> the differences in the land, and the circumstances in which they moved
> to the colonies in the first place. The conflict with the colonies was
> bound to happen.

Parent Responses

The parents who accompanied us on the trip answered the following
questions:

1. Of what value is it in your opinion to have your son or daughter
    learn about the conflict and the nature of conflict in a high school
    class that focuses on American history? Why?

2. Do you think it is valuable that Americans know the circumstances
    under which the United States was born, particularly as it relates to
    colonial-English relations? Why?

The last two questions for the parents were the same as the students' questions two through four. Most of the parents said that for
them, it was a matter of having their sons or daughters understand that
in conflict people die and it is important to understand the reasons for
those deaths. One of the parents responded that he was struck by the
analogies between the British who fought against the crown (now Patriots) and modern-day revolutionaries who advocate armed opposition to the government of the United States, such as modern-day militia groups the government has confronted at Ruby Ridge, Montana,
and in Waco, Texas. In fact, in some of these circles the meaning of Patriot's Day had changed to something more sinister. It had been on Patriot's Day in 1995 that the Murrah Federal Building in Oklahoma City
had been bombed, and it had been Patriot's Day in 1993 when federal
agents attacked the Branch Davidian compound at Waco, Texas. Many
of the modern-day militia groups claim the mantle of those who fought
in April 1775 against the crown and at least in my estimation the commemorative meaning has been scarred in those New England states
that offer Patriot's Day as a holiday. Another parent offered this:

Conflict, more specifically, the ability to manage conflict on either an individual or societal basis is the key energy which drives us forward. The sooner conflict's constructive side is understood, the sooner maturity will emerge.

One mother put it this way:

Since Mary Beth has ancestors who supported the American Revolution, it is especially important for her to understand how America's "conflict" directly affected our family. Learning about America's history, she's learning about her family's history.

At some level, every American family is affected by conflict and the particular path upon which it takes us, whether it is a history of involvement in World War I or World War II, the Civil War, Korea or Vietnam, the Persian Gulf or some other dispute.

An Interdisciplinary Approach

The curriculum for some of my courses, in particular advanced placement and survey courses, requires a global, chronological approach. Generally I use a variety of media to teach this material, and it has become an increasingly interdisciplinary approach. I repeat the historiography lesson around Paul Revere and use the Doolittle prints as well as the 1775 broadside, but in a different way.

Students in my regular survey class read *April Morning* (Fast 1961), and we talk about character development and the life of a teenager on the eve of rebellion in Massachusetts. In some ways, using historical fiction is better than using the "stuff" of real history to make important connections with secondary-age students. I agree with Juliet Whitman, a frequent book reviewer for the *Washington Post's Book World* that, "The best historical novels communicate a sense of history as complex, constantly changing and connecting seamlessly with the present. They flesh out the simple outlines of events we remember from school; they revise stereotypical understanding; they show that those who lived before us were both exactly like us and profoundly different." (*Book World* July 16, 2000) Howard Fast's novels, of which *April Morning* is a classic, resonates well with students. Fast, who is no stranger to conflict in his personal life (among other things he was blacklisted during the period of McCarthyism) uses conflict as the basis of most of his novels. His characters, in the case of *April Morning*, Adam and Moses Cooper, Gideon Jackson in *Freedom Road* (1944) or Evan Feversham and Hans Pohl in *The Hessian* (1972) all encounter life tied up within the framework of personal and communal conflict. I will address the latter two books in subsequent chapters.

Students also read *The Lexington-Concord Battle Road Guide,* and we compare and contrast that historical narrative with Fast's fictional account. The novel seems to help students understand the time period better than the guide does, though the guide provides students with a better historical framework. *April Morning* also works well with middle school or junior high students as does the time-honored classic by Esther Forbes, *Johnny Tremain* (1971) and *Private Yankee Doodle* by Joseph Plumb Martin (1989), an exceptional and easy-to-understand memoir of the entire War for Independence.

Liberty *and "Great Minds of American History with Gordon Wood"*

When I teach the American Revolution in my survey courses, I always discuss the economic roots of this war. The epigraph at the beginning of this chapter reflects my belief that the roots of many conflicts can be found in economics. Certainly, there is no way of avoiding it when discussing the background causes of the American Revolution. For this, I like to use the PBS video series, *Liberty* (1997). Not only does this exceptional program outline the economic causes, but it also explores in depth the social causes of the war. The film is six hours long, but I only use the first two episodes and the last as they meet my academic needs. The genius of this series is that it combines actors portraying significant players of the historical events with reenactments and period illustrations. Students respond very well to the content and the context. In addition, there is a first-rate educational package that can be purchased to accompany the video sequences. The handouts, which can be reproduced, include primary-source material, historical commentary offered by leading scholars such as Pauline Maier and Gordon Wood, and visuals. Additionally, the program and ancillary support materials are reflective of the changes in historiography and American diversity. African Americans as well as women make up the landscape of the video and the lesson plans. All combined, these make for effective teaching tools and are designed for activities that incorporate differentiation.

For advanced placement students, I would also recommend using the segment from the History Channel's *Great Minds of American History* series, "The American Revolution with Gordon Wood" (1998). This fifty-minute program encapsulates the essence of the American Revolution as interpreted by one of America's leading academics. It offers more sophisticated learners a deeper approach to the causes and effects of the American Revolution. This program helps advanced placement students to consider the complex elements of this event in preparation for writing lengthy and analytical essays.

One of the questions I ask all of my students to respond to in their journals is: "In your opinion, is the American Revolution over?" For this I use as an introductory prompt, John Adams' often-repeated quote, "The American Revolution was in the minds and hearts of the people. The War for Independence is over but the American Revolution has just begun." Bridgette, an African American student, replied:

> I agree with John Adams when he said the Revolutionary War was only an effect and consequence of the Revolution. The Revolution was not entirely an act of physical violence between two opposing parties, it was also the change of the ideas to fit the times. The question of its success and whether or not it is still ongoing is a question of opinion. Personally, I believe that the American Revolution was a success in what it stood for but not in its final results. As Americans we have not fulfilled our original purpose (all men are created equal). I feel that we are currently in the state of the American Resolution. In order for our journey as Americans to be complete, we must resolve all the issues that have hindered our development as a whole. The Revolution is over, but the resolution has just begun.

Bridgette's eloquence makes a great segue to talk about a source with which all American history teachers should be familiar: Eric Foner's *The Story of American Freedom* (1998). This is an important book in that it helps readers to understand the shifts over generations of the different interpretations of the meaning of the word *freedom*. What freedom means today and what it meant in 1775, or 1787 for that matter when the Constitution was framed, are entirely different. In fact, some historians have argued that the creation of the Constitution was actually a conservative step backward from the Declaration of Independence to define more narrowly the idea of "freedom" and "We the people." I have to constantly remind my students that, "We the people" did not mean all the people in 1787. In *Liberty*, Gordon Wood points out that Jefferson's phrase, "All men are created equal" really became a "permissive doctrine" that was latched on to by various groups over time and thus helped to create an event or series of events that continued to be played out. Reading Foner's *The Story of American Freedom* will nevertheless help you to recognize the ebb and flow in the American drama and dream. In particular, Foner's examination will help you to assist students in understanding the context of the Declaration of Independence and its subsequent interpretation. Foner's book is written in such a way that it could be used effectively as a supplemental tool for advanced placement students to read in concert with their standard American history text.

The Boston Massacre

The Boston Massacre of March 1770 is another event that is of interest to look at from the standpoint of conflict and the background to the War for Independence. I like to use the following activity with my students in my advanced placement and regular survey course because it helps them to see that events of this age were neither simple nor one-sided. For this I rely, in part, on the episode about John Adams from the television series *Profiles in Courage* (1966) about his defense of the British soldiers accused of murdering the five victims of the Massacre. The *Profiles in Courage* docudrama programs, based on John F. Kennedy's Pulitzer Prize–winning book of the same name, may look a bit campy, but I find them to be very effective teaching tools. The strength of this series is its ability to capture the idea in depicting personal conflict and struggle within the larger context of national conflict and struggle. What students come to recognize by watching these films is that conflict can take on very personal dimensions when explored against our national history. "John Adams" is a particularly good episode because it blends the fervor of the period of colonial dissension in Boston with the way evidence is presented to construct a particular memory or history—in this case the guilt or innocence of the accused British troops that are brought before the colonial Massachusetts court.

First we pick apart the word *massacre*. How is it defined? What qualifies as a massacre? Then I show the film, which is a drama and depicts the Massacre and subsequent trial. What students come to realize is that this event was really sparked by the actions of an unruly mob who threatened the British sentries outside the Massachusetts State House. Adams is successful in the defense of the soldiers and uses the laws of the period to help acquit them. Throughout the film, Adams continually defends his course of action in defending the soldiers even though he is an avowed member of the Sons of Liberty, because he wants to ensure that his cause of liberty is based on rule of law and not mobocracy, a term from the period used to describe government by mob rule. Once the film is finished, I share with students a transparency of the famous lithograph of the Boston Massacre engraved by Paul Revere. You can find a full-page, color illustration of this engraving in just about any good book on the Revolution. The Revere engraving is a clever piece of propaganda, depicting an orderly row of British soldiers firing a volley into a crowd of defenseless citizens. Of course nothing could be further from the truth. The film "John Adams," though a product of Hollywood, is much more accurate than Revere's lithograph. In studying the lithograph, I ask students to tell me what they see and to consider how this drawing may have incited tension and increased hostility in colonial Boston and the rest of the colonies. Then I share with students five different historical perspectives of the event and ask students to match the paragraphs to the correct sources. One source is an eyewitness in 1770, another source is that of a British historian, the third source an American historian, the fourth is John Adams, and the fifth is one of the British soldiers. After matching the sources, we talk about viewpoints and bias and how they play into interpretation and perspectives. This exercise can be updated by comparing these sources and this event to how people view contemporary events. It's often hard to determine the "truth" of an event until time and space have played their role in memory. I like to mention to students as a point of reference that it's often easy to make a historical judgment about a person or event *after* the event because we know how the event turned out. That's why critical or historical thinking skills are so important to instill in students. Teaching about conflict, whatever it is, can help to refine those skills.

My wrap-up of the material on the Boston Massacre is to show students a slide of the common grave site of the victims, including the mulatto, Crispus Attucks, located in Granary Burying Ground in downtown Boston. Not too far from their grave is that of Paul Revere.

Art and the War

For as long as I can remember, one of the best ways I came to understand the American Revolution was from the plethora of paintings and sculptures about people and events that illustrated the books I read. It should come as no surprise then that I've found ways to gather these images and use them in my teaching repertoire.

The Patriot Artist of the American
Revolution — John Trumbull

John Trumbull, a soldier in the Continental Army, was trained as an academic artist. Trumbull's *The American Revolution Series* is important in its documentation of significant events of the period. Four of his paintings were considered so important by Congress that when the US Capitol was rebuilt following the War of 1812, Trumbull was asked to enlarge these images for the new rotunda. Visitors to the US Capitol can see on a grand scale his paintings *The Presentation of the Declaration of Independence, The Surrender of Burgoyne at Saratoga, The Surrender of Cornwallis at Yorktown,* and *The Resignation of George Washington.* Congress selected these images because they marked seminal events in the creation of the nation, notwithstanding that one of them, *The Presentation of the Declaration of Independence,* is historical abomination (as I'll demonstrate shortly). The original eight paintings, on a much smaller scale, hang in the Yale University Art Gallery in New Haven, Connecticut, where Trumbull graduated. The other four paintings are *The Death of General Warren at the Battle of Bunker Hill, The Death of General Montgomery at the Battle of Quebec, The Surrender of Colonel Rall at the Battle of Trenton,* and *The Death of General Mercer at the Battle of Princeton.* It has taken me a while to gather slides of all the images from a variety of sources. I might suggest for your sake that you refer to any good picture history book on the American Revolution and take them to your local copy center and have them made into transparencies, as I did with the Doolittle prints.

The way I use these paintings is to provide students with a visual lecture about each image and its significance. I provide them with background information on Trumbull, including his military service, his apprenticeship under the artist Benjamin West, dubbed the "Father of American History painting," and his friendship with Thomas Jefferson. It's important to point out that most eighteenth-century individuals in Europe and America learned about historical events from paintings, the school of American History Painting created by West. Many American colonists, particularly those living in the coastal cities, were familiar with West's work. I also tell students that American art has always differed from European art in that American art, painting, and sculpture has always had a sense of "realism"—West took this realism and moved it to a grand scale. Trumbull, called the "Patriot Artist of the Revolution," furthered the tradition with his work. Trumbull's works are considered doubly important because they are primary sources about the events and also significant pieces of American art. There was a method to Trumbull's work. First he sketched mini-portraits of real participants of the events and then he painted these portraits onto his main canvas. He also conducted interviews with the participants to help create his story paintings. One can look at Trumbull's paintings and see the actors in the drama. In some cases, he embellished and his history may be a bit skewed. Many artists of the age were preoccupied with death, particularly combat deaths, and so four of his images deal with such themes. His painting, *The Death of General Warren at Bunker Hill* is significant because, if you look carefully at the painting, you will see two black Patriots, Peter Salem and an unidentified "Negro" servant of a Lieutenant Grosvenor, located near the bottom right edge of the image. Salem would go on to serve with distinction during the war and saw further combat at Saratoga and Stony Point. I make this very clear to my students, as the historical records supports the assertions of black participation in this engagement.

Showing the entire series helps students to get a sense of the time span of the war. In addition to the Bunker Hill image, I focus on the four other paintings that hang in the Capitol because they represent turning points in American history. The image concerning the Declaration of Independence is critical to study, not only because it commemorates the event that separated the colonies from Great Britain, but because it has shaped American perception of that event where it appears to be gospel truth. Before relating to students the story of this painting, I ask for a show of hands from my students to see how many are already familiar with the image. The vast majority of students raise their hands, and when I ask them where they have previously seen the image, most respond in history textbooks or books about the American Revolution. Trumbull shows all fifty-five signers of the Declaration of Independence in the room at one time; in fact, this never happened. Instead, the signing took place over a two-year time span. Although a copy was sent to King George III and Parliament, it did not look like the completely signed document that is enshrined in the rotunda of the United States Capitol. Providing students with this information helps them to understand the "politics of patriotism" and the role played by imagery in creating a national historical memory. One way of supporting this lesson with advanced placement students is to use Chapter 3, "Declaring Independence: The Strategies of Documentary Analysis," in James West Davidson's and Mark Hamilton Lytle's, *After the Fact: The Art of Historical Detection* (2000). In their book, these authors offer other ways of looking at this painting and its relationship to print documents of the period, including several drafts of the Declaration itself.

The two other battle paintings we examine in detail are the ones concerning the surrender of the British armies at Saratoga and Yorktown, two events that helped shape the direction of the war and the course of world history.

The final image of the series, the *Resignation of George Washington in 1783,* is important because in his resignation as commander-in-chief, Washington fulfilled the ideals of the meaning and cause of the war. He had done his duty, and now he was turning in his commission to become George Washington, citizen. Historians clearly believe that Washington was in the perfect position in 1783 to establish himself as a military dictator; he was popular among the people and had the support of the army. This gesture was perhaps one of the greatest acts of his life. When I show this slide, I explain to students that some of Washington's contemporaries claimed that he was an American Cincinnatus. Cincinnatus was a legendary Roman general who, when called by his countrymen to help defend Rome, left his farm and led the Romans to triumph. Upon victory, Cincinnatus was exalted by his countrymen and could have established himself as dictator. Rather, Cincinnatus chose to return to his farm to become, once again, a Roman citizen. Washington's officers were so caught up by their commander's action that they formed The

Society of Cincinnati, a hereditary organization composed of Washington's officers and their descendants.

Emanuel Leutze and Washington Crossing the Delaware

Probably the most famous picture depicting the American Revolution, and one of the best-loved images in all of American art, is Emanuel Leutze's *Washington Crossing the Delaware* (1851). The painting documents a critical moment in the war, when Washington, desperate for a victory, made a gamble to attack the Hessian barracks at Trenton on the morning after Christmas. The surprise attack worked. The Hessians, German mercenaries, paid by the British crown, were routed. The victory at Trenton inspired men whose enlistments were about to expire to remain in the fledgling Continental Army. Leutze painted several versions of this bombastic work. One of them hangs in the Metropolitan Museum of Art's American Wing in New York City. The gift shop at the museum sells slides of this painting, but again you can find it in any number of source books about the American Revolution and have a transparency made. Like Trumbull's painting about the Declaration of Independence, Leutze's work is primarily fantasy. Once again, I ask students to indicate if they are familiar with this image and again most of the hands in my class go up. There are many inaccuracies in the painting. First, Washington never would have stood in the boat. Second, this event took place in the dark of night, not the light of day; remember, it was a surprise attack. Third, the flag in the painting did not become the banner of the Revolution until the following summer. Aside from these inaccuracies, I like to point out that one of the oarsmen in Washington's boat is black, tradition holding that it is a man by the name of Prince Whipple, from New Hampshire. In another painting of the same subject, painted in 1819 by Thomas Sully, there too appears a black individual near Washington. The fact is that blacks served in the Continental Army on a nonsegregated basis. Leutze and Sully were sensitive enough to the historical record to include blacks in their paintings. Sully's painting can be compared to Leutze's, and you can have students discuss which painting is more realistic in terms of its depiction of the event.

In addition to the paintings, you can show students the excellent film produced by the History Channel, *The Crossing* (1999), a dramatic rendering of Howard Fast's novel of the same name, and compare the film to both Leutze's romantic interpretation and Sully's more realistic image. The film runs about ninety minutes. All of this provides good food for thought for students to consider the "whys" and "hows" of certain interpretations. Teaching with such activities permits students to see the complexity of history and conflict and how stories about such events have been passed down from one generation to the next.

Minute Man *by Daniel Chester French*

One of my favorite works depicting the American Revolution is the sculpture that was unveiled in 1875 at the Centennial Celebration of the fight at the North Bridge—Daniel Chester French's *Minute Man.* This statue, located on the bank of the Concord River from where the Minutemen in 1775 returned the volley of the British, commemorates the heroics and sacrifices of the Minutemen. Over the years, this piece has come to symbolize the idea of the American citizen soldier. Here we see the farmer with one hand grasping his musket, the other hand resting on his plow, striding off to defend liberty. Residents of nearby Acton like to lay claim that this image is really of Isaac Davis and that French used the original Davis plow for his model. In fact, that plow is on display in the Acton Town Hall.

Probably no other American sculpture, with perhaps the exception of the Statue of Liberty, has been used to represent in public and private arenas the image of what it means to be a vigilant American. I like to show my numerous slides of this image and have students compare and contrast the image with some of those "borrowed" by various advertisements. Edward Linenthal's book, *Sacred Ground: Americans and Their Battlefields* (1991) has a chapter on Lexington and Concord that has pages showing some of these advertisements using the image of the *Minute Man.* We hold class discussions about the appropriateness of such use of imagery. Some students, generally those from military families, occasionally have trouble with the idea, while others see it as just a part of American capitalism. This lesson activity gets students to at least recognize that some images become timeless and take on a life of their own.

I developed a lesson on the *Minute Man* that incorporates written primary-source material of French's recollection on the fiftieth anniversary of the unveiling of his sculpture along with visuals of the statue. The lesson can be found in the Organization of American Historians/National Center for History in the Schools publication, *Commemorative Sculpture in the United States* (1998). It takes only about twenty minutes to teach effectively in the classroom. This lesson allows students to analyze the image within the context of the American Revolution and to examine the artist's intent of the piece within a framework of the passing of time. Lessons such as this engage students in a way that permits them to establish their own interpretation of the past based upon a set of provided criteria, while at the same time recognize the power of enduring iconography. It's also helpful to guide students to an understanding that sometimes the most enduring images of American history represent violence as a means of defending national principles or ideas. With sophisticated students, you can also explore how these images may move from iconography to propaganda, as was done during the

Second World War when French's *Minute Man* became part of the landscape of wartime posters.

The American Revolution Scrapbook

Although the activity described here was done with one of my advanced placement classes, it can be easily modified to work with regular survey students as well. In fact, the historical scrapbook that I assigned works with other time periods just as effectively.

The participants in the American Revolution represented a diverse group of individuals, so I needed to be sure that varied materials would be available for students. I made certain that the list of names provided for students to research represented a good cross section of the men and women of the period. I selected specific participants such as John and Abigail Adams, Nathaniel Greene, Henry Knox, Phillis Wheatley, and Joseph Brandt. But in some cases, I wanted a specific *type* of person researched, so some students investigated a Hessian soldier, a British Grenadier, an American Loyalist, or a black soldier in the Continental Army. In these instances, students were able to create a person, but everything about their fictitious personality had to be historically accurate. Individuals selected represented both sides of the conflict, including William Franklin, son of Benjamin Franklin and Loyalist governor of New Jersey, and Benedict Arnold. When I assigned the project, I had students pick their individual's name from my tri-cornered hat. Students were given the opportunity to trade the names they selected with each other. One student, David, had a real personal investment in this assignment: one of his ancestors, John Hager, was in fact a Hessian soldier who served in America.

Students assembled a minimum of a ten-page scrapbook that might have been compiled by their participant, and at least each year of the conflict had to be represented in the scrapbook. They could use period images where appropriate, but the finished product had to have an "authentic" look. I did not want a scrapbook that looked like it had come from the shelves of Staples. Each scrapbook had to document the person's experiences during the war. Specific and historical events needed to be examined and documented. The pages had to include this person's reflections or reactions to events. If the personality was fictitious, then students had a bit more leeway, but still had to be historically on target. I asked that the scrapbooks *not* be bound via modern technology—staples or paper clips. Consequently, many students dipped plain paper in tea to get the right antique feel and resorted to using string or twine to bind their pages. Figure 1–4 shows a collection of scrapbooks.

Figure 1–4
American Revolution Era Scrapbooks

Students were given two months to complete their research and work. On the due date, I collected not only the finished scrapbook, but also a list of resources, of which at least one had to be primary. Only two sources from the Internet were permitted. Finally, students submitted a summary sheet that examined how the conflict generated by the American Revolution and the War for Independence affected the person they had studied.

Student Samples

I mentioned my student David and his Hessian ancestor. David pored through family records to compile his narrative and here is what he wrote:

> The Revolutionary War affected John Hager and many other Hessians more than any other personalities involved in the War for American Independence. Many Hessians, including John Hager, had their worlds

turned upside-down by a war in which they should not have fought. Many of the Hessians had never served in the army before, and most had never ventured more than a few miles from their homes.

Because of the extreme distance between America and Germany, many Hessians felt as if they were betrayed by their King and Country. Morale was drastically decreased by this and many other factors, one of which was that they never heard from their families again after their departure. Sometimes this was not just because families didn't write, but because letters were captured by the Americans, withheld by the British, or lost at sea during the long journey it took to reach the colonies. This, too, made the Hessians feel as if they had nothing to lose by desertion.

John Hager also had to learn the English language, and how to survive on his own. He also lost two of his brothers to the war, and after the war he lived in America, something which on his birth (December 26, 1759) would have seemed impossible to his family before the war. Later he married Mary Shrader somewhere on the Maryland-Virginia border, a member of a highly respected German family formerly from Pennsylvania. She bore him six sons and one daughter. He also volunteered to fight under General Anthony Wayne in his battles against the Indians as a matter of curious adventure to know their mode of warfare, being as he had already fought for and against the Americans and the British. John Hager died in 1819, never having expressed the desire to leave this country which he had adopted as his home.

Elizabeth created a scrapbook for and wrote about the war's impact on the African American poet Phillis Wheatley. According to Elizabeth:

While Phillis Wheatley came into the prime of her life, from 1765–1782, the Revolutionary War was raging across the colonies of the soon-to-be United States of America. If the War of Independence had never occurred, Wheatley may never have become a major historical personality. However, she also may not have died as early as she did, at the age of only 31. The war seems to have intensified her life at the expense of longevity.

Phillis Wheatley came into the public eye with an elegy written for Reverend George Whitefield. However, most of her precious poems were politically grounded, commenting on such events as a fatal conflict between a Tory and a Whig ("On the Death of Mr. Snider Murder'd by Richardson") and the Boston Massacre ("On the Affray in King Street, on the evening of the 5th of March, 1770"). Had these events never taken place, Wheatley may have lost her inspiration for writing and have been devoted to being an obedient slave by the time of Whitefield's death. It is also likely that she could have found inspiration in other circumstances, being poetically gifted. However, her political poems struck a chord with the revolutionary populace, who demanded more. Her controversial poem addressed to Earl William Legge at the time of his appointment as Secretary of States voiced sentiments for freedom that had never before been proclaimed so strongly and openly by a woman, let alone a slave. The colonists thrived on such assertions, which encouraged their belief that their cause was supported by others. Wheatley's popularity might not have been as great if she had simply written pretty verse describing springtime and flowers.

Not only did Phillis benefit socially from the war, she benefited emotionally too. The excitement of the period fed her spirit, and inspired her to write and achieve more than the average slave. Had the country not harbored an overwhelming desire for freedom, Wheatley's spirit might have been broken. As a slave, she longed for the day that she and her people could be liberated from bondage. Seeing proof in the battles of the Revolutionary War that such an event was possible gave Phillis the strength to continue hoping and striving for her own independence. Even after she personally gained freedom, she did not stop encouraging the emancipation of all slaves.

As much as Wheatley seemed to benefit from the War for Independence, her life was at the same time crippled by it. The inflation and hard economic times caused by the war were very detrimental to a single free black woman. She was only able to earn money by selling her poems, and as financial hardship settled over the nation, fewer people had the money or leisure for a book of poetry. One of her only options was to get married, which she did. Her marriage to John Peters was a direct product of the war; from all accounts it seems to have been born of necessity instead of love. This marriage may have even hurt her more than it helped her, for the strain of bearing three children and losing two caused irreparable damage to her already frail health. John Peters disappeared in 1784 to debtor's prison, leaving Phillis to fend for herself for a time. All the gains she had made earlier in the war seemed to have been forgotten by 1783, and Wheatley died in 1784 almost unknown; no one even attended her funeral.

Despite all of the fame, admiration, and emotional stimulation brought on Phillis Wheatley with the onset of the Revolutionary War, the financially difficult conditions of wartime lead her to an early, unhappy grave. If it seems that the negative side of the war overcame any advantages it might have given to Phillis, we must consider if the journey was more important than the destination. Sometimes it is better for one to accomplish much and feel things intensely for a short time than for one to lead a long but monotonous and uneventful life never having realized one's full potential.

By engaging in such personal and hands-on work associated with the intense human experience of war, students come to recognize that humans do not live in a vacuum and that life can be fragile when confronted with conflict. Many students develop a kind of historical empathy that puts them into the skins of the person whose life they have entered. In a way, these ghosts from the past help students to understand the very real experiences endured by these individuals. Students are able to grasp that not only is the world at large shaped by conflict, but so too are the lives of individuals. While some people endure and prevail, others do not. An in-depth activity such as the scrapbook not only hones research skills, but it also provides students a window through which they can measure their own lives.

Shortly after our Applied History sojourn returned from the 225th Anniversary Commemoration of Lexington and Concord, I picked up the phone and called the head of the modern-day Acton Minutemen and fulfilled a childhood dream, by becoming a member. It seems, too, that this middle-age veteran teacher wants to look into that window and live a glimpse of the past so as to make a measure of the present.

Resources

Books

Andrews, Joseph L. 1999. *Revolutionary Boston, Lexington, and Concord.* Concord, MA: Concord Guides Press.

Ayres, William, ed. 1993. *Picturing History: American Painting 1770–1930.* New York: Rizzoli.

Bailyn, Bernard. 1967. *The Ideological Origins of the American Revolution.* Cambridge: Harvard University Press.

Bobrick, Benson. 1997. *Angel in the Whirlwind.* New York: Simon and Schuster.

Calloway, Colin G. 1995. *The American Revolution in Indian Country: Crisis and Diversity in Native American Communities.* Cambridge: Cambridge University Press.

Fast, Howard. 1943. *Citizen Tom Paine.* New York: Grove Press.

———. 1944. *Freedom Road.* Armank, New York: M.E. Sharpe.

———. 1961. *April Morning.* New York: Crown.

———. 1965. *The Crossing.* New York: Crown.

———. 1972. *The Hessian.* Armank, New York: M.E. Sharpe.

Fisher, David Hackett. 1995. *Paul Revere's Ride.* New York: Oxford University Press.

Fleming, Thomas. 1997. *Liberty.* New York: Viking.

Forbes, Esther. 1971. *Johnny Tremain.* New York: Bantam Doubleday.

French, Allen. 1992. *Historic Concord and the Lexington Fight.* Concord, MA: Friends of the Concord Library.

Galvin, John R. 1989. *The Minute Men.* New York: Pergamon-Brassey's.

Graymont, Barbara. 1975. *The Iroquois in the American Revolution.* Syracuse, NY: Syracuse University Press.

Gross, Robert A. 1976. *The Minutemen and Their World.* New York: Hill and Wang.

Hallahan, William. 2000. *The Day the American Revolution Began: 19 April 1775.* New York: Avon Books.

Higginbotham, Don. 1983. *The War of American Independence.* Boston: Northeastern University Press.

Jaffe, Irma. 1975. *John Trumbull: Patriot-Artist of the American Revolution.* Boston: New York Graphic Society.

Kaplan, Sidney, and Emma Nogrady Kaplan. 1989. *The Black Presence in the Era of the American Revolution.* Amherst, MA: University of Massachusetts Press.

Ketchum, Richard. 1962. *Decisive Day: The Battle of Bunker Hill.* New York: Henry Holt.

———. 1973. *The Winter Soldiers: The Battles for Trenton and Princeton.* New York: Henry Holt.

———. 1997. *Saratoga: Turning Point of America's Revolutionary War.* New York: Henry Holt.

Maier, Pauline. 1992. *From Resistance to Revolution.* New York: W. W. Norton.

Martin, Joseph Plumb. 1989. *Private Yankee Doodle.* Eastern Acorn Press.

Martin, William. 1999. *Citizen George Washington.* New York: Warner Books.

Quarles, Benjamin. 1973. *The Negro in the American Revolution.* New York: Vintage.

Sizer, Theodore. 1998. *The Works of Colonel John Trumbull: Artist of the American Revolution.* New Haven, CT: Yale University Press.

———, ed. *The Autobiography of Colonel John Trumbull: Patriot Artist, 1756–1843.* New Haven, CT: Yale University Press.

Tourtellot, Arthur B. 1959. *Lexington and Concord.* New York: Norton.

Wills, Gary. 1978. *Inventing America: Jefferson's Declaration of Independence.* Garden City, NJ: Doubleday.

———. 1984. *Cincinnatus: George Washington and the Enlightenment.* Garden City, NJ: Doubleday.

Wood, Gordon S. 1992. *The Radicalism of the American Revolution.* New York: Alfred A. Knopf.

———. 1998. *The Creation of the American Republic, 1776–1787.* Chapel Hill: North Carolina University Press.

Videos

April Morning: Producers: Robert Halmi, Jr., and Delbert Mann; Director: Delbert Mann. 90 Minutes. Robert Halmi, Inc., 1988.

The Crossing: Producer: David Coastworth; Director: Robert Harmon. 90 minutes. A & E Television, 1999, videocassette.

George Washington—The Man Who Wouldn't Be King. Producer: Donald Sutherland. 60 minutes. PBS Productions, 1994, videocassette.

Gordon Wood on the American Revolution. Great Minds of American History series. Producers: Steve Atlas, Tim Smith, and the History Channel. 50 minutes. Unipix Entertainment, 1998, videocassette.

Independence: Producer: Joyce and Lloyd Ritter; Director: John Huston. 30 minutes. National Park Service, 1975, videocassette.

John Adams: Producer: Gordon Oliver and Robert Saudek; Director: Robert Stevens. 50 minutes. Robert Saudek Associates, 1966, videocassette.

Liberty: The American Revolution. Producers/Directors: Ellen Hovde and Muffie Meyer. 420 minutes. Middlemarch Films, 1997, videocassette.

1776. Producer: Jack L. Warner; Director: Peter H. Hunt. 141 Minutes. Columbia Pictures, 1972, videocassette.

Chapter Two

Survivors of Custer's Last Stand—Indians, Anglos, and the West

Know the power that is peace.

—Black Elk, Lakota Sioux

Standing on the hill, looking down past the ravine toward the river, you can almost see it unfold before you. If you close your eyes and let your imagination take hold, you can imagine the sounds associated with that hot Sunday in 1876. Those sounds would be a mixture of noise combining the shrieks of men, the crack of rifle fire, and the whinnying of horses. You would be hearing one of the most widely written about events in American history, the Battle of the Little Bighorn, known in popular American culture as "Custer's Last Stand." Snapping back to the present, you would see covering this pristine land the pockmarks of white marble markers denoting the places where each of the 260 Seventh Cavalry troopers met their fate. Mixed in among the markers for the soldiers are the markers for four civilians, two of whom were relatives of Custer's. The markers that are scattered over Last Stand Hill, called Greasy Grass Ridge by the Indians, are all the same with the exception of the marker of Lieutenant Colonel George Armstrong Custer. Affixed to his is a black shield, separating Custer in life, death, and myth from the rest of the men of his fabled cavalry regiment.

It's hard not to be overwhelmed by what you see when you visit what is now called Little Bighorn National Battlefield Monument. For years, this place was designated by the United States Department of the Interior as Custer National Battlefield. In 1991, under increasing pressure from the American Indian community, Congress voted to change the name. Edward T. Linenthal (1991) asserts that of all of America's battlefields, this one is the most contentious in terms of public memory and enduring mythology.

Just as many Americans who were living in 1963 can tell you where they were and what they were doing when they heard the news that President John F. Kennedy had been assassinated, many European Americans living in 1876 would be able to clearly recall where they were and what they were doing when they received the news of the events that unfolded in Montana Territory on Sunday, June 25. The timing of this event was a national calamity. When word that America's most celebrated soldier of the day had been defeated and killed by a combined force of Sioux, Cheyenne, and Arapaho Indians, the nation was on the eve of celebrating its centennial. A dark pall clouded the premier event of the year, the centennial celebration in Philadelphia. European Americans were outraged and shocked. How could the finest officer in the armed forces of the nation have been defeated by a band of "savages," they asked. For the Indians, this was a single victory in a long line of defeats, and in the end it really was a pyrrhic victory, as the wrath of a nation saw to it that there would be no rest or quarter given to the Indians who roamed the Great Plains. In 1890, the Plains Indian Wars came to a bitter end when hundreds of Sioux were gunned down at Wounded Knee, South Dakota. How ironic that this event would take place in the same year in which the national census would be interpreted such that the American frontier was considered closed. Even more ironic was that it would be the Seventh Cavalry who would be behind the guns on that cold day in South Dakota, in a way exacting revenge for the events of fourteen years earlier.

For nearly one hundred years, the popular history of the Battle of the Little Bighorn would record that there were no survivors. No living Indian dared to speak or come forward to acknowledge that there were indeed survivors of Custer's Last Stand—the Indians.

Standing next to the monument over the mass grave of soldiers that adorns the crest of Last Stand Hill, I drew some needed inspiration. It was early August and school would be starting in a month. Casting about for some ideas as how to reinvigorate my Applied History curriculum, I found them in eastern Montana. Prior to this family vacation out West, I had never really paid much attention as a teacher to the history of the West. I knew it was there, but I had no tangible link with which I could connect. Our two-week trip to the West and its dramatic scenery and vistas changed my view of history, our country, and my teaching. Before we even pulled out of the parking lot of Little Bighorn National Battlefield Monument, I knew I was headed in a new direction.

A Multifaceted Teaching and Learning Approach to Little Bighorn

Shortly after returning to Virginia, I began to pull together extensive material to develop my new unit on the Battle of the Little Bighorn. I had decided to make this unit as dynamic as possible and knew that, based on the wealth of materials available, it would be possible to create a teaching and learning experience that could work well with high school seniors as well as some younger students. Knowing that there were numerous Hollywood interpretations of Custer's Last Stand, I turned to David Smith, our principal, and asked him if he would fund the purchase of seven of the various-length films dealing with this event. I received a hearty green light. (It's great having a principal who is a former history teacher.)

As I continued to pull resources together, I spoke to Brian Pohanka, noted Civil War and Little Bighorn historian. Pohanka, who annually speaks to my Applied History class and understands my approach to teaching history, liked my Custer/Little Bighorn ideas but suggested that as part of this assignment I have students conduct original, primary-source research using 1876 newspaper accounts found in the Library of Congress. I contacted the head of the Newspaper and Periodical Division of the Library of Congress. He sent me a complete list of all the 1876 newspapers that were in the library's collection and advised me as to how to get my students permission to use the material. (Students sixteen or older may use the collection of the Library of Congress with permission of the curator of the Newspaper and Periodical Division.)

Pohanka also suggested that I look at an Arts and Entertainment Network Biography episode on Custer called *George Armstrong Custer: America's Golden Cavalier* (1996). I ordered the film. The film included interviews with a number of historians, and shortly after watching the film, I contacted them at their various colleges and universities. I was not only having my students explore the conflict, but also study the mythmaking of this event. It was important to me that they understand how "winners" have the means and necessity of constructing a particular version of history. Not only did I want my students to study the event, but I wanted them to look at the history of the interpretation of the event, through film, artwork, and music.

One of the sources to which I was directed were back issues of *Montana: The Magazine of Western History*—in particular the Winter 1991 issue featuring Paul Andrew Hutton's article, "Correct in Every Detail:

General Custer in Hollywood" and the Autumn 1996 issue and the article "What Valor Is: Art and the Mythic Moment" by Brian W. Dippie. "Correct in Every Detail" is an analysis of the plethora of films that tell the story of Custer's Last Stand. This line, "correct in every detail," the last line in the film *Fort Apache* and spoken by John Wayne, seems to resonate throughout any serious research or scholarship about the Little Bighorn, as for over 125 years historians have been trying to unravel what took place in Montana in 1876. It begs the question where does fiction end and history begin? Knowing that I could not show all of the movies related to the battle of the Little Bighorn, I settled on the best-known films and, using the money provided by Smith, purchased *The Plainsmen* (1937); *They Died with Their Boots On* (1941); *Fort Apache* (1948); *Sitting Bull* (1956); *Custer of the West* (1968); *Little Big Man* (1970); and *Son of the Morning Star* (1991).

I decided that I would break the class into groups of students who would watch each film in teams and then report their findings to the class as a whole. I chose the previously mentioned films because they seemed to represent a fairly good cross section of Hollywood interpretations. The films range in their interpretation of the battle from *They Died with Their Boots On*—a rousing patriotic expression of this tale on the eve of American entry into World War II, to *Fort Apache*—a piece about the many sacrifices made by America during World War II, to the much darker *Little Big Man*—a film that is really more about American participation in Vietnam, starkly set during the Plains Indian Wars and reflecting a more cynical view of the American West and the United States military. You can find a synopsis of each film in Appendix A and Appendix B.

I was able to locate slides of various artistic renderings of the battle in the collection of the Buffalo Bill Historical Center in Cody, Wyoming. Referring to the article by Dippie as well as his book, *Custer's Last Stand: The Anatomy of an American Myth* (1994), I knew which specific images I wanted to use, particularly the famous *Custer's Last Fight* (1896) by Otto Becker, which was mass produced by the Anheuser-Busch Company and sold to bars and saloons all over the United States, and Edgar S. Paxson's 1899 interpretation of the battle. These two paintings are housed at the Buffalo Bill Historical Center, and I was able to obtain slide images of them as well as two other artistic renderings, including a poster from Buffalo Bill's Wild West featuring Custer's Last Stand as the climax to the program. I was even put in touch with artist Eric von Schmidt, whose painting *Here Fell Custer* (1976) is considered the most realistic and historically accurate image. Von Schmidt was kind enough to send me a copy of the painting because I would be using it for academic purposes only. Enlisting the support of the former chief historian of the National Park Service and Little Bighorn Battlefield National Monument,

Robert Utley, and noted American Indian historian Herman Viola, I proceeded with my planning. Utley agreed to participate in a telephone conference with my students, and Viola agreed to meet with my class as a guest speaker. A phone call to the National Park Service office and staff at Little Bighorn National Battlefield Monument garnered me some additional educational material.

Finally, I rummaged through some old vinyl records I had and found a copy of a 45 rpm recording of the 1960 hit song, *Mister Custer* sung by Larry Verne. This is a humorous song about the battle and uses images in the lyrics that today we would find offensive. My idea of using it was to demonstrate to my students the range of material affected by Custer's Last Stand. I went to the Internet and was able to download the lyrics. During my visit to Little Bighorn, I purchased a music compact disc of Seventh Cavalry songs, including two of Custer's favorites: "Garryowen," which he adopted as his regiment's tune and "The Girl I Left Behind Me." Using the Internet, I was also able to find copies of these lyrics. Providing students with lyrics of the songs I play allows them to follow along and to understand the words. At a local music store, I uncovered a hidden gem, a music compact disc of American Indian songs, including the Indians' victory song over Custer. By the time November arrived, I had put in four solid months of preparatory work and was ready to launch the unit.

Teaching the Unit

Providing students with background information to put the project in historical context is essential. Granted, seniors who are enrolled in Applied History should have the basic background premise from their US history curriculum, but because this conflict is, like most conflicts, complicated, it warrants student preparation.

Student Preparation

On the first day, I provide each student with a copy of the *National Park Service Guidebook to Little Bighorn* by Robert Utley and a folder that contains the following:

1. a detailed, class-by-class work plan outlining our approach to the topic

2. two worksheet/video guides for the two documentary films I will show in class, the A & E Custer biography I have previously discussed and the film from the American Experience series, *Last Stand at the Little Bighorn*

3. a copy of a handout provided to me by Fort Laramie National Historic Site that provides important background information relative to the 1868 Treaty of Fort Laramie, which is crucial in understanding why the Plains Indians Wars took place

4. copies of the articles by Hutton and Dippie

5. a list of the 1876 newspapers that students will examine

6. a list of the Hollywood movies to be watched

Students are also directed to read the chapter, "A Sore from America's Past That Has Not Yet Healed: The Little Bighorn" from Linenthal's *Sacred Ground: Americans and Their Battlefields* (1991). In addition, the folder includes a complete set of directions on how students are to approach this assignment and what the final project, a research paper, should reflect. Students will write a research paper broken into several sections including an essay on Custer's life; an analysis of artwork— paintings and other visuals—relative to the topic within the context of mythmaking; an analysis of their selected Hollywood film regarding its interpretation of the historic event and a reflection as to how the film mirrors the time in which it was produced; an analysis of their selected newspaper account; and a conclusion. The paper must be documented internally with an annotated bibliography. Generally students have six to eight weeks to finish their work. Much is presented in class, and students respond to various aspects of the unit through journal entries that I require them to keep. The whole process works like a series of building blocks—what I discuss and show in class helps students to understand both the big picture of the Little Bighorn as well as specifics related to the actions on June 25, 1876. The independent research forces them to pull everything together and draw their own conclusions.

Teaching the Unit

On the first day of the unit, I show slides that I took while visiting the site. (You can access these images on my website *www.wshs.fcps.K12.va .us.*) These images include photographs of the battlefield; markers; and archival images of Custer, his adjutants, and Indian chiefs Sitting Bull, Gall, and Red Cloud, who lined up against Custer's command. There are no images of Chief Crazy Horse because he refused to ever have his photograph taken. Slides of these photographs can be purchased from the National Park Service at the Little Bighorn site. Images can also be found on the American History Laserdisk. While showing these slides, I describe the events as they unfolded on that Sunday in June 1876. As best as I can, I provide a slide tour of the battlefield highlighting different places through my lecture. I relate to students the fact that it is very critical to understand the topography of the land to grasp the picture of what occurred. The final slide shows the grave of Custer and his wife in the cemetery at West Point, New York. Custer's wife, Elizabeth (Libbie), arranged with the federal government to have her husband's remains exhumed in Montana and buried with full military honors at West Point. She then spent the next fifty years promoting her husband and his legacy, generating much of the mythology that surrounds this event.

Over the next few class periods, I show the two videos and ask students to use the worksheets I have provided as a guide. The worksheets can be found in Appendix B. The A & E Biography covers the essential life information about Custer and his wife and explores at some level the Custer myth. The second film, *Last Stand at the Little Bighorn*, produced by James Welch and Paul Stekler, examines the Indian side of the battle—it provides a needed balance for the other material I use. Students respond to this film in their journals, noting the difference in perspective that this aspect of the story brings to bear. It is important for me to be certain that they examine both sides of the story so they recognize that this event did not happen in a vacuum.

As we continue our classroom journey back to the Little Bighorn, I play the music I have discussed with songs "Garryowen" and "The Girl I Left Behind" used to create atmosphere. I use "Mr. Custer" to make a point and to reflect not only on Custer's Last Stand and popular culture, but also on Indian stereotyping. While providing some humor about a cavalryman's misgivings about the campaign, the song casts negative images of American Indians, principally through the use of the term "Redskin" and the often-misunderstood practice of scalping (scalps were taken by both sides). The song provides a perfect vehicle to examine Indian stereotyping and how it played into the myth we are studying and how that myth, in turn, came to reinforce the stereotyping. We talk about the name of our local National Football League franchise, the Washington Redskins—and the efforts of some to change the name. There's some discussion of colleges that have changed their Indian mascots or names. I relate the story of Chief Nokahoma, an Indian who used to dance for the crowds at Atlanta Braves' games every time a Brave player hit a home run. Thankfully, the practice is no longer in place. Students are quick to pick up on these issues and are eager to talk about them in mature, objective dialogue. Over the years, we have had good, frank conversations.

Having the students read Linenthal's chapter helps them to see how this event is still contentious in different academic and cultural circles. He explores the controversy that surrounds this battlefield and takes the reader on a historic journey relative to the public memory of the

Little Bighorn while placing it in context of the bigger picture of clashing cultures. I point out that there are plans underway to erect a memorial to the Indians who fought there, but even that has come under fire from all concerned. I ask students to consider why an event that took place in 1876 still resonates with strong feelings today. Why does it have such a hold on our imagination in a way that reflects cultural perspectives? Why should we care? What does it say about being an American?

It takes about a week and a half to present all the aspects of the Little Bighorn that I need to cover in class, including looking at the paintings and hearing our guest speakers and commentators. Robert Utley takes the view that you cannot judge people of the past based on the conditions and parameters of the present. Herman Viola takes a more sympathetic view of the Indian side of the story. Utley and Viola are friends, and it's good for students to see that friends can respect each other and their opinions and yet hold countering viewpoints on the same topic. When Viola comes to my class to speak, he brings slides of Indian paintings of the battle that totally counteract the images painted by white artists at the end of the nineteenth century. He also provides students with a glimpse of Plains Indian culture, which I believe is essential for them to understand the culture clash that was involved with this episode in American history. His slides of Indian drawings of the battle and its aftermath clearly show a different view from what was offered by white artists one hundred years ago.

I like to point out how after the battle Indian women scoured the battlefield and mutilated the dead, not out of disrespect, but rather in an effort to send a message to the dead soldiers in the afterlife to remind them that they had committed a wrong in their present one. For example, Indian women ran sewing awls through both of Custer's ears so that in the next life he would hear better. According to the Cheyenne, Custer failed to heed a warning that was directed to him about the price he would pay should he attack the Cheyenne nation in the future.

When we examine the paintings of the battle, I point out that not only are the nineteenth-century paintings off-base historically (forensic evidence gathered over the years clearly refutes these interpretations), but that the Otto Becker image, by which most Americans learned visually about the battle, is replete with errors—most notably that the Indians are dressed like African Zulu warriors and that Custer is seen dressed in buckskin and brandishing a saber. Custer and his men did not carry their sabers with them on campaigns in the field because they were too cumbersome and would have rattled, making needless noise. The best artistic interpretation we have is the Eric von Schmidt painting, which was completed after almost twenty years of extensive research. It is also unusual in that the painting is from the view on top of Last

Stand Hill—it's from the perspective of Custer's men. No other artist devoted nearly as much painstaking time to try to get the story right.

Student Work

After all the classroom instruction has been completed, it's time for students to select their newspaper accounts and decide who will watch which Hollywood film. The students pick their newspaper from a hat, and I let them form teams and choose which film to watch. For the next month, students are on their own conducting their research. I have books placed on reserve in the school library, students have the option to use some records from the National Archives, and they do their newspaper research at the Library of Congress. I am available to assist them or monitor their progress if they so desire. One way you might approach this aspect of the assignment is to have students research newspaper accounts from your community covering the event or to create a similar kind of assignment using records from your local library or historical society. In addition, the old news journal, *Harpers Weekly,* is on microfilm and can be easily secured at many local public libraries or through Inter-Library Loan.

The papers are due in mid-January, and the students are expected to present their film as a group, sharing with classmates their analysis of the film's interpretation of the Last Stand. Students also complete two additional entries in their journals about their working with 1876 newspapers and on what they learned from the entire assignment. By the time the due date arrives, students have worked through a complex multilayered narrative of a landmark event in the nation's story. What they take away from the assignment is an appreciation for how history is often recorded or not recorded. They recognize that in the construction of the past, some things are not equal.

This is not to say that all students reach the same conclusion about the interpretation of the event. Some students have a difficult time accepting Indian oral history traditions of the battle because that kind of historical memory is generally not provable with empirical data. However, Herman Viola has published some recent scholarship about the Indian side of the story as told to white photojournalist Edward S. Curtis in 1907 by some of Custer's Crow scouts. This dimension of the story can be found in his book, *Little Bighorn Remembered: The Untold Indian Story of Custer's Last Stand* (1999). Curtis, who was out in Montana recording various accounts of Indian life for President Theodore Roosevelt, happened to meet some of Custer's aged Crow scouts. Their side of the story seemed to indicate Custer's poor judgment in approaching the battle and his failure to support some elements of his command that were already engaged. Curtis sent his findings to Roosevelt, who instructed Curtis not to publish the story because it would besmirch the reputation of a great American soldier and hero. When my students learn this from Viola, they have to weigh why Roosevelt would have prevented part of the truth from being told and compare that to the general treatment and regard given to Indians by a large portion of the white population of the time. Many of the students are quick to point out that the language used in the newspaper accounts is somewhat heavy-handed—describing the Indians as savages and beasts.

The papers that are submitted for evaluation reflect serious scholarship. Students are able to grasp the big picture and recognize that this event is a microcosm of the attitudes and government policy of the times. What also works well are the presentations matched to the various Hollywood films. Each group gets five minutes to encapsulate their film and share with classmates the film's nuances and subtleties. By the time they share the films, they are quite aware of the producer's intended subtext. This is best illustrated through the films *They Died with Their Boots On, Fort Apache,* and *Little Big Man.* These films are more than docudramas of Custer's Last Stand and the Indian wars; they are all classic reflections of the times in which the movies were made. Students also get to be in a way historic forensic detectives because they are so immersed in the historic reality of the subject that they are able to level all kinds of historical criticism at their films. For example, those students who watch *Sitting Bull* (1956) are quick to point out that the battle sequence is far from any sort of historical reality—often they laugh as they make their presentations because this film ends with President Ulysses Grant shaking hands with Chief Sitting Bull in the aftermath of the battle, not to mention the cumbersome romantic subplot between a cavalryman and his intended wife. We all can equally share in their laughter.

I also like to have students compare notes on their newspaper accounts because they all research different newspapers. It is not surprising that Custer and his men received press that glorified him and made the Indians savage and deplorable, when taking into account the sense of Manifest Destiny and racism that had swept the country in the last part of the nineteenth century. Custer and his men became martyrs and their deaths symbolized the beginning of the end of the Plains Indians. When Robert Utley was asked if the Custer myth would fade away, he replied, "It will not fade away—it will always remain in many aspects a mystery. That will keep it alive." I also like to have students compare and contrast the different newspaper reporting because it reflects various regions of the country. This, too, provides them another window to interpretation and bias.

As mentioned earlier, students keep ongoing journals that follow their progress. As a concluding journal response, I ask students to write about what they have learned as the result of this assignment. This is a good way for me to get important feedback as to how I might best modify the unit from year to year. Priya wrote:

> The first thing I learned from the story of Custer is that he just won't die. This is important because Custer is one of those American icons that existed but I never knew much about. In general I learned how frustrating research can be, through my visits to the National Archives and the Library of Congress. I particularly enjoyed this assignment because it allowed me to incorporate aspects from previous papers (we had done in class) into one that was well organized. I can truly say that Custer's Last Stand allowed me to see that finding connections between the past and the present over time is extremely useful in putting together a puzzle that can produce surprising conclusions. Overall I learned that Custer is a legacy that is just one part of American culture that has expanded and changed through the game of telephone over time.

Ellen related in her journal:

> This paper was not only a lesson about Custer, but a lesson in historical interpretation and analysis. The most beneficial part of this paper was having a chance to compare multiple—and often contradictory— opinions of the same event. By analyzing each interpretation I was able to understand the process of weeding out the parts that were obviously fiction from the parts that were fact. I was given the chance to view the same event from at least a dozen perspectives.
>
> At the same time I was able to refine my objective thinking skills. I learned to pay attention to interpretation based only on fact. I took into account personal biases and cultural effects—especially in the movie evaluation. All of this led to a better understanding of the Battle of the Little Bighorn, but also a clearer view of the changing perceptions of history.

The American West

In my advanced placement and regular survey United States history classes, we look at mythmaking in American history, as it is tied to the overall story of the closing of the American frontier and its impact on the native nations of the Great Plains.

To start the unit with these classes, I introduce students to a famous photograph of a mountain of buffalo bones and skulls that was taken in the 1880s. The photograph, which is in the holdings of the Detroit Public Library, can be found in James Welch and Paul Stekler's book, *Killing*

Custer (1994). It takes a few moments for students to let their eyes adjust to the photograph. Once I start hearing comments such as, "That's so gross," or "No way. That can't be a huge pile of bones," I know I have made my point. It's a great exercise in getting students to focus on a historical reality. By some estimates, there were twenty million buffalo on the Great Plains in 1865. By 1900 that number had dwindled to less than one thousand. Using the photo combined with the statistical information provides fertile soil to launch teaching about the closing of the West and the clash of cultures among American Indians and European Americans and the federal government.

Background Teaching

From the beginning of the school year, my classes examine the whole issue of Indian-Anglo relations from the colonial period to the present. Students study the pattern of encroachment on Indian lands, and we stop to look in detail at issues such as the policy of Andrew Jackson and the subsequent removal of the Cherokee nation, known as the Trail of Tears. Additionally, we look in depth at the idea of Manifest Destiny and its implications with the settlement of the West. The Buffalo Bill Historical Center in Cody, Wyoming, has an excellent outreach program through which they give schools educational packages related to western history. I show the Center's program on "The Mystery of Medicine Wheel," which helps to lay the foundation for understanding American Indian spirituality. Thus, by the time we begin talking about the Plains Indians, students are well grounded in this area of American history. What is really important is to get students to recognize that the federal government put much energy into their dealings with the various Indian nations. From their perspective, it was for the good of a nation that was rapidly industrializing and increasing in population.

By the time our unit on the West is over, I want all my students to have a content-based foundation in which they recognize the following essential knowledge:

- culture clash between Indians and whites, including the differing ideas of land ownership and spirituality;
- assorted legislation and treaties such as the Dawes Act and the treaties of Fort Laramie;
- the role of the railroad and telegraph in bringing an end to the Indian way of life;
- the federal policy of reservations;
- the influence of immigration;
- the eradication of the buffalo;

- the Indian Boarding School program;
- important military engagements;
- significant personalities on both sides;
- the implication of the Turner Thesis (1893); and
- an understanding that there were some reform-minded whites who did have what they thought were the best interests of the Indians at heart.

Once students get a handle on this information, I am ready to proceed with the extension activities tied to the unit.

Getting Started

I begin with a brief lecture covering the important concepts as just described. Depending on how your school day is arranged, you can get through this material fairly quickly by using a couple of methods. The Center for Learning has published some wonderful reproducible lesson plan books for both advanced placement and regular survey students. They offer a range of self-contained lessons from which you choose. The Social Studies School Service catalog carries the Center for Learning material. I also like to use slides of two paintings that capture nineteenth century white romantic ideas about the West, namely Emanuel Leutze's *Westward the Course of Empire Takes Its Way* (1856), which is located on the Senate side of the United States Capitol, and George Caleb Bingham's *Daniel Boone Escorting a Band of Pioneers West* (1852). These two paintings capture so vividly the preconceived ideas that Americans held at the time about the Westward movement. Showing them helps students to see how attitudes were formed and how these attitudes were translated into art. They serve as excellent prompts for exploring the foundations of mythmaking in American history.

I also like to show the film *In the White Man's Image* (1991) from the American Experience series. This moving film chronicles the history of the Indian Boarding School program operated for close to fifty years by the federal government. It is an intense look at the accepted idea that was held by many whites of the late nineteenth century that it was best to "kill the Indian and save the man." It's a powerful film that can get students to recognize the extremes to which the government went in an effort to deal with the Indian question. Some students express outrage, others sadness.

Once we are underway, I provide students with a copies of the handout from Fort Laramie National Historic Site to give them a perspective and background of the treaty arrangements between the Indians and the government. They read the handout for homework, and then we discuss it the following class period. I am careful to have them note that the 1868 treaty specifically stated that the Black Hills in the Dakota territory were off limits to white encroachment.

Buffalo Bill and Frederick Jackson Turner

In some ways, this unit was inspired by a film I also showed one year. My department had purchased the video set of the History Channel's production of the series, *Great Minds of American History*, in which Roger Mudd interviewed well-known and influential historians. The segment "Richard White on the American West" (1998), takes an excellent look at the historiography of the Westward movement and its subsequent interpretation. White, who is a professor at Stanford University, explains how the settlement of the West has been mythologized, and he offers two reasons as to how and why this happened: "Buffalo Bill's Wild West," which was never referred to by Buffalo Bill as a "show" because he believed he was providing audiences an authentic, living document of the West; and historian Frederick Jackson Turner's 1893 thesis "The Closing of the Frontier in American History." I also located a book called *The Frontier in American Culture* (Grossman 1994), which contains an essay by White.

With White's essay in hand, I met with our school reading specialist, Marlene Darwin, and asked her if she would be willing to help me help my students pull the important information from White's essay. She was more than willing to help. We met several times before she spoke to my classes and culled what we thought were the main points. White argues in both the *Great Minds* program and his essay, "Frederick Jackson Turner and Buffalo Bill" that these two men did more than any other western figures to shape how Americans came to perceive the West in the American narrative. He examines how Jackson set in motion a pattern for scholars to consider the closing of the laboratory of democracy as being the end of a three-hundred-year historical pattern and that the availability of land and open space shaped American history. Based on his reading of the 1890 census, that pattern was then closed. Though no longer accepted in academic circles, White is quick to say that the Turner thesis in its own way became part of the mythology of the West. As for Buffalo Bill, White asserts that Cody, through his "Wild West," brought a particular view of the West to mass audiences, a view that validated their preconceived ideas of the West. In his narrative, Indians become the aggressors, whereas in reality it was whites' moving in on Indian land and territories—it's sort of a flip-flop of historical reality. Hollywood merely took Cody's vision and interpretation and brought it to the next level.

Darwin pulled together a template program from Inspiration software and created a schematic that students could fill in based on their watching White's film and reading his essay (see Figure 2–1). We gave the students several days to work through the activity. The next step was to go over with them what they had extracted from their reading and viewing and make sure that they had the right information filled in on their templates. Once students had the basic understanding of the ideas expressed by White and his view of the West, we were ready to move on. I was particularly interested in having students hook on to White's notion that Hollywood film interpretation can offer a view of the Indians as either aggressors or victims of this conflict depending on the film, the time period during which the film was produced, and the director's bias. Again, relying on Hollywood as a tool, we dove in to create our own interpretations of the West. The A & E Biography film *Buffalo Bill* (1996) also helps students grasp the topic.

I had students watch one of several classic Westerns to see if they could pick up the trends in their film as it related to what they had learned in the introduction of this material. The motion pictures I chose were *Stagecoach* (1939), *Fort Apache* (1948), *She Wore a Yellow Ribbon* (1949), *The Searchers* (1956), *Cheyenne Autumn* (1964), and *I Will Fight No More Forever* (1976). Certainly there are many more films from which you could choose, but I settled on these for their length and their classic quality.

Again, students self-selected groups and picked the name of their film from a hat. They would have to spend one afternoon after school viewing their film. Prior to showing the films, I went to the Internet and downloaded a copy of their generic film analysis worksheet from the website *www.teachwithmovies.org*. This worksheet, based on Bloom's taxonomy, helps students to focus during the film. I simply adapted it to fit the theme of the Western films.

Because music makes up a big part of my teaching repertoire with this material, I usually have Indian music playing on my classroom stereo, generally the Indian flute music of R. Carlos Nakai. His haunting sounds set a kind of tone. One year, my student Matt introduced me to the Dave Matthews song "Don't Drink the Water." The music video and lyrics were in the spirit of the unit and my objectives. I decided I would also dovetail a song from the musical "Annie Get Your Gun," the story of Annie Oakley. In the original Broadway show and in the 1966 revival, there was a song called "I'm an Indian Too." It's a song laced with stereotypical imagery of American Indians. I obtained a copy of the music and lyrics and put together a lesson comparing and contrasting the Dave Matthews song to Irving Berlin's piece. I gave students copies of lyrics for both songs and played them. What followed was an intense discussion. They really liked the Dave Matthews song, and Amanda, a Dave Matthews fan, excitedly remarked, "I love that song, but never listened to the lyrics. Wow!" Students also picked up on the derogatory nature of the lyrics to "I'm an Indian Too." I explained that

Figure 2–1

Frederick Turner Jackson/Buffalo Bill Template

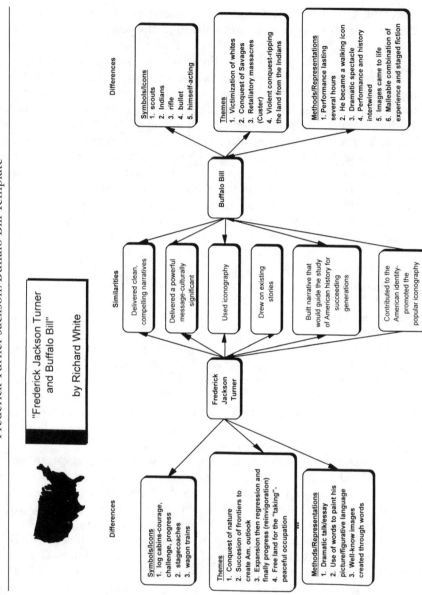

the song had been eliminated from the most recent revival of the show—the main Indian character in the musical, Sitting Bull, had been changed from being a figure of comic relief to a character of dignity. Again, I wanted students to see that nothing historical stays the same over the shifting attitudes of time. It was a great way to launch our film component.

The afternoon of the festival, the students shuffled in at 2:30 and I dispatched them to different classrooms to watch their films. I'm amused when I hear students' initial negative comments, and then see their attitudes soften as they watch their films. One year, Jessica whined about having to watch *Stagecoach*. "Man, Mr. Percoco," she said. "This is black and white. I'm going to die." Two hours later she had changed her tune, telling me that it was a really good movie.

Before students watch their selected films, I instruct them to look for patterns of how Indians and whites are depicted. In particular, I want them to determine if the Indians are viewed as either aggressors or victims. Students should be prepared to observe the following:

1. the plausibility of the film's plot
2. the physical appearance and countenance of the Indians and whites
3. the settings in which violence erupts with a keen eye toward who started the violence
4. the use of language by both Indians and whites as they describe themselves, each other, and the world
5. the use of music during particular scenes

I ask students to select one clip from their film that depicts the film's interpretation and be ready to share it with the class as a whole, including their explanation of the film and the scene.

During the next class period, students make their presentations to their classmates. As part of their presentation, they have to explain the film's plot, and identify the director, characters, and stars. Students present the films chronologically according to when they were produced. I want them to notice that the first five films are all John Ford productions and that initially his view of Indians was as aggressors; but by the time he made his last film, *Cheyenne Autumn*, he had changed his interpretation of Indians to being victims. We discuss the possibilities of what caused such a dramatic shifts in perspectives. This shift is most noticeably present when the students present the film *I Will Fight No More Forever*, the tale of the Nez Perce tribe's attempted flight to Canada, which was produced in 1976, well after the American Indian Movement was underway. In this film, the Indians are seen as the objects of the pursuit of the federal army in 1877. At one point, the character Captain

Wood, played by Sam Elliot, who is sympathetic to the Indian's cause, offers a reflection on the way the Indians have been treated, suggesting that in a hundred years Americans will be ashamed of what they did to the Indians. This film is capped by a moving rendition of Ned Romero's recitation of Chief Joseph's famous, "I will fight no more forever" speech. I think it's one of the best films a teacher can show, and the film was hailed by American Indians when it was produced as a television film.

Follow-Up Tasks

There are several more activities to follow up student learning and put closure on the unit.

Movie Posters   Students make a movie poster of an original film about this topic that they would produce if they had a chance to do so. Andrew's poster is shown in Figure 2–2. They submit a plot summary of their film with the posters. I want them to make connections with their learning. Students then present their posters to the class and I display them on the wall outside my classroom. Some of their film titles have included *White Savage, Battle for the Black Hills, The Victims,* and *The Journey to the Buffalo*. The plots they create for their films are often sensitive tales of relations between Indians and whites, filled with all manner of big picture issues and microcosmic conflicts among characters, government policy, and cultures.

Sculptures and Monuments   As we bring the unit to a closure, I put up on the screen in my room several slides of different public monuments of Indians. You can also find these images on my website. The statues I use are Cyrus Dallin's *Appeal to the Great Spirit* (1909) located in Boston; James Earle Fraser's *The End of the Trail* (1915) found in Waupun, Wisconsin; and Glenna Goodacre's *He Is, They Are* (1992) in Rapid City, South Dakota. Each of these sculptures is a powerful image of Indians coping with defeat. My students are always fascinated with the statues and what usually follows is a solid class discussion based on some prompts I ask them, including:

1. What do you see?
2. What impression or emotion does each sculpture convey?
3. If you could name each piece what would you call it? Why?
4. What connection can be made between what you have learned and these images?
5. Why do you think that white artists made sympathetic sculptures of Indians?

Figure 2–2
Andrew Explaining His American West Movie Poster

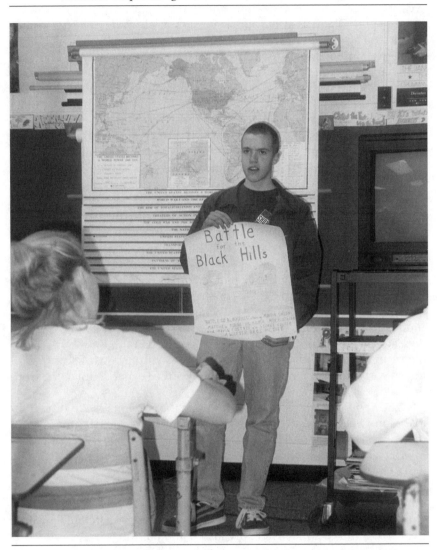

Then I fill students in with the story of each sculpture. Dallin's piece is part of a larger series called the *Epic of the Indian,* which chronicles the relationship between Indians and whites, the last figure being an Indian chief with raised head and hands asking the Great Spirit, "Why?" Fraser's piece, perhaps the most-recognized Indian sculpture in America, depicting a worn-out Indian chief and his pony, was originally to be placed on a cliff in San Francisco overlooking the Pacific Ocean, having literally reached the end of the trail. Finances were a problem and a wealthy local resident of Waupun bought the statue and had it placed in a city park. There is also a plaster version of *The End of the Trail* located in the Cowboy Hall of Fame in Oklahoma City, Oklahoma. Both Dallin and Fraser used Indian models in creating their sculptures, and they both had long-standing, positive relationships with Indian peoples, Dallin actually having been raised near an Indian reservation in Utah. The final work, *He Is, They Are,* is an Indian figure that from the front looks like he is walking forward with his head bowed, his arms behind his back. Many students say that he is meditating or lost in deep thought. Some are sharp enough to suggest that the reason his arms are behind his back is that they are bound, which is the case. I then show them a close-up slide I took of his hands. All of the sculptures reflect a kind of sensitivity toward the Indian plight and as a class we consider why this could be found in art but not necessarily in reality or motion pictures.

I also have on occasion compared these Indian sculptures to those sculptures of cowboys by Frederick Remington, specifically his only public monument, *The Cowboy* (1909), located in Philadelphia's Fairmount Park, and some of his smaller bronze parlor pieces such as the *Bronco Buster* (1895) and *Comin Through the Rye* (1902). Using Remington's work in juxtaposition to the sculptures we have looked at about Indians, I ask students to suggest why these statues of cowboys might appear to be more heroic or more exuberant than the figures of the Indians. It's important to point out that many of these works were produced within the generation immediately after Turner claimed the frontier to be closed.

The United States is filled with public monuments of American Indians, and for that matter cowboys and trailbusters. If you want to complete your own investigation, I suggest that you log on to the Inventory of American Sculpture, at the Smithsonian in Washington, DC, and work your way through their records to see if you can pull up some images that may be near you. I would also suggest that you take a look at James Loewen's book, *Lies Across America* (1999), which also has some vignettes related to Indians, public monuments, and related historic sites across the country. There are also many paintings in American art galleries that you could use to augment these lessons. Try checking with some art galleries or institutions in your vicinity. Again, go online and look up artists such as George Catlin or Charles Russell.

Political Cartoons and Journal Entries   For the next activity, I pass out a political cartoon by *Los Angeles Times* political cartoonist Paul Conrad (see Figure 2–3). The cartoon, from 1995, depicts a solitary Indian holding a sign saying "Deport Illegal Immigrants." The irony of

Figure 2–3
Paul Conrad Political Cartoon

BY CONRAD FOR THE LOS ANGELES TIMES

the image is not lost on the students. Students record their reactions to the cartoon in their journals.

Finally, students respond in their journals to the questions: Could anything have avoided this conflict? and What have you learned from this unit? To the former, Lexie reported:

> I believe it [the conflict] could never have been avoided due to the expansion to the West by Americans. I think the Indians were victims because this was their land and we took it away. Also, most of the Indians did what the white men told them to do, until they would be pushed off their land so far that they had no where to go. Many of the Indians also fought the white man because they were upset. If someone kicked me out of my home, then put me in another place, then still kicked me out of that place, I would be pretty upset, too, and after

a while would want to fight back. The dishonest ways of the white man also added to the conflict because the one thing that the Indians did not like was a liar and a cheater. Overall, I think that conflict between the white man and the Indians was inevitable so long as there was land in the West and expansion to that land. But even though it couldn't have been avoided it could have been dealt with better.

Chris wrote:

Due to the westward expansion there was a great deal of conflict between the Indians who had lived there for centuries, and the white settlers. I do not think that this conflict could have been avoided. Unless of course the Americans just would have stayed where they were and left the Indians alone. It could not be avoided because eventually the Indians would have to confront modern civilization. It is impossible to stay totally isolated forever. Now I do think the situation could have been handled much better. I don't agree with what the Americans did to the Indians at all. I understand why they did it but it still is wrong. I guess for a while they could have built around them and given them space. Why try to totally destroy or relocate them? Even that, though may not have been enough to prevent conflict.

To the latter question, Amanda contributed:

I have learned so much from this unit. I never sat down and thought about the [W]est and its expansion. The Indians were treated so poorly it makes me feel for them. All of their sufferings were because the Native American race and the white race could not get along. The Native American culture was so different from the American culture, we believed they were savages, but in truth because of the government's dishonesty and the way the government controlled food and water supplies we made some of them become savages. . . . I had never really studied the West before so this (a lot of it) was new to me. I wish we could go further with this unit.

It seems as if the students' reactions mirror the words of what was said over one hundred years ago by then secretary of the interior Carl Schurz, a man who sympathized with the Indians but whose government policy did not: "It is a matter of historical experience that nothing that is wrong in principle can be right in practice. People are apt to delude themselves on that point, but the ultimate result will always prove the truth of the maxim. A violation of equal rights can never serve to maintain institutions which are founded upon equal rights."

What works so well with both the units and lessons described in this chapter is how they lend themselves not only to a connection with historical empathy, but also to differentiation activities and alternative modes of assessment. The material can be taught on a number of levels and the levels within the particular content reach all learners. The unit on the West is taught to a wide range of learners, running the gamut from advanced placement to English as a Second Language. I think what makes this kind of learning powerful and relevant is that it reaches a wide population through a variety of means by demonstrating the big picture of American history without sacrificing its human dimensions.

Contemporary History and Indians

I think it is important at some point in your curriculum when dealing with the Indian issue to incorporate stories or lessons about recent historical events and their place in Indian and Anglo memory. One song that has been successful for me in achieving this is Johnny Cash's, "The Ballad of Ira Hayes." Hayes was one of the American Marines to help raise the flag atop Mount Surabachi on the island of Iwo Jima during World War II. I like to play this song with a slide of the *Marine Corps Memorial* on the screen. Cash's song raises many of the issues raised in this chapter regarding the relationship between Anglos and Indians. Hayes was a Pima Indian, a small tribe in the Southwest. Like others from America's minority groups, he served in the military during World War II. As a result of Joe Rosenthal's famous photograph, Hayes returned to the United States near the end of the war a hero. However, he had difficulty adjusting to his newfound status, particularly given the impoverished conditions of his tribal community. Unfortunately, like so many American Indians, Hayes succumbed to alcoholism and was found dead in a ditch on the Pima Reservation. Students respond well to the music and the image.

If you are going to talk about contemporary American Indian questions, you should also discuss with your students the Indian Civil Rights movement and the objectives of the organization, American Indian Movement. Have students conduct outside research into AIM and their onetime leader Russell Means. For one lesson, have a group of students research and use images from the *American History Videodisk* (1996) and the CD-ROM program, *Who Built America?* (1993) that focus on the Massacre at Wounded Knee in 1890. These students can present this episode to your class. Then have another group of students research the 1973 uprising on the Wounded Knee Reservation and present their findings to the class. These students would benefit from watching the PBS film *The Spirit of Crazy Horse* (1992), which explores Indian militancy of the 1960s and 1970s. After both events have been presented, lead students in a discussion in which they can draw inferences and conclusions related to each separate event, but at the same time recognize that both events are tied to a greater whole.

They say that sometimes, at night, when the sun is dipping below the horizon, you can see several spirits of mounted Indian warriors on the crest of Greasy Grass Ridge. Perhaps it was their voices I heard beckoning me to reflect on my prior teaching experience, one that was not nearly so rich until I stood on a little hill in Montana.

Resources

Books

Ambrose, Stephen E. 1975. *Crazy Horse and Custer.* New York: Doubleday.

Bernstein, Alison R. 1991. *American Indians and World War II.* Norman, OK: University of Oklahoma Press.

Billington, Ray Allen. 1973. *Frederick Jackson Turner: Historian, Teacher, Scholar.* New York: Oxford University Press.

Bradley, James. 2000. *Flags of Our Fathers.* New York: Bantam Books.

Brown, Dee. 1970. *Bury My Heart at Wounded Knee.* New York: Holt, Rinehart, and Winston.

Cody, William F. 1979 (reprint). *The Life of Honorable William F. Cody.* Lincoln, NE: University of Nebraska Press.

Connell, Evan. 1984. *Son of the Morning Star.* San Francisco: North Point.

Custer, Elizabeth B. 1913. *Boots and Saddles.* New York: Harper and Brothers.

Deloria, Vine. 1969. *Custer Died for Your Sins.* New York: Macmillan.

Dippie, Brian W. 1994. *Custer's Last Stand: The Anatomy of an American Myth.* Lincoln, NE: University of Nebraska Press.

———. 1996. "What Valor Is: Art and Mythic Movement." *Montana: The Magazine of Western History.* (Autumn).

Faragher, John Mack. 1994. *Rereading Frederick Jackson Turner.* New Haven, CT: Yale University Press.

Fenin, George N., and William K. Everson. 1973. *Westerns: From Silents to the Seventies.* New York: Grossman.

Garfield, Brian. 1982. *Western Films: A Complete Guide.* New York: Rawson Associates.

Grossman, James R., ed. 1994. *The Frontier in American Culture.* Berkeley, CA: University of California Press.

Hammer, Kenneth, ed. 1990. *Custer in 76.* Norman, OK: University of Oklahoma Press.

Hardy, Phil. 1983. *The Western.* New York: William Morrow.

Hutton, Paul Andrew. 1991. "Correct in Every Detail: General Custer in Hollywood." *Montana: The Magazine of Western History* (Winter).

———, ed. 1992. *The Custer Reader.* Lincoln, NE: University of Nebraska Press.

Kassom, Joy S. 2000. *Buffalo Bill's Wild West*. New York: Hill and Wang.

Leckie, Shirley A. 1993. *Elizabeth Bacon Custer and the Making of a Myth*. Norman, OK: University of Oklahoma Press.

Linenthal, Edward T. 1991. *Sacred Ground: Americans and Their Battlefields*. Urbana, IL: University of Illinois Press.

Loewen, James W. 1995. *Lies My Teacher Told Me: Everything Your American History Textbook Got Wrong*. New York: New Press.

———. 1999. *Lies Across America: What Our Historic Sites Get Wrong*. New York: New Press.

Marquis, Thomas B. 1976. *Keep the Last Bullet for Yourself*. Algonac, MI: Reference Publications.

Neihardt, John G. 1979. *Black Elk Speaks*. Lincoln, NE: University of Nebraska Press.

Panzeri, Peter. 1995. *Little Big Horn 1876*. Oxford: Osprey.

Rankin, Charles E., ed. 1996. *Legacy: New Perspectives on the Battle of the Little Bighorn*. Helena, MT: Montana Historical Society Press.

Rosa, Joseph G., and Robin May. 1989. *Buffalo Bill and His Wild West*. Lawrence, KS: University Press of Kansas.

Russell, Don. 1960. *The Lives and Legends of Buffalo Bill*. Norman, OK: University of Oklahoma Press.

———. 1968. *Custer's Last*. Fort Worth, TX: Amon Carter Museum.

Sorg, Eric. 1998. *Buffalo Bill: Myth and Reality*. Santa Fe, NM: Ancient City Press.

Steltenkamp, Michael F. 1993. *Black Elk: Holy Man of the Oglala*. Norman, OK: University of Oklahoma Press.

Turner, Frederick Jackson. 1894. "The Significance of the Frontier in American History," *Annual Report of the American Historical Association for the Year 1893*. Washington, DC: US Government Printing Office.

———. 1920. *The Frontier in American History*. New York: Henry Holt.

Utley, Robert M. 1973. *Frontier Regulars: The United States Army and the Indian, 1861–1891*. New York: Macmillan.

———. 1988. *Cavalier in Buckskin*. Norman, OK: University of Oklahoma Press.

———. 1993. *The Lance and the Shield: The Life and Times of Sitting Bull*. New York: Henry Holt.

———. 1994. *Little Bighorn Battlefield*. Washington, DC: National Park Service.

———, ed. 1977. *Life in Custer's Cavalry: Diaries and Letters of Albert and Jennie Barnitz, 1867–1868*. New Haven, CT: Yale University Press.

Viola, Herman J. 1990. *After Columbus*. Washington, DC: Smithsonian Books.

———. 1999. *Little Bighorn Remembered: The Untold Indian Story of Custer's Last Stand*. New York: Times Books.

Welch, James, with Paul Stekler. 1994. *Killing Custer: The Battle of the Little Bighorn and the Fate of the Plains Indian*. New York: W. W. Norton & Company.

Wert, Jeffrey D. 1996. *Custer*. New York: Simon and Schuster.

White, Richard. 1993. *It's Your Misfortune and None of My Own: A New History of the American West*. Norman, OK: University of Oklahoma Press.

Yost, Nellie Snyder. 1979. *Buffalo Bill: His Family, Friends, Fame, Failures, and Fortunes*. Chicago: Sage Books.

Videos/Films

Buffalo Bill: Showman of the West. Producer: Robert Kirk. 50 minutes. Greystone Productions, 1996, videocassette.

George Armstrong Custer: America's Golden Cavalier. Producer: Craig Haffner. 100 minutes. Greystone Productions, 1996, videocassette.

Great Minds of American History: Richard White on the American West. Producers: Steve Atlas, Tim Smith, and the History Channel. 50 minutes. Unapix Entertainment, 1998, videocassette.

In the White Man's Image. Producers: Christine Lesiak and Matt Jones. 60 minutes. Native American Public Broadcasting and the Nebraska Educational Network, 1991, videocassette.

Last Stand at the Little Bighorn. Producers: James Welch and Paul Stekler. 60 minutes. Midnight Films, 1994, videocassette.

The Spirit of Crazy Horse. 60 minutes. Frontline Productions, 1992, videocassette.

Chapter Three

The Central Dilemma
Race in American History

*There can be no perfect democracy curtailed by color, race, or poverty.
But with all, we accomplish all, even peace.*
—W. E. B. DuBois

I was going to see Wild Man's. That's all I knew as I eased my car across the train tracks into the small village of Kennasaw, Georgia. I had been advised by a friend of my father's that it was a must to visit Wild Man's before leaving the Atlanta area. What or who he was, I had no idea. No clues had been given, except for my host's wry smile. As I crossed the railroad tracks and entered the small town, I could see before me a row of buildings that looked as if they were right out of the antebellum South. Clearly, they were vintage nineteenth century. Recalling my Civil War history, I knew that this community was known for one small incident that took place here during the Civil War: the beginning of Andrew's Railroad Raid, made popular by a Walt Disney film in the 1960s. Nearby was Kennasaw Mountain, the site of an important battle during William T. Sherman's Atlanta Campaign in the summer of 1864. Still, I had no idea that I would shortly have to sort through some awkward feelings—feelings that still exist in modern America that were not resolved when Lee surrendered to Grant at Appomattox.

As I parked the car, I felt as if I should be tying my horse to a hitching post. The name "Wild Man's" was hanging over the front of a small entrance. In the window, my eyes caught a large white sign, edged in gold and with large gold letters that read, "We Celebrate National White History Year." Struck by these words and what they implied, I immediately knew that I was going to be entering an establishment that would be totally foreign to me. Before I entered the portals to Wild Man's, I noticed a beat-up old station wagon with bumper stickers affixed to the body, mostly of Confederate battle flags and pro-South, pro-gun, and pro-white slogans. As I entered the store, my senses went reeling as a pungent, earthy odor caught my nose. Behind the counter sat a burly man, who I presumed to be Wild Man. Walking through the small, seedy shop I was first taken by a sign on one of the bookshelves that read something to the effect, "If you're not buying then stop looking. This ain't no library. You want to browse, go there." I was a bit amused at the candor.

Scattered among the Civil War ephemera of swords, kepis (Civil War era infantrymen's hats), and Confederate uniforms, and not at all inconspicuous, were an assortment of racially charged items or knick-knacks. Inside a glass display case were statuettes of sambos and mammies, a poster was for sale with a photo of Hitler exhorting a German crowd with the phrase emblazoned across the top, "I'm Coming Back. And This Time I Won't Be Such A Nice Guy." In another box there was a poster of a stereotypical black male, bug-eyed, looking at a noose. Another poster had another stereotype drawing of a young black male with big lips, drooling over a piece of watermelon. I had never imagined that places like these really existed in contemporary America. What bothered me most was how blatant it all was. There was no pretense that I was in a bastion of segregation and racism. Time seemed really compressed as I tried to take in everything I saw and at the same time beat a hasty retreat back to my car. Only the day before, I had visited the Martin Luther King, Jr., Center for Non-Violent Social Change and the Martin Luther King, Jr., National Historic District. I had stood before King's final resting place, reading the words inscribed on his sarcophagus, "Free At Last. Free At Last. Thank God Almighty, I'm Free At Last." Standing outside of Wild Man's, I really began to wonder just how free "we" really were.

Was I really that naive? Sure I had seen racism rear its ugly head on the television news. The terrible television images of the events that led up to and exploded in the Rodney King Los Angeles riot were all familiar; so, too, were the other litanies of racial strife and injustice documented by the evening news, such as racial profiling, problems of exclusion, exploitation, and cultural or physical violence; but as long as they remained on the television, they remained distant and remote. In Kennasaw, I had the wind knocked out of me.

Every year since I have had this encounter, I have related this story to my students. For some, it is shocking; but for those who have felt the sting of racism and bigotry, it resonates quite differently. The world is not the same for all of us. And so each year I find myself confronting the demon of racism time and time again. I agree with what DuBois said nearly a century ago, that "the problem with America in the twentieth century is the problem of the color line." Here it is at the sunrise of a new century and DuBois' words still echo across the barrier of time.

The story about my visit to Wild Man's may be seen as a story of prejudice and racism. On another level it's also a story about a racial construct, that process by which people acquire cultural traits that are racially linked, that tends to reinforce bigotry and that has shaped our history for many generations.

Dealing effectively with race in the classroom is not easy. It does not come overnight. For me, the journey has had many bumps along the way. I've had to examine my own prejudices and value system. I've had to question America's prejudices and value systems, and I have had to remain open so that I can continue to learn. My teachers have been more than the Frederick Douglasses or Ida B. Wellses of the world, but other people of color including my colleagues at work, parents, college friends, professionals in the world of the academy and public history, and many of my students. To them I owe a great deal, as they have shared with me in various settings their particular struggles.

When teaching about race and its role in American history, I want to ensure that students of all races understand that the differences between us are learned and shaped by culture, not biology. Our students' sense of their racial identification is a product of our history. For white students in particular, it's important for them to be cognizant that white does not equal "normal." As one historian put it, "In our society white has been the cultural default." Most texts and films assume that the normative American is "white" and that other people are variations or diversions. We need to challenge our students to consider the following question. What would it take for us to see American as normatively a person who is of African origin, or Korean, or of African, Irish, Thai, and Indian origin as is Tiger Woods, for instance? Our students' sense of their racial identification is a product of our history. Race is not black/white, it's a rainbow. A song that works well with students, tied to this theme, is "Black Man" by Stevie Wonder from his album *Songs in the Key of Life*. This song, written for the nation's bicentennial, evokes the lives and accomplishments of many Americans, reflecting our national pool of different races, ethnicities, and religions. Some of the people mentioned in the song are Benjamin Banneker, Sakajawea, Thomas Edison, Dr. Charles Drew, and many others. The lyrics can be found on the album or CD jacket. I like to use this song at the beginning of the school year to generate discussion about the people we will encounter in our study of history during the course of the year.

One of the things that marks the history of the United States is that we have never been a homogeneous nation. We have always been a nation of immigrants. This provided the United States with a unique set of racial and ethnic problems that never confronted most nations. Maps showing immigration have had a bias to emphasize east to west migration to the exclusion of important migrations from Mexico and Central America and Pacific rim nations. Some historians argue that the United States truly became a multicultural nation upon the conclusion of the war with Mexico, when the United States absorbed much of the West and Southwest that had been populated by Mexicans and European Hispanics.

My hope here is to provide you with some models of what has worked for me in dealing with this sensitive topic. If you are a white educator, this will mean something entirely different than if you are a black educator or an educator from another minority group. From the outset, I must emphasize that I can only speak from my frame of reference, which is white and male. Anyone who is serious about working in any arena of history must recognize that everything contains some sort of bias. We bring to our study what we believe and value. This helps to shape our understanding of who we are as well as of the past. Additionally, the idea of truth is not immutable. What I see as truth may be something totally different from your vision of truth. If we can agree on this, then perhaps that is the best place to start.

In that twenty-plus years I have taught here, West Springfield has changed as have much of the demographics of the area and nation. When I first arrived, our school was 92 percent white with a 2 percent African American population and the remaining 6 percent split between Asian and Hispanic American students. Today it is roughly 75 percent white with a 25 percent racial mix among blacks, Asians, Latinos, and students with a Middle Eastern background.

Where to begin? I start right from the beginning of American history, incorporating lessons that reflect my need to have inclusion-based instruction provided to my students. At the outset of my classes, I advise students that we will be looking at race throughout the year. The history of America is a sweeping narrative that chronicles the interaction of all peoples at all times. No one lives, works, or plays in a vacuum. History should not be taught as such. However, I still recognize the need to have educational programs such as Black History Month. While it may seem to be "legislated," it's important to realize that attempts to reach the public through such forums are valuable simply because the issue of whether or not we have created a society in which a level playing field is available to all of its citizens has yet to be resolved. Several African American friends of mine have confided that they would rather there not be a formal program such as Black History Month, but that it needs to be in place until we reach the day when that playing field is indeed level.

Beginning the Year

Over the course of the last three or four years, I have begun the school year showing one of two films: either Ken Burns' documentary *The Statue of Liberty* (1985) or Charles Guggenheim's *The Shadow of Hate* (1995). Using these films helps me to set the tone for the year. Gauging student reaction to the films and the subsequent discussions and journal entries that they submit helps me to get a feel for how mature the students are as well as prepare them for the kind of instruction that they will receive in my classroom. Both films can be used effectively to teach not only specific moments in American history, but to provide a forum for dialogue.

Showing *The Statue of Liberty* works well because the concept and definition of liberty is explored from multiple angles. The power of this film evolves from the individuals who make assorted statements about what the Statue of Liberty means to them. Along with the parade of immigrants (some notable like Milos Foreman), who were in some way touched by seeing the statue for the first time, the montage includes statements from writers like James Baldwin who states that "For Black Americans the Statue of Liberty is nothing more than a bitter joke." This kind of prompt makes a good place from which to launch a discussion with students after the film about the merit of Baldwin's remark. Is it valid? I raise this question with students. What kind of perspective does he bring to the narrative and from what frame of reference is he approaching the idea of liberty?

Burns also included comments from former Texas Congresswoman Barbara Jordan, an African American who speaks with a different kind of authority and tone. Jordan's take on liberty is that it is something that needs to be tended to every day or it will erode away. Good discussions can emanate from looking at both Baldwin's perspective and Jordan's, comparing and contrasting the views of two influential African Americans. This helps students to recognize that even within groups there can be differences.

Generally, I ask students to make their first journal entry before I show these films. I ask them what their expectations are of this class. What do they want to learn? What do they want to have accomplished by June? David, an African American student, responded to the effect that he wanted to learn more about the Black American experience than he had learned before. He clearly felt that this aspect of American history had been ignored in his previous academic experiences.

I came across the film *The Shadow of Hate,* while leafing through an issue of *Teaching Tolerance,* the magazine published by the Teaching Tolerance Institute, a branch of the Southern Poverty Law Center in Montgomery, Alabama. Copies of the film were free and came with a teaching kit.

Guggenheim's film is very powerful. It takes the viewer on an odyssey of hate that has crossed cultural and racial lines from the Colonial age to contemporary America. All aspects of hatred are examined, including violence and intolerance leveled at gender, sexual preferences, religion, and race. Prior to pushing the play button on the VCR, I inform students that some of the scenes will be quite graphic, in particular shocking images of African Americans who were lynched. Students will also hear racist language as part of the dialogue. It is always important when showing a film containing sensitive material to prepare students for what they are about to see and hear. Because it is the beginning of the year, I advise my classes that much of our history is filled with such images and language and that my teaching this material is within a historical context. During a film such as this, I like to watch the faces of my students—you can learn a great deal about them by watching their reactions. The narrative of the film is in chronological order and it makes sense to show the film at the beginning of the year, though I could also see the value of the film being shown as a kind of closure activity to a yearlong survey course in American history. Not all of my students feel comfortable with this film. Occasionally I will hear a muffled negative comment float from a student in the class, but generally I have found most of my students open to learning from the message of the film. So as not to deny students a voice, those students who may find objection to the film have the forum of their journals to express their ideas—students only have to share journal entries if they so desire—in this way, privacy can be maintained.

One year, Bridgette, an African American, expressed her thoughts on the film. She thought that it was very appropriate to show and discuss the film, because it dealt with issues that were often swept aside. For her, it was important that all Americans understand that the issues that face African Americans reach far beyond the topic of slavery. I was very glad that she shared her views because I wanted my students to recognize that one of my objectives in class is to raise issues surrounding the dark side of American history during the course of the year. I am not interested in placing blame or making inappropriate historical judgment. It's not my intention to create a sense of guilt among my students about the negative aspects of American history but rather to create a kind of community where we can talk about our differences in a respectful environment. For students to embrace the past and truly learn, particularly when dealing in the arena of sensitive topics, it is important to build a climate in which tolerance and respect are hallmarks of instruction and learning. The lessons that I develop and then teach around this particular theme are specifically designed with this idea in mind.

As one scholar put it to me as I was trying to make sense out of all of this with the intent to be a better informed and more effective teacher, "I think it's important to clarify that *empathy* means having an understanding of why people acted as they did, but not excusing their harmful behaviors. Understanding is not exculpation." She continued, "The issue is not prejudice; it's accepting uncritically power structures and representations that sustain racial hierarchies or looking for those structures and behaviors and trying to change them. Prejudice emphasizes one's values; I'd rather emphasize behaviors."

Much of my teaching is centered around experiential learning, whereby genuine and historical empathy can be developed by students. So, for example, watching a film about Frederick Douglass or reading a diary entry from a member of the United States Colored Troops during the Civil War can elicit from students a response that stirs within them a sense of what it might like to be in the skin of someone else, particularly in the face of oppression. This can be a powerful teaching tool that not only imparts good history, but fosters in students sensitivity to others and their experiences.

A source you might want to consider consulting to prepare you for teaching about race is the book, *An American Dilemma: The Negro Problem and Modern Democracy* (1944) by the Swedish economist Gunnar Myrdal. In 1938, Myrdal and his associates, including Ralph Bunche and Kenneth B. Clark, began a two-year study of African Americans and their condition in the United States. What they concluded was that there was "an ever-widening gap between the American principle of equality and the reality of African American lives." It was recognized at the time as a landmark book that sold more than 100,000 copies and remains an influential work today. However, while many of its findings are out of date and have been altered by subsequent scholarship, the book remains historically significant. At the end of the chapter you will find a wealth of recent scholarship listed in the references.

A film you might want to consider showing or using to acquire background information on race and prejudice is the classic film *A Class Divided* (1985). In 1968, shortly after the assassination of Martin Luther King, Jr., Jane Elliot, a third-grade teacher in Riceville, Iowa, deliberately divided her class into "blue eyes" and "brown eyes" for the purpose of demonstrating the degrading nature of discrimination and segregation. The experiment lasted several weeks. To one group she gave all the rights and privileges they needed to live a normal life—this was the power group. The other group received little or no rights or recognition. Within hours, students in the group with limited or no rights physically and emotionally withdrew. All you need to do is look at their body language. *A Class Divided* is a frightening film because it also demonstrates how racism is a learned behavior. The students in the power group acted as if they did indeed have the power in their relationship to their peers. This is a powerful film that I have used on student leadership retreats because it depicts in a very real way the brutality of segregation.

One of the techniques that has been very successful for me to employ is to have students create historical bumper stickers as part of their assessment. These bumper stickers are intended to be an enjoyable activity that pulls together knowledge that students have learned and to present that knowledge in creative ways. I provide students with a sheet containing some specific directions including "dos" and "don'ts." On these guide sheets, which have grown into actual rubrics, I explain to students that they can't make fun of or malign any group or individuals. It's clearly spelled out. Several years ago I was really put to the test. That year, I began with the use of the film *The Statue of Liberty*, followed by discussion. When I read the journals of several of the students, I was appalled. These journals were outright offensive in tone and language. It was the first time I had run into such an obstacle. The next class session, I reminded students that journals were a freewrite, but that I would be reading them. I thought I had delivered the message clearly. I was also trying to deal with my own beliefs that students should have a vehicle in which to express themselves as long as it was done respectfully. But as September rolled into October, tension between me and this group mounted, until finally one day I exploded. There was a lot of chest pounding on their part and muttering about not having to listen to this "stuff" as they stormed out of the class when the bell rang. My head ached. In frustration, I turned the issue over to an assistant principal who spoke with these students. For a time, things calmed down and got better until I gave out the assignment to create their own bumper stickers. One of the stickers created by these students said "Freedom for All. No Slavery," but juxtaposed on either side of the slogan was a picture of a member of an African tribal group (from *National Geographic*) and a white business executive. The other bumper sticker had something in a similar vein, but the student incorporated a drawing of what is known as the Klan Well. This time I went right to our principal with the issue. She also saw through the students' charade and immediately suspended them for three days, based on their disrupting the educational environment of my classroom. Naturally, we held parent conferences. It was sad to see one of the students' mothers break down when I shared with her his journal entry about *The Statue of Liberty*. But for me it was most important that the other students in this class see just how serious I was about the issue at hand.

This of course was not the only time I witnessed intolerance raise its ugly specter at West Springfield. In one class, white students produced a video in which they role played African Americans talking about the injustices of slavery in light of the Declaration of Independence and Constitution. The problem was that they blackened their faces. I had never had any previous problem with student video productions and previewing student work was not part of my repertoire. I was taken by surprise by what I saw. These students did not mean to offend anyone, they just wanted to make their video seem accurate. As they were from a contemporary era, they did not understand the implications of blackface and how it was perceived by a black student in the classroom. It turned ugly quickly when one of the two black students in the classroom was offended and ran out of the room crying. After much class discussion and meetings with school-based administrators and parents, it was agreed to develop a set of criteria for students and teachers to use in helping guide them when developing video productions. For the white students directly involved, as well as the other white students in the class, it was a lesson about perspective, different viewpoints, and the tantamount place that race has in modern America.

Studying Slavery: Understanding "We the People"

Until about twenty years ago, most high school survey courses dealt with slavery as a phenomenon limited to the South and generally dealt with the issue within the context of the Civil War. In fact, most standard United States history textbooks usually only mentioned Harriet Tubman and Booker T. Washington in passing. But students today are learning that slavery was practiced well into the nineteenth century, both north and south of the Mason-Dixon line. The idea that the institution of slavery was linked to just about every serious economic endeavor also needs to be examined—for example, New England seafarers and New York businessmen and merchants were just as guilty as southern plantation owners of building fortunes upon the backs of slave labor. Slaves were bought and sold until the 1850s within view of the United States Capitol building, which was in fact also built with slave labor—the very building that we think of as the home of "We the people." It seems to me that the central issue to teaching American history is to understand the shifting notion over time of just what is meant by the phrase, "We the people." Clearly it means something far different today than it did two hundred, one hundred, or even fifty years ago.

One of the best tools to use to give students an idea of the historical ramifications and long-standing history of slavery is to use a clip from the movie musical *1776* (1972). There's a marvelous sequence sung by actor John Cullum as the South Carolina delegate to the Second Continental Congress, Edward Rutledge. He sings a powerful song, "Molasses to Rum to Slaves," which points out the hypocrisy of the northern colonies in their attempt to keep a slave clause in the original draft of the Declaration of Independence. It is a highly dramatic piece that keeps students' attention and forces them to consider the entire system of slavery and the slave trade within the context of early American history. One scene from the film also contains dialogue with the character of Thomas Jefferson, who claims that he has already resolved to free his slaves. Nothing could have been further from the truth—Jefferson only released a few of his slaves upon his death, the rest being sold to pay off his long-standing debts.

This is the kind of juncture in class when you can discuss Jefferson and his relationship with his slave mistress, Sally Hemmings. It's the perfect place to point out that the old maxim "truth is the daughter of time" plays out in a very real sense. In this case, history joined with modern science to lend credibility to the argument that Thomas Jefferson did, in all probability, sire at least one child with Sally Hemmings. Here in Virginia, this story has received a great deal of attention as has the role of the Thomas Jefferson Memorial Foundation and his home, Monticello, as they have had to struggle with evidence that runs counter to the position that they held for many years. And even though I teach things to this generation of students that were never taught to me, I take solace in that perhaps we have matured somewhat as a nation to be able to square off with our history. As Richard Kluger so eloquently points out in his Foreword to his wonderfully monumental book, *Simple Justice* (1977), about the history of the 1954 *Brown v. Board of Education* decision, "Only lately . . . has the dazzle of America's achievement dimmed enough for people to sense the need to distinguish their conceits from a set of humbling truths." This sentiment of inclusion as opposed to exclusion can now be found within the realm of public history. For example, Colonial Williamsburg and the National Park Service can be found at the forefront of instituting interpretive programs for the public regarding slavery and race in America. I encourage you to at least read Kluger's Foreword, perhaps with your students, at the beginning of the school year if you intend to take an honest and direct look at the history of slavery. Additionally, Kluger's second chapter, "Original Sin," is an excellent place for you to find a concise but accurate historical treatment of the politics of slavery and race between 1787 and 1860.

There are numerous lessons that can be developed around the complex institution of slavery. Images of slave ship diagrams and photographs of slave life (including one taken in 1863 in Baton Rouge, Louisiana, showing the back of a slave, named Gordon, covered with scar tissue resulting from the lash) can be found on the *American History Videodisk* (1999). Slave narratives, too, can go far in helping students to understand the kind of life that slaves endured either on the Middle Passage (the horrific journey from Africa to the Western Hemisphere) or on the plantation. I have used the photograph of Gordon a number of times, and each year I hear gasps from my students when they see the picture and understand its content. In some ways that photograph sums up for many students—black, white, Asian, and Hispanic—the absolute horrors of slavery. When preparing students for such lessons and related activities, sometimes the shock method works. In this case, you need to have a feel for your classes. At other times, gradually bringing your students to terms with the full implication may be more appropriate. Certainly, you can fill your curriculum with ample stories about the Underground Railroad. All kinds of rich resources abound, from music to docudramas to narrative accounts. Try playing some slave songs, such as "No More Auction Block for Me" and "Swing Low Sweet Chariot" and ask students to decipher their meanings. The folk group Kim and Reggie Harris produced an entire music CD called *Steal Away: Songs of the Underground Railroad.* All of the songs on the album, be they Negro spirituals, ballads, or contemporary pieces written by the singers/songwriters, are very appropriate for the 7–12 classroom. You can access Kim and Reggie Harris' website at *www.KimandReggie.com.* Give students an opportunity to plan an escape off of a plantation and plot a journey north. This will also help build geography skills because students will be forced to deal with terrain such as mountains and bodies of water just like the runaways had to. It is vital to make sure that students understand that, although the Underground Railroad was a multiracial and quasi-religious movement, its core was the black community and the resources that they brought to bear to bring people out of bondage. One year I played the contemporary song by Stevie Wonder and Paul McCartney, "Ebony and Ivory" and asked students to make links between that song and the actions of people involved with the Underground Railroad. Another idea would be to compare a runaway slave wanted poster from the nineteenth century to a modern law enforcement wanted poster. Examples of runaway slave wanted posters can be found on the *American History Videodisk.* You could compare and contrast the content, language, and images on these posters.

Honest discussions and discourse about the nature and place of slavery in American history also can provide a vehicle for an examination of the often-asked question, "Did racism cause slavery, or did slavery cause racism?" Again, skill, sensitivity, and maturity of your students should serve as benchmarks as you probe this question. Howard Zinn, author of *A People's History of the United States, 1492–Present* (1995), believes that, "Like so much in the American system, it [slavery] was not devilishly contrived by some master plotters; it developed naturally out of the needs of the situation." In this case, the situation was a need for cheap labor.

As I alluded to in my Introduction, sometimes "good guys" often do "bad things." This is one of the central points I try to transmit to my students. Hearing this, particularly for the first time, students sometimes react like little children when they have to down bad-tasting medicine. A number of white students over the years have told me in their journals that they feel guilty for the behavior of people who lived so long ago. This confusion is natural. I assure students from the outset that doing a bad thing doesn't mean that you are a bad person. People who lived before us had difficult choices to make, and followed their own self-interests and maintained their power base without really meaning to harm another person; nevertheless they did.

To try and impart this message to your students, I suggest that you read to them the following excerpt from the novel, *How Few Remain*, by Harry Turtledove (1997). Turtledove, who got his start as a science fiction and fantasy writer, now fashions himself as the "Father of Alternate History." Some of his novels deal with the notion, "What if?" *How Few Remain* is the story of a Second American War Between the States, in the 1870s. The Union lost the first war and the Confederacy remained a nation based on slaveocracy. Now they are at odds again. There is an interesting exchange between Frederick Douglass and Thomas "Stonewall" Jackson, now head of the Confederate military. Douglass, ever still a foe of slavery, is a northern reporter who gets captured behind the Confederate lines. Douglass is released to the North where he is reunited with his family; they hold the following conversation:

> Lewis Douglass asked the question his father had known he would ask: "What was it like, sir, coming up before Stonewall Jackson?" . . .
>
> "It was frightening." He held up a hand before his son or wife could speak. "Not in the way you think, either. It was frightening because I found myself in the presence of a man both formidable and, I judge, good, but one who believes so deep in his heart in things utterly antithetical to those in which I believe, and who reasons with unfailing logic from his false premises." He shivered. "It was in every sense of the word, alarming." . . .
>
> As Lewis put the last suitcase behind the seat, he remarked, "You have said before that it is possible for a slaveholder to be a good man."
>
> "Yes . . . It is possible, but it is not easy. Jackson . . . surprised me."
>
> "I reckon you surprised him, too." Anna patted her husband's arm. (493)

Inclusion Rather Than Exclusion

I like to tell the narrative of American history as the ebb and flow of human interaction. This approach works for me, but it has also required me to think well beyond the standard school resources. There are all kinds of gems that can be used to illuminate and enrich your classes beyond basic instruction. Over the years, I have compiled an extensive slide collection of articles, primary sources, historical paintings, and public monuments. Using such devices has helped immeasurably in augmenting the story of America. Generally, I sort material according to particular themes.

African American War Memorials

My favorite public sculpture is the *Robert Gould Shaw and Fifty-Fourth Massachusetts Infantry Memorial* created by the American sculptor Augustus Saint-Gaudens and unveiled in Boston on Memorial Day in 1897, which honors black soldiers of the Civil War. However, I found an equally compelling war memorial to black soldiers in Chicago. It's simply called *The Victory Monument,* and it pays tribute to black soldiers from the Chicago area who served in World War I, specifically the Eighth Regiment of the Illinois National Guard. When I first found out about the work, I immediately contacted the Chicago Department of Parks. They were kind enough to send me a good photograph plus a handout of the history about the sculpture. In the case of *The Victory Monument,* "the black community began petitioning for a suitable monument befitting the valor of the 'Fighting Eighth.' By the mid-1920s proposals for the erection of a permanent monument in the Parkway of Grand Boulevard were met with stiff opposition by the South Park Commission which had control over the boulevard system. The South Park Commission maintained that there was no space available for such a monument, but relented after the *Chicago Defender* (the city's chief black newspaper) began actively promoting a 'vote no' campaign against the commission board, urging blacks to defeat any project backed by the South Park Commission until due recognition of the community's war heroes was realized." This story speaks legions to students about the enduring poor treatment of African Americans well after slavery had been abolished. Students can see quite plainly that here were black soldiers fighting in a war that President Wilson claimed was "making the world safe for democracy," and yet when these soldiers returned home they were still treated as second-class citizens. The sculpture is quite unique. It consists of a cylinder on top of which is a black doughboy from the period. But what really makes the monument compelling are the allegorical figures around the cylinder, including a black warrior, a black woman symbolizing motherhood, and the figure of Columbia holding a tablet on which is recorded the combat record of the regiment.

Pennsylvania honored its black veterans of World War I with a memorial dedicated in 1935 called *The All Wars Memorial to Colored Soldiers and Sailors*. Actually, this public monument honors black Pennsylvanians who fought in all of America's wars between the War for Independence and the then-called Great War (World War I). It is a period piece depicting World War I soldiers, sailors, and marines, some holding the American flag, around a central plinth. Unfortunately for viewers, this memorial was placed in an obscure part of Philadelphia's Fairmount Park. In 1992, after being restored, the sculpture was moved to a much more prominent place along the Benjamin Franklin Parkway near Center City, Philadelphia. Images of both the Chicago *Victory Monument* and the *All Wars Memorial to Colored Soldiers and Sailors* can be found on my website, as are other black military memorials to the Buffalo Soldiers and the Tuskegee Airmen. I like to show these monuments when we are studying World War I.

After sharing these images with my classes, I then read them a story that really angered me from Kurt Piehler's important book, *Remembering War the American Way* (1995). When World War I was over, the government of the United States gave families of American dead a choice to either bring the remains home or leave them buried in French soil. Many families chose the latter, including African American families. Mothers of American dead were formed into groups known as the Gold Star Mothers. This organization still functions today. Gold Star Mothers of those American servicemen whose remains were left in France were brought to Europe by ship at government expense to see the graves of their kin. White Gold Star Mothers sailed on cruise ships, black Gold Star Mothers crossed the Atlantic in steamers. Many students react very strongly to this little known episode in American history, particularly after we have been discussing a war in which Woodrow Wilson claimed the United States had to fight "in order to make the world safe for democracy." Students are sharp and the irony is not lost. I also tell students that the popular post–World War I song, "How You Going to Keep Them Down on the Farm" was really about the anxiety felt by white Americans now that thousands of black soldiers had fought in France and thousands of others had moved north, filling in jobs for men who had left to go to war during the war in the Great Migration. This story is important to share because it demonstrates how blatant the government was in expressing its view toward African American servicemen, despite them having fought in a war, "to make the world safe for democracy."

Asians and the American Civil War

When I take my students on our annual trek to Gettysburg, Pennsylvania, I like to bring them into the National Park's Visitor Center and show them the "Wall of Faces." On this wall, viewers can look at hundreds of photographs of men who saw combat during the Battle of Gettysburg. One of the images is of Joseph A. Pierce of F Company of the Fourteenth Connecticut Volunteer Infantry. What is very interesting is that Pierce is Chinese. Intrigued, I did some further research in the park's library and found documentation of several Union soldiers who fought at Gettysburg who were Asian. Pierce is the best-documented soldier of Asian origin. In 1842, a New England seafarer named Pierce found a boy at sea off the coast of Japan. He brought the boy to Connecticut and raised the young "Joseph Pierce." I like to show my students this image as well as relate Pierce's story to demonstrate the complexity and the place of diversity in our history.

Chinese and the Building of the Continental Railroad

By far the biggest impact of Chinese Americans in our nineteenth-century history is tied to the story of the building of the Transcontinental Railroad, particularly the Union Pacific stretch from California east to Utah. *The Shadow of Hate* as well as *Us and Them* detail the anti-Chinese sentiment on the West Coast. The film *The Iron Road* (1991), part of the *American Experience,* also examines in detail the role of the Chinese in building the Transcontinental Railroad. Both films document the fact that Chinese lives were considered expendable as they were given the most dangerous tasks to complete as the railroad inched its way through the rugged Sierra Nevada Mountains. Many Chinese lost their lives as a result of explosions and cave-ins. What you can do with students when discussing the building of the Transcontinental Railroad is to explore with them attitudes and behaviors held toward the Chinese that would justify such exploitation. Have students consider what drives people to such negative behavior.

As closure, I like to show students the famous photograph taken at Promontory Point, Utah, documenting and celebrating the completion of the railroad. The photograph can be found in many books on the history of the Transcontinental Railroad and also on the *US History Videodisk.* When I show students the photograph, I ask them to look carefully at what they see and tell me what is missing. It's very clear that there are no Chinese in this picture, yet they played a vital part in the construction of the railroad. My query to students is, "Why don't you think there are any Chinese in this photograph?" Then I ask, "Do you think the Chinese were deliberately excluded from this picture?" What this lesson beautifully demonstrates is how history can be constructed by certain players, specifically the ones in power.

Race and National Policy

To show how race can alter national policy, you can consider using any of the following episodes from American history to make the point that sometimes the government has used race as a means to legally limit individuals' rights.

The Japanese Internment Issue

In February 1942, shortly after the United States entered World War II, President Franklin Roosevelt signed into law Executive Order 9066. Under this law natural-born citizens of Japanese ancestry were rounded up on the West Coast and placed in internment camps. The premise for the government action was the sneak attack on Pearl Harbor by the Japanese. Many officials felt that the Japanese Americans could not be trusted because they might support the Japanese Empire as opposed to the United States.

Given forty-eight hours to sell their homes and businesses, thousands of Japanese Americans were trucked or bused to these camps well inland from the Pacific coast. The camps were crowded, fenced in by barbed wire, and maintained by the War Relocation Authority, a branch of the United States Army.

There are plenty of educational materials available on the question of Japanese internment and the subsequent Supreme Court decision in *Koramatsu v. the United States* (1944), which upheld the constitutionality of such camps. Teachers can explore with students the use of racist anti-Japanese propaganda produced during World War II, including excerpts from the Frank Capra film *Know Your Enemy: Japan* (1945) or other venues produced by either Hollywood or the motion picture branch of the War Department during the Second World War. The National Archives has extensive coverage of the plight of Japanese Americans in their Teaching with Documents Kit, *World War II: The American Homefront*. This resource includes related text, primary-source documents, photographs from the camps, and related lesson plans. Their other World War II kit, *1944: America at War*, also includes lesson plans and material on Japanese American units that fought in Italy during the war. One unit, the One Hundredth Infantry Battalion and the 442nd Combat Team, from the all Japanese American "Go for Broke Division," received more battle citations than any other American units during the Second World War. *1944: America at War* also contains an eight-minute, government-produced film called *Japanese-Americans* that documents these two combat units and that is also a backhanded apology for government policy. By 1944, most Americans had come to believe that the internment of Japanese Americans was plain wrong. And shortly after the war ended, historians agreed that this sad affair was one of the grossest miscarriages of justice in American history. The film *The Shadow of Hate* as well as the magazine *Us and Them* also explores the Japanese internment issue.

An excellent Hollywood film that can be used to raise issues of anti-Japanese sentiment is the Spencer Tracy classic, *Bad Day at Black Rock* (1951), which is a fictional story about a white GI who wants to present a medal to the father of the young Japanese American soldier who saved his life. The problem for Tracy is the encounters of hostility he meets when he comes to the town Black Rock, New Mexico, where the father, Mr. Komoko, lived. There's a great deal of action that students will find entertaining, but the bottom line is a stark depiction of just how deep race and hatred can go in destroying not only the victim but also the victimizer.

The American History Videodisk also includes some wonderful photographs taken by Dorothea Lange for the War Relocation Authority. These photographs document life in the relocation centers. They are moving, as they depict faces of real people who committed no crime yet had their rights denied—the young as well as the old. Some of the most powerful photographs show children. One image in particular shows young Japanese American boys and girls reciting the "Pledge of Allegiance." Showing students this particular image forces them to consider the hypocrisy of the government's policy.

One way you could approach teaching this material is to show the images from the videodisk and read to students an excerpt or two from *Farewell to Manzanar* (1983) by Jeanne Wakatsuki Houston and James D. Houston, which is a heartfelt memoir written by a young interned girl.

It is also important to raise with students the question, Why was this action taken against Japanese Americans, but not German Americans? (There were some, but not many, Italian Americans placed in camps.) What does this fact have to say about attitudes and behaviors held by Americans and our government at the time?

In the National Archives' Teaching with Documents Kit *The Bill of Rights: Evolution of Personal Liberties,* you can find the extensive lesson plan, "The Internment of Japanese-American Citizens: The Bill of Rights Outside of the Fence and Inside of the Fence." The documents in this lesson plan include President Franklin Roosevelt's Executive Order 9066, which authorized the creation of the camps and the internment of Japanese Americans.

The Case of Felix Longoria

An interesting case to have students study is that of the World War II serviceman Felix Longoria, a Mexican American from Texas. He was killed in combat during the war but was denied burial in his local cemetery on the grounds he was Mexican American. The congressman from Longoria's congressional district, Lyndon Johnson, intervened in the case and made arrangements for Longoria to be buried with full military honors in Arlington National Cemetery. Again, the film *The Shadow of Hate* can assist you with instruction about this topic.

Other Attitudes and Government Policy Toward "Others"

The Longoria material can make a great segue for you to study other government policies aimed at exclusion. Go to the Library of Congress' Internet site (*LOC.gov*) and click on the *Thomas Site*. This site is dedicated to American legislative history. From this site you can download such laws as the Chinese Exclusion Act (1882) and the National Origins Act of 1924. Have students read the documents and then in their textbooks review the section on the Know-Nothings. Ask students to consider why there has been a pattern of hostility generated against immigrants, particularly those who are not of Anglo stock. Other questions might include:

1. Why has the power structure in America been mostly in the hands of whites?
2. What fears might be generated among whites that would lead to legislation and behavior that excludes others?
3. How did these excluded groups react to such policies and subsequent behavior toward them?
4. What does all of this say about our democratic principles and traditions?

Luis Jimenez—Mexican American Sculptor

In the film *Public Sculpture: America's Legacy* (1995), there is an eight-minute sequence on the New Mexico sculptor Luis Jimenez. Jimenez discusses his Mexican roots and how that background has shaped his art. He likes to use fiberglass instead of bronze or stone because it is a contemporary material and reflects different colors. In the film, Jimenez discusses his belief that Mexicans and Mexican Americans are discriminated against, particularly in the area of immigration. He takes offense that his parents were called illegal aliens, as if they came from outer space. He dedicated his sculpture *The Border Crossing,* shown in the film, to his parents. The sculptor also discusses the ways in which he integrates Mexican literature and oral story traditions into his work. In showing this film, you can ask students to discuss how a person's race or ethnicity is depicted in his or her work or daily life. Have them consider how one's roots affect daily life, particularly if those individuals are recent arrivals in the United States.

The Alamo

One of the great epics in American history is the siege and battle of the Alamo in San Antonio, Texas. If you believe Hollywood, the mission church was defended by an entirely white group of Texicans. One of the enduring images in American history is Davey Crockett, fighting to the last. However, a more thoughtful approach will indicate that there were also Mexican defenders of the Alamo, called Tejanos. Their story, too, is splendidly recounted in the CD-ROM *The Alamo: Victory or Death* (1995). This interactive CD-ROM is quite easily adapted for classroom use. The narration is excellent and the graphics first rate. One of the ways you can use this film is to dovetail it with a showing of the climactic battle sequences from films such as *The Alamo* (1960), starring John Wayne as Davey Crockett, or the television miniseries *Thirteen Days to Glory* (1994). Have students consider the differences between the more accurate CD-ROM and these Hollywood productions. Why would a CD-ROM produced in 1995 be more accurate than Hollywood films? What does this say about shifts in historical interpretation?

The War with Mexico

PBS produced an outstanding television series, *The US-Mexican War* (1998). Have students make note of the name and compare the film title with what the war is often called in history textbooks: The Mexican-American War. Ask the students what implications can be drawn from the difference in titles. "Mexican-American War" suggests that the Mexicans were the aggressors. Now most historians have reached the consensus that the United States was the aggressor in 1845. The PBS film includes both Mexican and American historians discussing the war and its ramifications for both countries, ramifications that still are in place today given the frequent discord in United States–Mexican foreign policy.

One of the little-known episodes from the war is the story of the San Patricio Brigade (Saint Patrick's Brigade). These were Irish immigrants who joined the American army, only to desert and fight for the Mexicans. To these Irish, the American cause was wrong. They saw it not only as a war to extend slavery, but also a war against Catholicism.

When the war was over, those San Patricio's who had survived were ex-ecuted by the United States. This would make a really interesting re-search project for students.

Other Topics Related to Hispanic Americans and Latinos

Until recently, there was very little work done in the area of the Chicano Civil Rights movement. Now you can find a great deal of information about this important movement in which many Mexican Americans and immigrant people from Central and South America participated. You could certainly break your classes into two groups, having one group research the Black Civil Rights movement and the other group the Chicano Civil Rights movement. As part of their work, they would need to compare and contrast both movements in terms of goals, mo-tivation, and action. An offshoot of this could be an examination of the life of Cesar Chavez and his work with the United Farm Workers Union. Students can explore how he helped to bring the Chicano civil rights to the forefront of American life.

You can check various newspapers online. In particular, the *Los An-geles Times* often runs major stories on issues of importance to Hispanic Americans and Latinos. Based on recent articles, students might be able to investigate how far the Hispanic Civil Rights movement has come and where it wants to go.

A good book for you to direct students to is *Standing Tall: The Stories of Ten Hispanic Americans* (1994) by Argentina Palacios. This young-adult book contains minibiographies of people such as Jaime Escalante, Gloria Estefan, Roberto Clemente, and Admiral David G. Farragut, among others. Some students might read a biography and role play that person's life for classmates. Other students might write a newspaper obituary for one of the people about which Palacios writes. With a vivid imagination and a broad vision that extends you and your students be-yond the classroom, the possibilities are endless.

Race and Confederate Iconography

Students are always interested in a discussion of race and Confederate iconography, namely the Confederate battle flag and Southern war memorials. A good place to start is a reading of Tony Horowitz's *Con-federates in the Attic: Dispatches from the Unfinished Civil War* (1998). This book is alternately humorous and scandalous. Essentially, Horowitz ex-amines the southern Civil War subculture that remains alive and well today. During his travels through the South, he encountered all kinds of people, white and black, young and old, and recorded their reactions to this subculture, his investigation, and to each other. It is really a unique piece of sociology and historiography. We enter Horowitz's world as a class by my reading numerous passages of his book to students. There are so many rich discourses between Horowitz and people and Horowitz and himself that really shed light on this aspect of American culture. The book contains a treasure trove of rich anecdotes from which you can pull to share with your students. In fact, *Confederates in the Attic* is a popular book on our AP United States history summer reading list. A number of my colleagues have also read the book and swapped impressions during lunchtime conversations. We like to share with each other our related personal readings and discuss our findings with each other and to explore their relevance to our classroom instruction. For me, the most compelling chapter is "Kentucky: Dying for Dixie" in which Horowitz chronicles the 1996 story of a black youth who shot a white high school youth for flying the Confederate battle flag from his truck. Reading assorted excerpts from this chapter generates so much energy on the part of students that it becomes quite easy for me to lead them into an exploration of an issue that still, at this writing, strikes the nerve of black and white Virginians. In this Commonwealth, the Civil War still is unfinished business. In 1996, this dichotomy was witnessed in Richmond, the state capital, when a statue honoring tennis great Arthur Ashe was unveiled on Monument Avenue, which for a century had been ground sacrosanct for heroes of the Confederacy.

Using a series of articles and editorials from the *Washington Post* in conjunction with slides I've taken, I've been able each year since the statue was unveiled to explore with students dimensions of race that are not only close to home, but also tied to one of my favorite subtopics, public memory. Students respond in a variety of ways: David, an African American sixteen-year-old, wrote the following in his journal: "I feel that the Arthur Ashe statue is out of place being on the same street as Robert E. Lee: The two were fighting against each other in a sense. The whole issue of the South trying to rise again is in essence them being sore losers." Ellen, who is white, wrote: "I find the placement of the statue to Arthur Ashe on Monument Avenue to be inappropriate. I think it does a disservice to the memory of Ashe. I agree with those who want to place the statue by the tennis courts where Ashe experienced discrimination. I think this would better show his triumph as an African American in a predominately white sport."

Following the discussion on the Ashe statue was a discussion and writing exercise on the issue of the Confederate battle flag flying from the domes of certain state capitol buildings, in this case the South Carolina capitol. Ellen again responded:

I see Southern iconography to be rather strange. I don't see why whites support flying the battle flag of their losing side. It's amazing how the bitterness of whites felt after Reconstruction has survived for 130 years. While I don't have a problem with memorials to great military leaders (Lee, Stuart) I think that these defenders of slavery should not be raised to Christ-like status. People should probably accept that the South will probably not "rise again." It seems like a section of the population is still acting like sore losers 100 years after the fact.

David, another white student, took something of a different approach:

Even though the Civil War has been over for more than a century, some of the turmoil that has risen from the ashes of this bloody war still has to this day been not resolved. Many of the icons from the Civil War are sore points to many people and some icons are misinterpreted as meaning something totally different. For instance many people believe that the Confederate flag is a symbol of racial prejudice, an icon for white supremacists to rally around. In a few cases this can be true. However, many people from the South are not prejudiced and they view it as their heritage. I ask this: who is more prejudiced? The Southerners, or the Northerners who make these assumptions about people they have never met?

But David, the African-American student, sees the Confederate battle flag in a completely different light when he says:

Flying the Confederate flag over the South Carolina State Capitol is just like spitting in the face of black people and those who fought for the cause just alike.

Students have the option to share journals and often are quite willing to engage in good, meaningful conversation with me and their classmates over this issue. If you have created an atmosphere of community in your classroom, where student and teacher self-expression are not threatened, then the debate will be productive. As a wrap-up, I put on an overhead transparency a copy of a Herblock cartoon that appeared in the *Washington Post*. You can see the cartoon in Figure 3–1. This cartoon helps me to demonstrate to students that history is not something confined to ancients, but rather is very much alive as we speak.

A book that you might find of use is James Loewen's *Lies Across America: What Our Historic Sites Get Wrong* (1999). Loewen, in his latest myth-bashing testimonial, presents some pretty compelling and often humorous anecdotes about sensitive issues such as the Confederate flag or southern Civil War memorials. I like to share with students what he has written about the Confederate memorial on Stone Mountain, Georgia. Again, I dovetail this reading with slides that I have taken of this huge bas-relief sculpture to Robert E. Lee, Stonewall Jackson, and Jefferson Davis, none of whom were from Georgia. Loewen points out

Figure 3–1
Herblock Political Cartoon

"IT'S A TRIBUTE TO THEIR HISTORIC STAND AGAINST THE FEDERAL GOVERNMENT WAY BACK IN THE '60s — THE 1960s, THAT IS"

©2000 HERBLOCK

Copyright 2000 by Herblock in The Washington Post

that Stone Mountain was a Ku Klux Klan shrine for a time—a kind of altar for their organization. He raises the question, how is it that one of the largest public monuments in this country is dedicated to the defenders of the institution of slavery? Again, all of this provides great food for thought to raise with your students. I discovered something even more intriguing when I visited Stone Mountain for the first time.

Every summer evening a laser show program is held on the mountain as a tribute to the state of Georgia. During the show, there are all kinds of patriotic images flashed on the mountain representing American and southern history. Along with images about nearby Atlanta's sports franchises, including a large tomahawk chop, at the end of the show the three figures on the mountain "come to life" via laser and ride off the face of the mountain. What I found most interesting was that the crowd in attendance, which numbered several thousand people, was mutltiracial. For a site that is so obviously pro-South, in the Civil War context of the term, the evening's festivities were enjoyed by a wide cross section of the public.

Ironies like this occur all over the country and I think speak to a particular vein about what it means to be an American. Several years ago when I was in Austin, Texas, I visited the Texas State Cemetery. Individuals buried in this cemetery have to be "Texas Patriots" and heroes to qualify for interment. Buried here in a large and ostentatious wrought-iron mausoleum is one of Texas' heroes from the Civil War, General Albert Sidney Johnson, who was killed in April, 1862, at the battle of Shiloh, Tennessee. Some historians believe that had he lived, he would have made a better general than Robert E. Lee. Johnson's grave sits on a knoll overlooking row upon row of Confederate dead, almost as if he was at the spiritual head of his legions. Inside the mausoleum is a marble figure of a recumbent Johnson wrapped in a shroud. It is very Victorian in appearance and feel. Not far away is a more contemporary grave marker, a simple vertical plinth with a medallion affixed to its surface. Chiseled into the plinth are the words "Barbara Jordan—Patriot." How ironic and how totally American. Barbara Jordan was one of Ken Burns' interviewees in his film *The Statue of Liberty*—students may need to be reminded of this. This is a good time to discuss the dichotomies that we as Americans seem to embrace.

As you can see by now, I like to share with my students what I am reading. This is an important strategy I employ to demonstrate to students that I am serious about keeping current with issues as well as to signify that learning is a life-long journey. One year I was reading a very unusual novel and I shared the book, or at least my reaction to it, with my students. The book is *The Guns of the South* by Harry Turtledove (1996). In this novel, he skillfully combines history with science fiction. *The Guns of the South* is based on the notion that white supremacists from South Africa develop a time machine that takes them back to Civil War Virginia in 1864. The objective of these white supremacists is to arm Robert E. Lee's and other Confederate armies with AK-47 automatic weapons, turn the tide of the war and history in favor of the South, and establish a Confederate States of America based on white supremacy. But the book is really more about what happens after the South wins.

The plot line is very compelling and Turtledove does not take the easy way out as the story builds to its conclusion. At one level, the book is quite entertaining, but Turtledove wants readers to be more than entertained. He wants them to consider the role of race in our national legacy. Granted, the premise of the book is far-fetched, but I believe that anyone with a serious interest in race relations, or in teaching American history, should read *The Guns of the South*. It provides excellent food for thought and, though long, might spark students to think about the legacy of that war and what it means today.

Provocative Lesson with a Provocative Photograph

I sometimes like to jar my students' senses when I teach. Visuals can help me to achieve this by really getting students to focus on something at hand. I have employed this technique in a number of ways. It has been used when preparing my students for their reading of DuBois' *The Souls of Black Folk* (1996). I've used it as part of instruction on the Civil Rights movement. When my students are being introduced to Howard Fast's Reconstruction-era novel, *Freedom Road* (1944), I've found it to be equally powerful. I use one photograph in particular, taken by Stanley Foreman of the *Boston Herald-American* (see Figure 3–2). The photograph was awarded a Pulitzer Prize in 1977. I found the photograph in the book *Moments: The Pulitzer Prize Photographs* (Leekley 1978). I made a transparency and class set of handouts. As students shuffle into my classroom, I display the photograph on the screen so that it is the first thing that they encountered for the day's lesson. I provide each student with a copy of the image. Then I pass out a worksheet for them to complete based on their observations. The worksheet is titled, "A Provocative Photograph with Provocative Questions." The questions in order read:

1. What do you see in this image?
2. What do you think may have caused the behavior demonstrated in the photograph?
3. Where do you think, city, state, region of the United States do you think this photograph was taken? What's your rationale?
4. In what year do you think this photograph was taken? What's your rationale?
5. If you could title this photograph, what would you call it? Why?

After giving the students about ten minutes to make their observations and complete their worksheets, we hold a discussion. Generally, students are able to point out what they see: a white man, holding an

Figure 3–2
Students Examining Stanley Foreman's
Pulitzer Prize–Winning Photograph

American flag on a flag pole, lunging, using the flag pole as a spear, ramming into a black man who is being held back by another white man. Students offer a variety of responses to the second question about what might have caused this incident to occur. Some say that perhaps an argument started the fight. Other students offer the possibility that maybe it was taken during a large riot. As to where the photograph was taken, most students respond, Birmingham or Montgomery, Alabama; Memphis, Tennessee; Atlanta, Georgia; or as one student once said, "You know, down South where all that civil rights stuff happened." With regard to the date, there is a wide array of answers ranging from 1870, to 1900, to 1950, to the 1960s and 1970s. Some students are able to use the clothing on the people as contextual clues. Then I ask, "What would you title it?" Some students respond, "The Flag Kills," "America at Its

Worst," "Civilization Torn Apart," and "Stab of Injustice," "America: The Heartland."

Once everyone has contributed something to the discussion I then read the following text from the book *Moments:*

> 1976 . . . America's Bicentennial year here in the cradle of liberty—Boston. [Generally this brings a mixture of gasps from my students.] Flags are flying everywhere. It is ironic that the Stars and Stripes is being wielded as a weapon in an act of frenzied hatred. Raw, ugly racism hides behind increasingly sophisticated masks. This time the issue is busing in South Boston. [I take time here to explain to students the meaning of and concept of busing.]
>
> Two hundred white students gather outside Boston City Hall, carrying signs and banners . . . chanting anti-busing slogans. They sweep into City Hall in an attempt to force a list of demands on the City Council, but find only empty chambers.
>
> A moment of group inspiration as they recite: "I pledge allegiance to the flag . . . with liberty and justice for all."
>
> Suddenly, a group of twenty splinters off from the main bunch, erupting in violence. "Get the nigger. Kill him."
>
> Stanley Forman of the *Boston Herald-American* is out cruising when his police radio alerts him to "trouble on City Hall plaza." He arrives just ahead of the police and sees Theodore Landsmark, a black lawyer, walking briskly toward City Hall, unaware of the imminent danger. "Suddenly they were all over him—punching, whacking, knocking him to the ground. Through my lens I observed the flagstaff, the flag unfurled about it, its pinnacle being thrust at the head of the helpless black man. He struggled up from the pavement, with his attacker restraining him as they would steady a target for the benefit of a marksman."
>
> Theodore Landsmark is treated at the hospital for a broken nose, facial cuts, and bruises over most of his body.
>
> It is not a proud day for Old Glory. (114)

Then I tell my students that the title of the picture is "The Soiling of Old Glory." My class is initially so quiet that you can feel the depth of reflection on all our parts. Then out stream the remarks: "Man. People are such jerks!" "This makes me sick!" "Why do people have to act like this?" "We are such hypocrites!"

I ask students to consider the location of this event with the purpose of getting them to recognize that American bigotry and racism is not and was not an exclusively southern phenomenon. I also ask them to consider the date, 1976. I remind them that this photograph was taken during the national bicentennial—a period of celebration for the creation of a nation based on a set of principles that continue to be defined at this very moment. In many ways, it makes the sometime hypocrisy of America very real. It's a perfect lesson in having students encounter the past within a very contemporary context.

The Souls of Black Folk

I use DuBois' classic book, *The Souls of Black Folk* with my advanced placement students. I have several rationales for having students read DuBois. First of all, I think students need to be exposed to a wide range of American writers and thinkers from a cross section of American life and culture. Second, I want students to wrestle with the issues that DuBois raises. I want them to consider his statement that the "problem of the twentieth century is the color line," and to reflect on how they see that observation within contemporary America. Some students struggle with the concept and the language. And every year I have students tell me that they don't like the fact that that DuBois is simply complaining. I ask them to consider when the book was written and to remember that life in the African American community when DuBois was writing was experiencing one of the worst episodes of racial hatred; *Plessy v. Ferguson* was handed down by the Supreme Court in 1896, the number of lynchings throughout the country, not just the South, was at epidemic proportions, scientific racism was employed by "educated" whites to justify their positions of power. I also tell students that in 1895 DuBois was the first African American to receive a Ph.D. from Harvard; and it was the same year that Frederick Douglass died. I remind them that in 1897 the *Shaw Memorial* was dedicated and unveiled in Boston. (Incidentally, the *Shaw Memorial* was restored by the citizens of Boston in 1982 in an effort to promote racial healing in light of the divisive busing issue.) In order for students to read DuBois in a true historical context, you need to provide them with important background about DuBois, who was a northern black, from Great Barrington, Massachusetts, who never experienced the institution of slavery. Students need this information to help them see the logic of DuBois' ideas. There is an excellent PBS video, *W. E. B. DuBois of Great Barrington* (1992) that can assist you in this purpose. To aid me in my preparation for dealing with this subject, I turned to a special copy of *The Souls of Black Folk* written for teachers and accompanied by a workbook and student guide.

Another part of my agenda is purely academic. I will be having these students write a document-based essay comparing and contrasting the strategies employed by DuBois and his contemporary, Booker T. Washington, to help blacks reap the full blessings of American life. So, as part of my instruction, I read Dudley Randall's poem "Booker T. and W. E. B." to launch them in their examination of the mind-set of the two significant Americans. We talk about Washington's 1895 Atlanta Compromise and his "accommodationist" philosophy. Students also read his Atlanta Exposition Speech, which can be found in the book *Soul of America: Documenting our Past—Volume II: 1858–1993* (Baron 1994a). I also provide a brief lecture on Washington's background as someone born into slavery who went on to achieve and write his landmark autobiography, *Up From Slavery* (1953), and establish Tuskegee Institute in 1881. His goals for African Americans are contrasted with DuBois'. Relying once again on my array of public monuments, I show students the sculpture of Booker T. Washington on his grave at Tuskegee, which the sculptor, Charles Keck, titled *Lifting the Veil of Ignorance*. This sculpture depicts Washington removing a covering from an allegorical figure of a slave or uneducated black man, awakening him to a new day and future. In an interesting twist, some radical blacks during the 1960s bitterly redubbed the statue, *Placing the Veil of Ignorance*. It's ironic that both Keck and DuBois use the metaphor of a veil. In Chapter 1 of *The Souls of Black Folk*, DuBois explains his concept of "the veil" that exists between blacks and whites and how that veil plays daily into the relationship between blacks and whites. Before students write their essay, I have them reflect in their journals about *The Souls of Black Folk*. Lawrence, a white student, wrote:

> During a time of extreme prejudice and racism one of the nation's brightest individuals tried to break through the "color line." DuBois attempted to explain the racial issue to whites or rather he tried to explain the black side of it. Unfortunately after all these years this problem still exists. There is still discrimination at the work place and bigotry in communities. Although it has lessened it still remains a constant reminder of our past. I don't see people as one color or devoid of color. But I still have friends who are black or Asian. I guess what I'm trying to say is that I still recognize that they're different but I don't let it bother me. The world won't ever be able to see everyone as a person first and race or religion next. Hopefully we can look past it to the person and not let it be a determinant to the advancement of the human race. The world has too many other problems to squabble over to let petty differences come between us.

May, an Asian American student:

> I was impressed with DuBois' powerful articulation and eloquence. As a minority expressing his thoughts in a white-dominated world, he was extremely clear and coherent in his explanations. The idea of a double consciousness, resulting from viewing oneself through the eyes of a prejudiced world, is unfortunate, but an undeniable reality both during DuBois' time and the present time. The conflict then evolves from this double-consciousness—the world tells the black man that he is

less, inferior to the white man, but the black man, viewing himself
knows in his soul that this inferiority is not true or moral. Thus the
black man is separated from the white world of thought, dominant because white means majority, separated by an unpenetrable veil. In
essence DuBois accused Washington of more harming than helping
fellow blacks because as a man urging financial stability over political
and social equality, Booker T. Washington basically refused to acknowledge the presence of DuBois' veil. DuBois wanted, strived to
obliterate the veil while Washington wanted to assimilate through the
veil before attacking it. DuBois nevertheless had an undeniable passion for equality which was supported by an impeccable education
and a gifted mind.

Discussions about DuBois and Washington are great places to talk
about black and white comfort levels, a setting where both blacks and
whites can safely discuss race. It's important that my students know
that Washington was able to move fairly freely among the white upper
class, socializing and meeting with individuals such as industrialist Andrew Carnegie. Washington was also chosen to be one of the keynote
speakers at the *Shaw Memorial* dedication and unveiling. I ask students
why he and not DuBois could do such things. Most students are quick
to point out that Washington was not a threat to white interests given
his stance of accommodation. He did not cause whites to feel uncomfortable, something that I sense DuBois can still do.

A DuBois Historical Head

For a closure activity, I have students create a W. E. B. DuBois historical
head. I think this is a great activity to help students develop historical
empathy because they have to try to get into the skin of DuBois. This
strategy makes students respond on a gut level to the kinds of things
DuBois experienced and observed. A historical head activity requires
that students fill in a hollow head profile template, which I provide, with
the thoughts, ideas, visions, and experiences of the person students
have been discussing. Generally, I ask students to include ten images,
inside the template and number them. They can either draw the images
freehand or use Clip Art. On the back of the sheet, students must identify in several complete sentences the corresponding numbered image.
In Appendix E, you will find such a template. Tony, a white student,
created the exceptional head that is shown in Figure 3–3a.

My African American students appreciate my using DuBois. He's a
different sort of black champion, not an athlete or entertainer, but an
intellectual. I sense for these students that this may be the first time that
they see white students wrestling with a perspective they had never
before considered: a black man demanding something that he should

Figure 3–3a
W. E. B. DuBois Historical Head

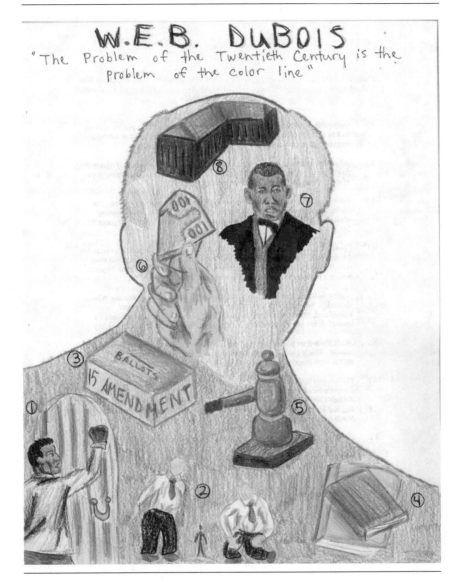

Figure 3–3b
W. E. B. DuBois Historical Head

Tony Jones
2nd period

The Souls of Black Folk
W.E.B. DuBois

1.)   DuBois wrote of Negroes being born with a veil, blocked from opportunities, and
       locked out of happiness. Slaves helped build America into a great power, and
       Negroes felt bitter that they did not get their fair share. (page 2)

2.)   When thrown into competition with rich, landowning, skilled whites, Negroes felt
       powerless to put up a fight. DuBois knew of the overwhelming depressed hopes
       of an impoverished people in a wealthy land. (page 5)

3.)   DuBois understood the great importance of the right for Negroes to vote. The
       fifteenth amendment was seen as the "chief means of gaining and perfecting
       liberty". The ballot was the great equalizer, leveling the playing field. (page 4,
       24)

4.)   Concerning the doings of the Freedmen's Bureau, DuBois was mostly critical, but
       did recognize one accomplishment. A great success of the Freedmen's Bureau
       were the great strides made in educating youths. Free schooling for all Negroes
       helped lay the foundation for high learning and rising up. (page 20)

5.)   A great failure of the Freedmen's Bureau were the tremendous injustices in law
       and order. When leaving the southern courts in-control, Negroes were
       intimidated, beaten, raped, and judged with a bias. Courts under the Bureau's
       control all too often made rulings simply to punish southern whites. (page 21)

6.)   While there were honest agents of the Freedmen's Bureau, some were selfish
       thieves. This led to a level of suspicion among Negroes, not knowing if the
       agents were friend or foe. (page 18)

7.)   DuBois was in direct opposition to Booker T. Washington and the ideas of
       compromise and submission to injustice. To radicals like DuBois, Washington's
       Atlanta Compromise was seen as a surrender of political equality. Instead of
       fighting for liberty, Washington was concerned with winning the admiration of
       North and South. (page 26)

8.)   DuBois found obvious paradoxes in Washington's arguments. While Washington
       preached self-respect, he advocated silent submission to civic inferiority.
       Washington founded Tuskegge Institute to train Negroes in common-schooling
       and industrial training, instead of pushing higher education. (page 31)

not have to demand. It's a lesson that can be applied on many different levels.

Another option for teachers to consider is using the outstanding film from the American Experience series, *Ida B. Wells—A Passion for Justice* (1989), which chronicles her important work in combating lynching of blacks through her exposé, the *Red Record*. The film also documents the work she and DuBois did together as part of the Niagara Movement and the eventual creation of the National Association for the Advancement of Colored People. Journals and historical heads also work well in tandem with *Ida B. Wells—A Passion for Justice*.

Howard Fast and *Freedom Road*

I do not want to deny my regular United States history survey students the same kind of intellectual and empathic learning exercises that I offer my advanced placement students. So I've turned to other means of instruction, no less powerful but more tangible for students in a regular history survey class.

When I was fourteen or fifteen, I read Howard Fast's *Freedom Road* (first published in 1944) for the first time, not for school, but for my own edification. I can still remember when I put the book down. When I finished the book, I sat in my reading chair, in my room, staring into space as if trying to comprehend what I had just read. That moment has remained fixed in my memory since then. *Freedom Road* is one of Fast's most widely read historical novels and has been translated into numerous languages. The power of this book is in its simplicity and its message. Anyone who is interested in the history of Reconstruction should read this book. When I discovered that it was available in a school edition, I knew I had to share it with my students. However, there was a catch: *Freedom Road* is laced with intense, racially derogatory language. I spoke with our principal about teaching *Freedom Road* and how to best approach it. He suggested I offer a second title for students to choose. Howard Fast has also written another historical novel, *The Last Frontier* (1941), about the treatment of the Cheyenne Indians by government policy in the 1870s. Fast's novels almost always deal with the issue of restrictions on freedom within the context of individual struggle against injustice. I reasoned that I could offer students the same underlying themes offered by Fast within the framework of these two novels. Additionally, I had the chronology of history on my side—both novels cover roughly the same time period, post–Civil War America.

When I presented the novels to the class, I also recounted to them how reading *Freedom Road* had changed my life. Letting them in on a bit of my past freed me to approach the book from a personal perspective. Upfront I told the students about the language in *Freedom Road* and offered them the choice between that and *The Last Frontier.* To my surprise, most students signed up to read *Freedom Road.*

Around the same time, I came across a book review in the *Washington Post* reviewing Randall Robinson's recent publication, *The Debt* (1999). *The Debt* is about Robinson's idea that America owes something to its black community in the way of reparations, much like the $20,000 that was provided by Congress to Japanese Americans who were interned during World War II. He believes that much of America's development and economic foundation was made on the backs of black people. I decided to use this review in class to start a dialogue. Digging through my slide collection, I came up with a famous photo of the 1930s showing two black men lynched in Indiana. I warned the students that the slide I was going to show them was graphic, but that it was entirely related to our course of study. There were some groans and hushed comments. This image is also on the *American History Videodisk* (1999). You can also turn to the recent publication, *Without Sanctuary: Lynching Photographs in America,* edited by James Allen (1999), and filled with historical commentary by noted historians. This photograph album of sorts includes images from the roughly 3–4,000 lynchings that took place between the late nineteenth century and into the second half of the twentieth century. Many of these images were turned into picture postcards that were mailed. It's a horrific montage that really depicts how cruel Americans could be at times to other human beings and fellow citizens.

I passed out the book review and had the students read it. What follows are some very thoughtful remarks both in writing and in class discussion. David wrote and then read his journal to the class:

> This review talks about the unfulfilled promise of 40 acres and a mule. The government makes promises to the black community but doesn't keep them. They give the Japanese Americans $20,000 for their losses and sufferings during World War II but not our 40 acres and a mule. The government tries to get rid of or cover their mistakes by using money to compensate but there is no true compensation. Trying to compare the Holocaust to slavery is a lost cause. Maybe many people were killed, but slavery lasted for over two hundred years. I like how Robinson puts it. "I was born in 1941, but my black soul is much older than that." I'm only 16, but I know how it feels.

David's fellow students listened quietly, but respectfully. In the discussion that followed, there was a lively exchange of ideas, with most students arguing that money can't make up for past injustices and that what really needs conversion are peoples hearts.

Returning to the historical setting of *Freedom Road,* I tapped into students' prior knowledge about Reconstruction, reviewing with them the successes and failures of government policies of the period. We re-examined the Thirteenth, Fourteenth, and Fifteenth Amendments to the Constitution and discussed the gains that African Americans had made in the South at the time, only to lose those rights in the years after Reconstruction ended. I gave the students a month to read their books, telling them that when they finished they would have to complete a historical head and present it to the class, write in their journals, and engage in a class discussion. Their journal entry would be a reaction to the book as well as an answer to the question, "If you could rewrite the ending, how would you conclude the novel book?" On the day the book was to be finished, I arranged the seats in the classroom in a circle, intent on building more community among students. We had such a frank discussion and in such a respectful atmosphere. It was incredibly moving. To my surprise, very few students would have rewritten the ending of *Freedom Road,* even though it is violent and tragic, and all the characters, the blacks and their poor white friends, young and old, are killed by the Klan. Students said that to rewrite the end would be changing the truth and altering history and that even though it's a powerful ending, it's historical reality.

We also discussed the language. Students said that given the time period in which the book takes place, they could understand why Fast used such terminology—it was real, it gave the book a certain historical legitimacy.

I once heard a compelling argument offered by respected scholar James Horton, Benjamin Banneker Professor of American History at George Washington University. He said that the issue of race is really a two-edged sword. He used the examples of the Negro Leagues in the 1920s and 1930s and the simple fact that white baseball players like Babe Ruth never consistently faced such great pitching as the kind thrown by Satchel Paige or Josh Gibson. This diminishes not only their greatness but the greatness of Ruth. Because Ruth and others only faced white pitchers, their true hitting skills were never put to the ultimate test. Thus, a fantasy created and organized by whites that maintained that whites were superior to black men in every way, including athletics, in the end cheated whites too, though in different ways than it cheated blacks.

I have barely scratched the surface in this chapter. There is far more material available to you than what I have been able to offer you in these brief pages. Programs and lessons that have worked for me and my students are presented here. The litany of racial abuses committed in the name of liberty and justice by Americans are too numerous to ignore. "If you want to destroy a country, destroy its memory," said novelist Milan Kundera. It is imperative that those of us who are engaged as the guardians of memory heed Kundera's words. You don't have to use exactly what I use. Find material with which you are comfortable.

Rely on your own creative and intellectual genius to enlighten your students. As adults, we need to remember that our youth can help us. Just because they are young doesn't mean that what they have to say is unimportant or of little or no value. Despite the bumps I've experienced along the way, I am convinced that a national dialogue about race rooted in classrooms of committed educators is the perfect forum to generate healing. Thomas Paine, no stranger to exclusion, once wrote, "We have it within our power to begin the world anew." Let's do it.

Resources
Books

Abdul-Jabbar, Kareem. 1996. *Black Profiles in Courage: A Legacy of African American Achievement.* New York: William Morrow.

Allen, James, ed. 1999. *Without Sanctuary: Lynching Photography in America.* Santa Fe, NM: Twin Palms Publishing.

Ambrose, Stephen E. 2000. *Nothing Like It in the World: The Men Who Built the Transcontinental Railroad 1863–1869.* New York: Simon and Schuster.

Bach, Ira J., and Mary Lackritz Gray. 1983. *A Guide to Chicago's Public Sculpture.* Chicago: University of Chicago Press.

Bain, David Howard. 1999. *Empire Express: Building the First Transcontinental Railroad.* New York: Viking Penguin.

Bennett, Lerome, Jr. 1988. *Before the Mayflower: A History of Black America.* Chicago: Johnson Publishing.

Berlin, Ira. 1998. *Many Thousand Gone: The First Two Centuries of Slavery in North America.* Cambridge: Belknap Press.

Boime, Albert. 1990. *The Art of Exclusion: Representing Blacks in the Nineteenth Century.* Washington, DC: Smithsonian.

Brack, Gene. 1975. *Mexico Views Manifest Destiny, 1821–1846: An Essay on the Origins of the Mexican War.* Albuquerque, NM: University of New Mexico Press.

Carnes, Jim. 1996. *Us and Them: A History of Intolerance in America.* New York: Oxford University Press.

Chan, Sucheng. 1991. *Asian Americans: An Interpretive History.* Boston: Twayne Publishers.

Chariton, Wallace O. 1992. *Exploring the Alamo Legends.* Plano, TX: Republic of Texas Press.

Cockcroft, James. 1995. *Latinos in the Making of the United States.* New York: Franklin Watts.

Crost, Lyn. 1994. *Honor by Fire: Japanese Americans at War in Europe and the Pacific.* Novato, CA: Presidio Press.

Davis, Marilyn P. 1990. *Mexican Voices/American Dreams: An Oral History of Mexican Immigration to the United States.* New York: Henry Holt.

DuBois, W. E. B. 1996. *The Souls of Black Folk.* New York: Modern Library.

Eisenhower, John S. D. 1989. *So Far from God: The United States War with Mexico.* New York: Random House.

Estell, Kenneth, ed. 1994. *African America: Portrait of a People.* Detroit: Visible Ink.

————. 1994. *The African American Almanac.* Detroit: Gale Publishing.

Fast, Howard. 1941. *The Last Frontier.* Armonk, NY: North Castle Books.

————. (1944) 1995 edition. *Freedom Road.* Armonk, NY: M. E. Sharpe.

Fox, Geoffrey. 1996. *Hispanic Nation: Culture, Politics and the Constructing of Identity.* Secaucus, NJ: Birch Lane Press.

Franklin, John Hope. 1994. *From Slavery to Freedom: A History of Negro Americans.* New York: McGraw Hill.

Gonzalez, Juan. 2000. *Harvest of Empire: A History of Latinos in America.* New York: Viking.

Gutierrez, Dave. 1995. *Walls and Mirrors: Mexican-Americans, Mexican Immigrants and the Politics of Ethnicity.* Berkeley, CA: University of California Press.

Hamanaka, Shelia. 1990. *The Journey: Japanese Americans Racism and Renewal.* New York: Orchard Books.

Hoobler, Dorothy, and Thomas Hoobler.1994a. *The Chinese American Family Album.* New York: Oxford University Press.

————. 1994b. *The Mexican American Family Album.* New York: Oxford University Press.

————. 1995. *The African American Family Album.* New York: Oxford University Press.

————. 1996. *The Japanese American Family Album.* New York: Oxford University Press.

Horowitz, Tony. 1998. *Confederates in the Attic: Dispatches from the Unfinished Civil War.* New York: Random House.

Horsman, Reginald. 1981. *Race and Manifest Destiny: The Origins of American Racial Anglo-Saxonism.* Cambridge: Harvard University Press.

Horton, James Oliver, and Lois E. Horton. 1997. *In Hope of Liberty: Culture, Community, and Protest Among Northern Free Blacks, 1700–1860.* New York: Oxford University Press.

Houston, Jeanne Wakatsuki, and James D. Houston. 1983. *Farewell to Manzanar: A True Story of the Japanese American Experience During and After World War II Internment.* New York: Bantam Starfire.

Inada, Lawson Fusao. 1993. *Legends from Camp: Poems.* Minneapolis, MN: Coffeehouse Press.

Johnson, Charles, and Patricia Smith. 1998. *Africans in America: America's Journey Through Slavery.* San Diego: Harcourt Brace.

Kanellos, Nicholas, ed. 1993. *The Hispanic-American Almanac.* Detroit: Gale Research.

Kitano, Harry. 1995. *The Japanese Americans.* New York: Chelsea House.

Kluger, Richard. 1977. *Simple Justice.* New York: Random House.

Leekley, Sheryle and John. 1978. *Moments: The Pulitzer Prize Photographs.* New York: Crown.

Lewis, Jan Ellen, and Peter S. Onuf, eds. 1999. *Sally Hemmings and Thomas Jefferson: History, Memory, and Civic Culture.* Charlottesville, VA: University of Virginia Press.

Little, Carol Morris. 1996. *Outdoor Sculpture in Texas.* Austin, TX: University of Texas Press.

Litwack, Leon F. 1979. *Been in the Storm So Long: The Aftermath of Slavery.* New York. Random House.

Loewen, James W. 1999. *Lies Across America: What Our Historic Sites Get Wrong.* New York: New Press.

Lord, Walter. 1978. *A Time to Stand: The Epic of the Alamo.* Lincoln, NE: University of Nebraska Press.

McGowan, Tom. 1995. *Go for Broke: Japanese Americans in World War II.* New York: Franklin Watts.

Miller, Robert Ryal. 1989. *Shamrock and Sword: The San Patricio Batallion During the Mexican War.* Norman, OK: University of Oklahoma Press.

Moguin, Wayne, and Charles Van Doren, eds. 1972. *A Documentary History of Mexican Americans.* New York: Praeger.

Myrdal, Gunnar. 1944. *An American Dilemma: The Negro Problem and Modern Democracy.* New York: Harper and Row.

Niiya, Brian. 1993. *Japanese American History: An A-to-Z Reference from 1868–Present.* New York: Facts on File.

Olmos, Edward James, Lea Ybarra, and Manuel Monterrey. 1999. *Americanos: Latino Life in the United States.* Boston: Little, Brown.

Painter, Nell Irvin. 1976. *The Exodusters: Black Migration to Kansas After Reconstruction.* New York: Alfred A. Knopf.

Palacios, Argentina. 1994. *Standing Tall: The Stories of Ten Hispanic Americans.* New York: Scholastic.

Patterson, Orlando. 1998. *The Ordeal of Integration: Progress and Resentment in America's "Racial" Crisis.* Washington, DC: Civitas/Counterpoint.

Piehler, Kurt G. 1995. *Remembering War the American Way: 1783–Present.* Washington, DC: Smithsonian.

Robinson, Cecil, ed. 1989. *The View from Chapultepec: Mexican Writers on the Mexican-American War.* Tucson, AZ: University of Arizona Press.

Robinson, Randall. 1999. *The Debt: What America Owes to Blacks.* New York: Dutton.

Rogers, Mary Beth. 1998. *Barbara Jordan: American Hero.* New York: Bantam.

Ruiz, Vicki. 1998. *From Out of the Shadows: Mexican Women in Twentieth-Century America.* New York: Oxford University Press.

Samora, Julian, and Patricia Vandel Simon. 1993. *A History of the Mexican-American People.* Notre Dame, IN: University of Notre Dame Press.

Savage, Kirk. 1997. *Standing Soldiers, Kneeling Slaves: Race, War, and Monument in Nineteenth-Century America.* Princeton, NJ: Princeton University Press.

Schlesinger, Arthur. 1992. *The Disuniting of America.* New York: Norton.

Shorris, Earl. 1992. *Latinos: A Biography of the People.* New York: Norton.

Stampp, Kenneth. 1984. *The Peculiar Institution: Slavery in the Ante-Bellum South.* New York: Vintage.

Stavans, Ilan. 1995. *The Hispanic Condition: Reflections on Culture and Identity in America.* New York: HarperCollins.

Suro, Roberto. 1998. *Strangers Among Us: How Latino Immigration Is Transforming America.* New York: Alfred A. Knopf.

Takaki, Ronald. 1993. *A Different Mirror. A History of Multicultural America.* Boston: Little, Brown.

———. 1998a. *A Larger Memory: A History of Our Diversity, With Voices.* Boston: Little, Brown.

———. 1998b. *Strangers from a Different Shore: A History of Asian Americans.* Boston: Little, Brown.

———. 2000a. *Double Victory: A Multicultural History of America in World War II.* Boston: Little, Brown.

———. 2000b. *Iron Cages: Race and Culture in 19th-century America.* New York: Oxford University Press.

Tateishi, John, ed. 1999. *And Justice for All: An Oral History of the Japanese American Detention Camps.* Spokane, WA: University of Washington Press.

Thernstrom, Stephan, and Abigail Thernstrom. 1997. *America in Black and White: One Nation Indivisible—Race in Modern America.* New York: Simon and Schuster.

Tuan, Mia. 1998. *Forever Foreigners or Honorary Whites?* New Brunswick, NJ: Rutgers University Press.

Turtledove, Harry. 1996. *The Guns of the South.* New York: Ballantine.

———. 1997. *How Few Remain.* New York: Ballantine.

Terkel, Studs. 1992. *Race: How Blacks and Whites Think and Feel About the American Obsession.* New York: Norton.

Washington, Booker T. 1953. *Up From Slavery.* Garden City, NJ: Doubleday.

Yancey, Diane. 1998. *Life in a Japanese American Internment Camp.* San Diego: Lucent Books.

Yoo, David, and Roger Daniels. 2000. *Growing Up Nisei: Race, Gender, and Culture Among Japanese Americans of California 1924–1949.* Urbana, IL: University of Illinois Press.

Videos/Films

The Alamo. Producer: Craig Haffner. 100 minutes. Greystone Communications, 1996, videocasette.

Bad Day at Black Rock. Producer: Dorey Schary; Director: John Sturges. 81 minutes. MGM Films, 1951, videocassette.

A Class Divided. Producer: William Peters. 60 minutes. Yale University Films and Frontline Productions, 1985, videocassette.

Freedom Road. Producer: Zev Braun; Director: John Kadar. 186 minutes. Zev Braun Productions, 1979, videocassette.

Ida B. Wells—A Passion for Justice. Producers: William Greaves and Louise Archambault. 60 minutes. William Greaves Productions, 1989, videocassette.

The Iron Road. Producer: Neil Goodwin. 60 minutes. Peace River Films, 1991, videocassette.

Public Sculpture: America's Legacy. Producer: Robert Pierce. 28 minutes. National Museum of American Art: Smithsonian Institution, 1995, videocassette.

1776. Producer: Jack L. Warner; Director: Peter H. Hunt. 141 minutes. Columbia Pictures, 1972, videocassette.

The Shadow of Hate: A History of Intolerance in America. Producer: Charles Guggenheim. 40 minutes. Teaching Tolerance, 1995, videocassette.

The Statue of Liberty. Producer: Ken Burns. 60 minutes. Florentine Films, 1985, videocassette.

W. E. B. DuBois of Great Barrington. Producer: Lilian Baulding. 60 minutes. WGBY-TV Productions, 1992, videocassette.

U.S.-Mexican War: 1846–1848. Producer: Paul Espinosa. 217 minutes. KERA Films, 1998, videocassette.

Electronic Resources

The Alamo: Victory or Death. CD-ROM. 1995. Dallas: Archimedia Interactive.

American History Videodisk. 1999. Annapolis, MD: Instructional Resources Corporation.

Who Built America? From the Centennial Celebration of 1876 to the Great War of 1914. CD-ROM. 1993. American Social History Productions. New York: Voyager.

Chapter Four

America's Second Reconstruction: 1954–1968
Exploring the Civil Rights Movement

I ain't gettin on, till Jim Crow gets off.
> —Montgomery Bus Boycotter

There comes a time in every young person's young life when he or she is suddenly aware that there is a world that exists beyond the boundaries of his or her home and family. On the evening of April 4, 1968, my father stuck his head inside my room and said to me, "When you go to bed tonight say an extra prayer for a very special man who has been killed, Martin Luther King, Jr." That night, cities burned across America. During the following days at school, I remember the nuns talking about King and his life and message. Watching the funeral procession in Atlanta on television I was struck by the simplicity of the mule-drawn wagon carrying the coffin in which King lay and the sheer size of the throng that followed beyond. Sixty-one days later I woke up one morning to find my parents glued to the television set in their bedroom watching the news reports that another great American had been gunned down: Robert F. Kennedy. I remember watching that funeral, too, as Kennedy's coffin moved slowly by train from New York City to Washington, DC, then on to Arlington National Cemetery. At age ten, in a few short weeks I had come to learn that there was a greater world that lay beyond my door at 14 Captain Brown's Lane. And in those same weeks, America lost two significant voices whose silence would affect the country for the next generation. Not only was I confused in 1968, so was most of America.

Starting with the *Brown v. Board of Education, Topeka, Kansas,* decision in 1954 through 1968, when Dr. King was assassinated, America underwent a profound change. It was a time of revolution and grassroots action. The dates of 1954 and 1968, and those in between, are etched on the surface of the Civil Rights Memorial in front of the Southern Poverty Law Center in Montgomery, Alabama. Along with the dates of major moments in the Civil Rights movement are chiseled the names of forty people, black and white, of varying religious denominations, who lost their lives in the struggle for civil rights in America. Beside the names of King and Medger Evers, notable players in the movement, are the names of average citizens who lost their lives. You will not find in any history textbook the names of James Reeb, Viola Liuzzo, and Jimmie Lee Jackson, among others. In most conflicts in our nation's past, most of those who make the sacrifices are forgotten.

When I teach the Civil Rights movement to my classes, it is very important to me that my students understand just how much of this movement was generated by ordinary people. Certainly, Martin Luther King, Jr., played an important role, but even historians David Garrow and Taylor Branch agree that the movement made King, not the other way around. Myung, one of my Asian students, wrote in one of his journal entries about the Civil Rights movement, "I have a little suggestion, I think we should change King's birthday holiday to a civil rights holiday since the movement made King. by changing the name we can remember all the other people whose lives were sacrificed."

While striving to help students remember the victims of the era, I also want my students to grasp the ideas of segregation that permeated the South and the legal implications of such a national and regional policy. In teaching the historical ramifications of the movement, it's important that young people also understand the politics and the social and economic justifications for such policies. Fortunately, with a proliferation of teaching material available, teachers can demonstrate to their students the complexity of the struggle at all levels—the individual, the regional, and the national—while remaining true to the central element of the time period that this was indeed a people's movement. In this chapter, I want to examine with you how one aspect of the history of race in America profoundly changed all of us, and that with those changes new ideas and a new national vision seemed possible, but that we still have to do our part to "keep the dream alive."

Background Reading

Before you begin teaching the Civil Rights movement, examine the variety of good, academic but well-written, historical narratives of the period; for example:

1. *Bearing the Cross: Martin Luther King, Jr. and the Southern Christian Leadership Conference* by David Garrow, 1986

2. *Eyes on the Prize: America's Civil Rights Years, 1954–1965* by Juan Williams, 1987

3. *Parting the Waters: America in the King Years, 1954–63*, 1988, and *Pillar of Fire: America in the King Years, 1963–65*, 1998, by Taylor Branch

4. *Walking with the Wind: A Memoir of the Movement* by John Lewis, 1999

5. *Simple Justice: The History of Brown v. Board of Education and Black America's Struggle,* by Richard Kluger, 1977

6. *Let the Trumpet Sound: The Life of Martin Luther King, Jr.* by Stephen B. Oates, 1982

Certainly, there are plenty of other books available for you to study, but these are the ones from which I have learned the most and that I have been able to dovetail into my curriculum. There are plenty of quotes that you can share with your classes and a plethora of stirring photographic images that can help you make your points.

Where To Begin

My approach to teaching American history is one of imparting the sweeping narrative of the nation to my students. The Civil Rights movement is an outgrowth of that narrative. It stands alone, but it is also part of the whole matrix of America. If you teach history in this fashion, it's only logical that the Civil Rights movement will follow closely on the heels of World War II, but by the time you reach this point, students should be familiar with the struggle blacks have had in the American past. Students should recall these aspects of American history beyond slavery, including the Dred Scott Decision, the Civil War, Reconstruction, *Plessy v. Ferguson*, W. E. B. DuBois, Jim Crow, and the Harlem Renaissance, among other topics. When I teach the Civil Rights movement, I like to have music of the era playing on my classroom stereo as the students walk into class, so it's not uncommon to hear songs like "We Shall Overcome" or "Get on Board," and other anthems of the period emanating from my room. The music helps to set the tone of what I will be teaching and what students will be learning.

    I generally like to begin talking about the Civil Rights movement with the story of Jackie Robinson and his breaking the color barrier in professional baseball in 1947. One of the things that I think is important to point out to students is just how much our triumph over Nazism in World War II played out in segregated America. At the end of the war in 1945, we had defeated an enemy whose primary goal was to eliminate another race. It was hard to reconcile that victory with the second-class-citizen status of black Americans. During World War II, the United States seemed truly united as a people and a nation. Everyone pitched in—people of all colors, races, and creeds. African Americans served in the armed forces in record numbers, and among their number counted the famed Tuskegee Airmen and the first black American general, Benjamin Davis, Sr. In Europe, black servicemen were treated as men, as race seemed to make little difference to the liberated French or Italians. However, when these American "heroes" returned home, they encountered, or reencountered, Jim Crow laws and segregation, but there was a difference this time—the hypocrisy of America could no longer be hidden or swept aside in light of our struggle with Germany. When Branch Rickey brought Jackie Robinson up from the Negro Leagues it was voluntarily—Major League Baseball was not responding to some court order. Shortly after baseball desegregated, President Harry Truman ordered the military and federal government to desegregate, and by the beginning of the 1950s, stirrings were taking place in America that would soon see a floodgate of social and political change.

I talk about Robinson because students can relate to the story. Sports figures have a kind of allure all their own. In 1997, the fiftieth anniversary of Robinson's breaking the color barrier, I showed my classes the film *The Jackie Robinson Story* (1950) and paired it with a set of editorials from the *Washington Post*. The timing was perfect because we watched the film during the same week that there was a great deal of media attention on the historic moment. But students also need to recognize that Major League Baseball was not always segregated. Prior to the 1890s, blacks played regularly on Major League teams. It was not until the *Plessy* decision in 1896 that segregation became a fixture of baseball. A book that you might want to consider having your students read is Troy Soos' *Hanging Curve* (1999). It's a baseball novel set in the early 1920s in the Saint Louis area. Soos has done his baseball and race history homework as the plot plays out against the Negro Leagues and the strain of race relations in America shortly after World War I. It is a very quick and easy read, one that will captivate students.

A Time for Justice

"Disturbingly powerful" is how May saw it. *A Time for Justice* (1992) is an excellent film to launch any study of the Civil Rights movement. Charles Guggenheim's film, produced for the Southern Poverty Law

Center, is much like his other film, *The Shadow of Hate,* in that he has created a stirring, haunting, and provocative film chronicling the story of the Civil Rights movement. Some students have told me that the film makes them feel uncomfortable. To those students, I respond that it is our discomfort that sometimes propels us to act and generate change. Using stark images and oral history testimony, the forty-minute film and an accompanying teacher's guide is provided by the Law Center at no cost to interested teachers. Even after watching it many times, I still find myself in the back of the classroom holding back tears as the film makes its way across images of the lunch-counter sit-ins; the freedom riders; Bloody Sunday in Selma, Alabama, in March 1965; and the subsequent march from Selma to Montgomery that brought about the Voting Rights Act of 1965. I can tell by watching the faces of my students just how moved they are. The journal entries submitted are in their own way moving and compelling. Brian wrote:

> I think this was a great movie that accurately displays the conflict of the country. It's amazing just to think about some of the atrocities committed against blacks during this time period. So many bad things happened, and so many people died, all over a cause that should not have had to been fought for. How can a peaceful demonstration such as marching to a capitol turn into a gruesome bloodbath? It's hard to believe that sheriffs of Southern towns could actually be active members of the KKK. This film really makes you think about what happened.

Mark wrote:

> I thought *A Time for Justice* was an incredibly moving and compelling film on the Civil Rights Movement. I learned of many things that I did not know occurred. The one line that sticks out in my mind from the film was when it was stated [by John Lewis] that everyone's beaten black body became living witnesses to the cause for human dignity. That hit it right on the nail. The most appalling of all the tragic events was the bombing that killed the innocent black girls attending Sunday school at the 16th Street Baptist Church in Birmingham. It has to be one of the most terrible and saddest things I have ever heard of.

I have used this film in a variety of ways with all of my classes. Sometimes I have students create a journal entry on the film based on a prompt from the teacher's guide: "The film begins and ends with a picture of Jimmie Lee Jackson's tombstone. Jackson was a young man killed by a state trooper while he tried to protect his mother and grandfather during a voting rights march. Imagine that you knew Jimmie Lee Jackson, and you were standing in that cemetery when his body was laid to rest. What are some thoughts you have? Write a diary entry for that day." Here's how David, an African American in my class, responded to that prompt:

Today they placed my good friend, Jimmie, to rest. It was an open cas-
ket funeral. I hate funerals. It seems as if there is one every week
around here. The Klan just lynched one man the other day. Don't know
what for, but they did. Jimmie and I had been friends since we were
little and them white men took his life because he was defending his
Momma. That bullet and that beating said something to the whole
world. Jimmie and I were best friends but now he's gone to a better
place. I'll miss him, but I still have a fight to win and as long as I am
alive and fighting I'll be thinking of him.

It is through writings such as those presented here that I am able
to create within students a kind of historical empathy that is rooted in
our common humanity. Reading journals such as this helps me to recognize that students are taking away from the class more than just
hard, cold facts. You might want to consider using similar prompts to
engage your students. Why not have them cover one of these episodes
from the perspective of one of the many black newspapers from around
the country like the *Chicago Defender* or the *Baltimore Afro-American*, or
from the NAACP's journal, *The Crisis*. Or perhaps you could have students role play live news coverage of one of these events. For other creative students, you might want to offer them the option of writing a
memorial poem or a eulogy.

The Civil Rights Memorial

On some occasions, before showing the film I have given students a
handout from the teacher's guide that has the timeline found on the
Civil Rights Memorial. I ask students to count and to look over the
names listed. Next, I ask them to tell me whose names they recognize.
Students recognize King's name and some know Medger Evers and
Emmit Till. But the other names are a complete mystery to my students.
By the end of this unit, it is my hope that they will have added a few
more names to their memory. Teaching like this is very powerful because it brings home quite clearly just how much this was a movement
of average people trying to make change, and in the end, despite terrible loss and hardships, succeeding. It might be interesting, at this point,
to muse with students about whether or not they think the movement
is over.

I always show images of Maya Lin's Civil Rights Memorial to my
classes. (Lin was also the designer of the Wall for the Vietnam Veterans
Memorial in Washington, DC.) This can be shown either through slides
or a four-minute clip from the video *Public Sculpture: America's Legacy*
(1995) in which the memorial and its purpose are explored in detail.
Dedicated in 1989, Lin's design incorporates not only the names and
dates of people and events, but also an excerpt from King's "I Have a

Dream" speech. On a wall overlooking the memorial tablet, one can read the statement based in part on the Old Testament book of Amos, "Until justice rolls like waters and righteousness like a mighty stream." Water flows over the face of the wall, then runs under the plaza and comes forth on top of the memorial tablet, where a "thin sheet of water which glistens with light reflects the image of the viewer." Maya Lin refers to her memorial as "a collective memory of history" that "is a very different memorial than most traditional memorials because it deals with direct, immediate relaying of historical facts. It relies on the power of the word" and is "a cool and tranquil place rich in the history of struggle and transformation." It is "a place to remember the Civil Rights movement, to honor those killed during the struggle, to appreciate how far the country has come in its quest for equality, and to consider how far it has to go." I want students to recognize, through these images, the power of simplicity in the memorial that mirrors a kind of simplicity that was vital to the core of the movement. As interdisciplinary learners, students need to understand the power and place of public art in a democratic society.

By and large, students like the design and think that it is an appropriate public monument that generates healing. One year I did a concluding activity in my classes in which students had to design a memorial to an American or event that we had studied during our survey of American history. I had several students offer their own design for a civil rights memorial, incorporating different aspects of the movement into their design concepts. One student designed a simple park; others offered figurative pieces of people and events like sculptures of Martin Luther King, Jr., or Rosa Parks. Space on the national Mall in Washington, DC has been reserved for a national memorial to Martin Luther King, Jr., and the design competition concluded in September 2000.

On some occasions, I provide students with different biographies to read from the supporting magazine *Free At Last* that comes with the film *A Time for Justice* as part of the teacher's kit. Each student selects a different biography and then reports out on how that individual played a role in the movement.

Using Music

As I've mentioned before, I try to incorporate music into my lessons when I can demonstrate a correlation between history and music. The Civil Rights movement has plenty of great music to offer that can be analyzed with students. Some of the songs are easily recognizable, such as Bob Dylan's "The Times They Are A-Changin'," as well as "Keep Your

Eyes on the Prize," and "Oh Freedom." But one of the real gems I like to use is Phil Ochs' song, "Here's to the State of Mississippi." It's a bit long, but its lack of subtlety and no-nonsense approach to conditions for blacks in Mississippi during the first sixty-some-odd years of the twentieth century and the attitudes toward race is not lost on the part of my students. Often you can go to the web and find lyrics to these songs. You can play "Here's to the State of Mississippi" without a lyric sheet because it is very easy to follow.

Another outstanding song is "Those Three Are on My Mind," also written by Ochs. This is a ballad about the 1964 murders, near Philadelphia and Meridian, Mississippi, of the three civil rights workers, James Chaney, Andrew Goodman, and Michael Schwerner. It's a song filled with metaphors about the lack of justice found in the South that skillfully blends a story of blacks and whites coming together and paying a terrible price for a human cause. I use this song as a kind of test to ensure that students have been focused during different lessons. I tell my students that we're going to listen to a song, but I'm not going to reveal the title or the summary of the song because I want students to reflect on some of the stories we have studied. Students already will have heard of or been taught about these three young men, so less than halfway through the song I can see the heads of students acknowledging that they have figured out the song's meaning. Playing this song while showing the scene of the three weeping mothers from *A Time for Justice* is powerful and conveys the multiracial dimensions of the story.

To counter the folksongs of the era, you can use Otis Redding's classic, "Sitting on the Dock of the Bay" to express the frustration that many blacks felt regarding the momentum and gains of the Civil Rights movement by the late 1960s. Again, the lyrics can be downloaded and passed out to students. Have students try to interpret the message that the song conveys and then compare it to other songs of the civil rights era. You might want to pose the question as to why Redding's song became a Top 40 hit when it was released, while many of the other civil rights songs remained relegated to the folk music industry's niche audience.

Norman Rockwell and Civil Rights

One summer, while traveling through western Massachusetts, I stopped at the Norman Rockwell Museum in Stockbridge. Most people know of Rockwell's skills at documenting a particular kind of "Americana" and that during the late 1950s and 1960s, he painted a number of images related to the Civil Rights movement. By this time, he was moving away from scenes characterized by a sweet, innocent vision of America to paintings that dealt with reality. His most significant and best known civil rights painting is *The Problem We All Live With* (1964) showing a little black school girl, Ruby Bridges, being escorted to a just integrated school by US Marshalls. On an opposite wall in the gallery hung an equally stark painting, *Southern Justice (Murder in Mississippi)* (1965), depicting the executions of civil rights workers Chaney, Goodman, and Schwerner. It is the moment of their execution by the Klan, of which local law enforcement officials were members and whose shadows are looming over the victims. Looking closely at the painting, you can see horns coming from the tops of the shadowy figures' heads. Chills ran through my body and my eyes filled. I think, in that moment, I came to really understand what this episode and this movement was all about.

In the summer of 2000, the traveling exhibition *Norman Rockwell: Pictures for the American People* was held at the Corcoran Gallery of Art in Washington, DC. The exhibition included the two paintings that I had previously seen in Stockbridge. For years I had wondered how I could secure these images to use in my classroom. Now I had a way. Fortuitously, the exhibition catalog of the same name included color plates of both images. By turning these images into transparencies, I can now share with my students not only my epiphany but the images that tapped a deep reservoir in my soul. In doing so I hope that my students come to see why it is important to have a vested interest in the study of history.

A Standards-Based Civil Rights Unit

As part of my professional development, I had volunteered to be trained as a member of West Springfield's Standards-Based Learning Team. A requirement of my training was to design an entire standards-based unit in my discipline. I was looking for something fresh to create. During this time, I was in Birmingham, Alabama. While there, I visited Kelly-Ingram Park, the site where many nonviolent demonstrators were hosed by Birmingham firefighters and where Police Commissioner Eugene "Bull" Connor's police officers used attack dogs to rout the protesters. I also visited the 16th Street Baptist Church, site of the bombing that killed four girls as they dressed in their choir robes, and the Birmingham Civil Rights Institute, where I was able to put my hand on the jail cell door that held Martin Luther King, Jr., when he wrote his famous "Letter from a Birmingham Jail." The visit galvanized my ideas into a huge, multifaceted civil rights unit that would culminate in a student recreation of the 1963 March on Washington. In developing the lessons for the unit, I drew on a number of resources at my disposal including the video, *A Time for Justice;* documents from the National Archives Teaching with Documents Kit, "Peace and Prosperity: 1953 to 1961"; King's

"Letter from a Birmingham Jail"; the Arts and Entertainment Biography video on King, *Martin Luther King, Jr.: The Man and the Dream* (1997); and assorted music of the era. The centerpiece would be an after-school film festival in which students could select from a series of Hollywood films about the Civil Rights movement. For assessment, students had to write a formal analytical essay, create historical bumper stickers, and create follow-up journal entries. One final element of the unit was to have students create placards and signs that were used by demonstrators during the actual march in 1963. These placards had to be historically accurate, so students were forced to do some outside research on photographs of the march to see just what kind of signs were used. I told them that this was 1963 and that Black Power slogans or phrases, which would have come later, would not be historically accurate.

The unit was designed to have students achieve the following goals:

1. analyze the ideas presented in King's "Letter from a Birmingham Jail" and the "I Have a Dream" speech
2. examine the Supreme Court in expanding civil rights
3. identify and evaluate patterns of Supreme Court decisions [*Brown v. the Board of Education of Topeka, Kansas,* (1954) among others], the role of key civil rights leaders, and acts of civil disobedience as catalysts for desegregation (national and state) of public accommodations, transportation, housing, and employment

I start out the unit much as I have laid out material before you in this chapter. We watch *A Time for Justice* and the King biography, listen to music, and read "Letter from a Birmingham Jail." However, an essential part of this unit incorporates primary-source documents from the National Archives. These documents, from the National Archives Teaching Kit *Peace and Prosperity: 1953–1961,* relate to different aspects of the Civil Rights movement and include:

1. *Brown v. Board of Education of Topeka, Kansas;* May 17, 1954 (Record Group 267)
2. text of presidential address released to the press regarding the Little Rock crisis; September 24, 1957 (Dwight D. Eisenhower Presidential Library)
3. House Resolution 6127; April 1, 1957 (Record Group 233)
4. House Report 291; April 1, 1957 (Record Group 233)
5. Morrow's memo to Eisenhower regarding the student protest movement in the South; March 7, 1960 (Dwight D. Eisenhower Presidential Library)

6. postal workers union resolution calling on President Eisenhower to conduct a civil rights fact-finding tour of the South; April 6, 1957 (Dwight D. Eisenhower Presidential Library)

7. tape recording of Dr. Martin Luther King, Jr., on CBS Network Program *Face the Nation* (Record Group 200)

8. a photograph of House and Senate leadership upon passage of the Civil Rights Act of 1957 (Dwight D. Eisenhower Presidential Library)

Students are given copies of all of these documents and work in small groups to determine the meaning and significance of each document in relationship to the struggle for civil rights. Of particular interest, I always ask them to take a long, hard look at the photograph of the House and Senate leaders. This is a classic lesson in looking for what *is not* in the photograph and how pictures can be used to record history sometimes by what is not in evidence. All the men in the photograph are white; there are no blacks in the photograph even though this is the most serious piece of congressional legislation on civil rights passed in over ninety years.

After this phase of the unit is complete, we move into the film festival portion of our learning. The first time I employed this activity, I teamed up with US government teacher Jamie Morris, who wanted his senior government students to participate because they were studying the political and legal aspects of civil rights. Students selected one film to watch and, on two different days, we showed each of the following films after school—students who were involved in sports or other activities, or who worked, could choose which day to attend.

1. *The Jackie Robinson Story* (1950)

2. *The Long Walk Home* (1990)

3. *Crisis at Central High* (1981)

4. *Ghosts of Mississippi* (1996)

Prior to showing the films, we gathered all of the students in the cafeteria where I spoke briefly about the purpose of this activity within a historical context and Jamie spoke about the relevance in terms of American government and politics. I reminded students that these were film-industry interpretations and that certain scenes were not necessarily accurate. It was quite a feeling to see these students engrossed in these different films after school.

When my classes convened again, students reported on the different films to their peers. This was done so that everyone could get a flavor of the different films. Several days before the march, I e-mailed my colleagues on the faculty the times of the re-created march. I wanted them to know what was going on when they saw and heard thirty or more students walking along the perimeter of the building chanting and carrying obvious protest signs.

As our march on Washington got closer, I directed my students to make sure that their placards were of a reasonable size, about that of a large poster board. For guidance, I suggested they go to sources like the book *Eyes on the Prize* (Williams 1987) to look at images of the march. There are plenty of photographs of people with placards in this book. On the morning of the march, students came to school early to drop off their signs. Sifting through the signs, I was impressed with what I saw—the students had really taken this topic to heart and created excellent replicas of the signs that were carried in 1963. There were signs proclaiming "Freedom Now," "No More Jim Crow," and "Equality For All."

We listened to some more civil rights music as each class gathered up their signs and headed out of the classroom to do living history. As we assembled on the front driveway, I had the students spread out so that they could get a sense of how big a march of this size really was. Students chanted various slogans from the march. Some students linked arms and began to sing, "We Shall Overcome." Although our march lasted a total of ten minutes, everyone felt unified with each other and with the marchers of 1963. The two photographs in Figures 4–1a and 4–1b show our march on Washington.

The re-creation clearly affected the students. One student, Elaine, shared with me an essay that she wrote as part of her college application:

> We shall overcome . . . End Segregation . . . Freedom and Justice. It was not a normal day at my suburban high school. We were engaged in a protest march around the perimeter of building and through the halls. Our signs looked authentic and our chants were similar to those heard during the Sixties. The only thing that gave away this flash from the past was our Nineties clothing.
>
> As we walked holding our signs proclaiming segregation as unjust, we received perplexed looks from most students. . . . That uncomfortable feeling was not one I had ever felt before. Even though many eyes were not focused solely on me, I felt as if I was making a spectacle of myself.
>
> It was at this moment that history came alive for me. I had an epiphany of the inner feelings of the 1963 protesters. True, their discomfort was from people not understanding the necessity of change, while mine was from witty students not understanding a protest for something that already occurred, but it was discomfort never the less.
>
> This re-creation of history affected me much more than reading the words out of a textbook would have. This one day at school influenced my entire outlook on comprehending not just the Civil Rights movement, but history itself History has a human side that cannot be learned

Figure 4–1a
Re-creation of 1963 March on Washington

by simply reading the facts. To grasp a true sense of history, one has to experience the emotions of the history makers, as I did during that fateful march.

Many students expressed a similar kind of sentiment after the march. They thought it had brought the issue home and given them a glimpse into the struggle of people many years ago. As a teacher, it proved to be a powerful day on which a lesson took on long-standing implications in a way that I had never before imagined possible. Students had actually re-created a moment from a time before their births and been able to grasp the power of uniting for a common purpose. They felt the energy that was needed to protest and march, even if it was for only a few short minutes. They left class with a sense of how people might have felt energized at the end of the march in 1963. With that in mind many came to realize that the purpose of the march is still to be fulfilled. Somehow they knew that the struggle for some still remains.

Figure 4–1b
Re-creation of 1963 March on Washington

Civil Rights Bumper Stickers

The final assessment tool of this unit is the student-created civil rights bumper sticker. Each bumper sticker must be 12 inches by 3 inches, and must deal with some aspect of the Civil Rights movement—something that might actually have been seen during the time.

That first year, students submitted all kinds of bumper stickers. Some consisted of quotes by King, others reflected the nonviolent posture of the period, some attacked attitudes held by southern whites, while still others were aimed at specific legislation, such as the Civil Rights Act of 1964 or the Voting Rights Act of 1965. Some simply reflected an appreciation of the various groups that played different roles, such as the Southern Christian Leadership Conference, Committee on Racial Equality, and the Student Non-Violent Coordinating Committee (SNCC). This activity gave students an opportunity to let their creative juices flow while providing me an opportunity to assess what they had learned. Two of my favorites are shown in Figures 4–2a and 4–2b.

A Civil Rights Surprise

After the march, the class had an enjoyable element to put closure on the unit. For the film festival, each student had a ticket that they were required to turn in for admission. Every class had a separate envelope for their tickets. I had told students from the beginning that there would be a raffle prize for each class. Shortly before the unit, Congressman John Lewis from Georgia had published his book, *Walking with the Wind: A Memoir of the Movement* (1999). As a young man and a member of SNCC, Lewis had been at the center of much nonviolent direct action. He was a lunch-counter sit-in demonstrator and a Freedom Rider. On Bloody Sunday in Selma, Alabama, he was badly beaten by law enforcement officers. I decided to contact his congressional office and ask how I could get signed copies of his book to give away as raffle prizes for our unit. His office aides told me that all I had to do was purchase the books, bring them to his office on Capitol Hill, and that over the weekend the congressman would sign the books. I could pick them up the following Monday. So I picked up the books, lugged them on the Metro to his House office, left them, and then picked them up several days later. All during the unit, I had been repeatedly mentioning Lewis' name. I would point his picture out on videos and even read to students his moving introduction to his book. Once I got back to school, I peeked to see what he had written in each book. Congressman Lewis had signed each book with an inspiring message to the recipients about keeping the faith in their dreams. In mine he had written, "To Jim Percoco, Thank

Figure 4–2a
Civil Rights Era Bumper Sticker

Figure 4–2b
Civil Rights Era Bumper Sticker

you for all your good work. With faith and hope, keep your Eyes on the Prize." The students who won these books in the raffle treated them like gold.

King's Letter from a Birmingham Jail

A document that I believe is vital for teaching the Civil Rights movement is King's famous letter to white clergymen of Birmingham, Alabama, penned when he was held behind bars in 1963. This letter, which can be found in either whole or part in most United States history textbooks, is something that all Americans should have to read. If it is not in your textbook, then look in any anthology of American political writing, in *Letters of a Nation* (1997), edited by Andrew Carroll, or in *Testament of Hope: The Essential Writings and Speeches of Martin Luther King, Jr.* (1986) edited by James M. Washington. I have used this document in several ways over the years. Sometimes I have had students read King's letter and then read the Declaration of Independence. When they are finished with both, I ask them to compare and contrast the ideas presented in both documents. What is King looking for that seems to be promised in the Declaration of Independence? Why is it that this letter had to be written in 1963, when the Declaration asserted that "all men were free and equal" in 1776? What does this disparity tell you about the process of American history?

In the film *A Time for Justice,* King reads part of the letter dubbed over images of snarling dogs and high-pressure firehoses knocking down peaceful demonstrators. Teachers can also use the letter to examine King's philosophy of nonviolent direct action and passive resistance. By reading King's words, students can see that King also addresses the issue of his vision for the movement versus the vision offered by the Black Muslims and their leader, Malcolm X. It's a good vehicle for students to examine differences within the black community as to how best to achieve similar goals. The role of religion in the movement is also an important component of the letter and provides a place to talk about the significance of the black church in the movement. In fact, one of my biggest objectives is to give students an understanding that even though this was a multiracial and multidenominational movement, it was primarily a black movement.

Sometimes I like to show the Arts and Entertainment Biography, *Martin Luther King, Jr.: The Man and the Dream* (1997) as an accompaniment to the letter. This film explores the complex dimension of King's personality and does not shy away from the personal insecurities and struggles he experienced during his public life. It's a good sixty-minute video that reflects on the life and role of King in mid-twentieth century America. We see King at his lowest when he is arrested and at his zenith when he delivers his "I Have a Dream" speech and receives the Nobel Peace Prize in 1964.

You can also play a more recent song about King's life, "Pride in the Name of Love" sung by the Irish rock band U2. The lyrics can be downloaded off the Internet and can serve as a prompt for discussing why a contemporary rock group would want to write a song about King. Another song that could also be played and discussed is the 1968 Dion ballad, "Abraham, Martin, and John."

A very short, but moving video clip that works well with students when discussing the death of King can be found in the video set, *Great American Political Speeches* (1995). On the night King was killed, Robert Kennedy, campaigning for the democratic presidential nomination, gave a stirring speech in Indianapolis to a crowd of predominately black residents. The crowd had yet to be informed that King had been assassinated, but Kennedy already knew. The remarks Kennedy planned to deliver were useless in this situation. Speaking entirely from the heart, with no planned text, Kennedy delivered a simple, but eloquent speech about King and his mission. That night, Indianapolis was the only major American city not to experience violence. When I show this film clip, I ask students to consider what Kennedy said and how his words managed to prevent an outbreak of hostility in Indianapolis.

After working on all or part of this King material, students are given a copy of the Epilogue from David Garrow's Pulitzer Prize–winning biography, *Bearing the Cross; Martin Luther King, Jr. and the Southern Christian Leadership Conference* (1986). Here, in part is what Garrow says;

> "By idolizing those whom we honor," writes black educator Charles Willie, one of King's Morehouse classmates, "we do a disservice both to them and to ourselves By exalting the accomplishments of Martin Luther King, Jr., into a legendary tale that is annually told, we fail to recognize his humanity—his personal and public struggles—that are similar to yours and mine. By idolizing those whom we honor, we fail to realize that we could go and do likewise."
>
> "You have a tendency to romanticize," Yolanda King notes, "when you are looking back on it." Andrew Young states that, "I think it's time to tell it all now," and Christine Farris, King's sister, says she wants to help demythologize one of our heroes. "My brother," she emphasizes "was no saint," but "an average and ordinary man." Indeed, many of King's colleagues worry, as Vincent Harding puts it, that people today are turning King into a "rather smoothed-off, respectable national hero" whose comfortable, present-day image bears little resemblance to the human King or the political King of 1965–1968. Hosea Williams says it bluntly: "There is a definite effort on the part of America to change Martin Luther King, Jr., from what he really was all about— to make him the Uncle Tom of the century. In my mind, he was the militant of the century."
>
> Ella Baker aptly articulates the most crucial point, the central fact of his life, which King himself understood: "The movement made Martin rather than Martin making the movement." As Diane Nash says, "If people think that it was Martin Luther King's movement, then today they—young people—are more likely to say, 'gosh, I wish we had a Martin Luther King here today to lead us.' . . . If people knew how that movement started, then the question they would ask themselves is, 'What can I do?'"

I like to have students respond to these ideas in a journal entry followed by discussion. Kendra wrote:

> I agree with the ideas of Garrow's Epilogue. I think that it is important that we honor Martin Luther King, Jr. for his accomplishments, but at the same time Americans are so focused on King the hero, we fail to see his humanity, his personal struggles that are the same as anyone else's. Americans fail to realize they can go out and do the same thing if they have enough heart and desire . . . this Epilogue encourages Americans to honor heroes but not to idolize them because anyone who wants to can be a hero.

Some students disagreed, though not vehemently, with Garrow's sentiments. These students saw King as someone who should be idolized because the world has too few heroes today and individuals like King are needed to be positive role models. One of my black students confided in me that when he had a racial problem with another student in our school and went to speak about it with his guidance counselor, the counselor said, "What do you think Dr. King would have done in this situation?"

King's letter and the film *Martin Luther King Jr.: The Man and the Dream* also open the door for discussion on racial terminology. It's important that students understand why people used the terms *Negro* or *colored* in either their writings or speeches. For instance, they should recognize that DuBois used the word *Negro* as a source of black pride, which then shifted to the term *black* in the 1960s as tied to the black power movement, and to African American in the 1980s as part of a national movement to heritage identity. I came across a wonderful quote by Henry Louis Gates, W. E. B. DuBois Professor of African American Studies at Harvard University who said, "When I was applying to Yale, the first sentence of my application said, "My grandfather is Colored. My father is Negro. And I am Black. Now my daughters are African Americans. Their kids, I bet, will be Neo-Nubians." I like to share Gates' quote with my students so that they see a living dynamic of how words and meanings can change over time. One time this led to a really strong, but positive, class discussion about cliques and groups self-segregating each other. This lively conversation led me to bring in and read to students the following excerpt from *Hanging Curve* consisting of a marvelous conversation between the white journeyman baseball player, Mickey Rawlings, and the black attorney, Franklin Aubrey, as they discuss the relations between whites and blacks. Aubrey points out:

> I mean no offense, but there are things about me that you will never truly understand, and things about you that I will never understand. One can never really know what it is like to live in someone else's skin. There are differences between us, and there always will be. There is no sense pretending otherwise. Negros are not looking to be the same as white people; we just want to be treated as human. (Soos 1999)

The point of reading this excerpt to my students was to let them see that the bottom line in any relationship is a fundamental sense of establishing respect for the other that not only recognizes and honors our differences, but celebrates our common humanity.

Dr. King and Malcolm X

To present a balanced view of the Civil Rights movement, I think it is important to have students compare and contrast the goals and objectives of Martin Luther King, Jr., and Malcolm X. Students need to recognize that they were contemporaries who essentially sought the same goal but that their approaches for the most part differed. This instruction can be achieved though a variety of strategies and techniques. If you don't want to lose class time by showing the two A & E Biography films of each man to all of your students, I suggest that you break your class into two groups and have one group watch the episode on King while the other group watches the segment on Malcolm X. Have students take notes while watching their film in order to prepare an oral presentation to the other group about the episode they watched. Students should be directed to explain the reasoning behind each man's strategies for achieving civil rights. King's and Malcolm X's motivations should also be explored. A comparison should be made between each man's background and upbringing and how that served to form each man differently.

For a role playing exercise, you could have your students play out a correspondence between King and Malcolm X. Pair your students and have one play King and the other Malcolm X. These students should write letters to each other from the frame of reference of the person they are portraying. These persuasive letters should address the author's belief system in an effort to convince the recipient that his particular strategy is more effective for the black community in achieving his goal. Students could share letters with the class.

Another approach would be to have students read selections from *The Autobiography of Malcolm X* (Haley and Shabazz 1965) and compare his writing with King's "Letter from a Birmingham Jail" or his "I Have a Dream" speech. Here you could again have students analyze each man's strategies and in a journal express their opinions as to whose writing is more persuasive.

Regardless of how you approach it and design your curriculum, it is in yours as well as the students' best interest not to bypass comparing King and Malcolm X. Each man was an important player. At times they played off one another. To dismiss this aspect of the movement does injustice to the men and their times and would be historically dishonest.

Powerful Images

If you are seeking additional images to use for your instruction, I suggest that you turn to the book *Powerful Days: The Civil Rights Photography of Charles Moore* (Durham 1991) or the film, *Simple Justice* (1993).

Powerful Days consists of photographs taken by the celebrated photographer, Charles Moore, who documented most of the significant events of the Civil Rights movement through his lens. These stark black-and-white images are easily turned into transparencies and can be used to generate discussion.

Another powerful teaching tool can be the film *Simple Justice*, which is based very closely on the book of the same name by Richard Kluger (1977). This two-and-a-half hour movie drama, produced for the PBS *American Experience* series, chronicles the legal struggle to overturn the 1896 Supreme Court decision of *Plessy v. Ferguson* in 1954. It is the tale of the close to thirty-year legal challenge that the NAACP brought before the highest court in the land culminating in the landmark case of *Brown v. the Board of Education of Topeka, Kansas*. The film works exceptionally well with students of all academic levels. It's one of those films that holds student attention for the duration and provides an inspiring message, while remaining true to history. As courtroom dramas go, you can show none better.

Before showing the film, I think it is important to lay some critical groundwork so that students have a foundation prior to watching the film. For starters, I get students to do some historical reminiscing. I ask them to think back to our study of Reconstruction and the various pieces of legislation and Constitutional amendments that were created in the years after the Civil War. Most specifically, I want them to recall the Fourteenth Amendment. Once we have reconnected with the past, I give each student a copy of the Fourteenth Amendment and ask them to read the Section One of the amendment and to paraphrase or summarize it. Section One defines citizenship and the rights and privileges of citizenship, complete with due process and equal protection under the law. Most students are able to understand what that means. Given that the Fourteenth Amendment plays a role in the rights they have at school, they can connect with it on a personal level.

This is followed with a brief lecture on the history of the *Plessy* case and an introduction to the workings of the Supreme Court. Students need to understand the idea of the court having a "compelling state interest" in order to hear a case. Next I provide students with a copy of the Majority and Dissenting opinions offered by Justices Henry Brown and John Marshall Harlan, respectively, in the *Plessy* case. After they read the opinions, I ask them to summarize what these two jurists offered as legal arguments for their positions.

Once we examine the two opinions, I ask students upon what basis does each position pose its argument. Brown's opinion essentially states that blacks by virtue of their color are different from whites and therefore not necessarily given the same protections afforded to white citizens. As such, it was reasonable to assume that "separate but equal facilities" in public accommodations, such as a railway car in this instance, were in fact constitutional. This smacks of the decision rendered in the Dred Scott case of 1856, in which Chief Justice Roger B. Taney argued that the Declaration of Independence and the Constitution were never intended for black inhabitants of the United States. Harlan argued that the framers of the Fourteenth Amendment were quite specific about the meaning of citizenship and were deliberate in providing to Americans of all colors the rights and privileges of citizenship status, particularly given that a war had been waged in which those rights were specifically gained for blacks. In Harlan's thinking, "separate but equal" undermined the Constitution. It is important to point out that *Plessy* was a split decision and the fact that there was one dissenting voice would play to the favor of blacks sixty years hence.

Finally, I give students a copy of Chief Justice Earl Warren's unanimous decision in the *Brown* case. Again, I ask students to read the decision and summarize its content. Then we discuss the implications of *Brown* and its importance in twentieth-century America. In particular, we are careful look at and recognize the significance of the unanimity of the judgment. When asked why this is significant, students can see that by having a unanimous decision, room could not be left open for future arguments.

All of this is played out quite dramatically in the film. *Simple Justice* is another one of those films where I enjoy watching student faces as they nod in unison when something is said in the dialogue upon which they all agree, or they cringe when Dr. Kenneth Clark successfully demonstrates, through his famous doll experiment, just how segregation can destroy one's self-image and engender self-hatred. When the final court verdict is announced, I can see just how satisfied students are that the decision came out the way it did. In fact, what makes it even more interesting is that students know what the decision was before I show the film. The portrayal of NAACP chief counselor Thurgood Marshall is crisp and adds to the sense of legal tension. Most students know who Thurgood Marshall was, but I have to check with them before I show the film to be certain that they knew he was later appointed by President Lyndon Johnson as the first African American justice to sit on the bench. *Simple Justice* works well because students get caught up in the human dimensions of the story.

David, an African American, responded in his journal:

This movie was very intriguing to me. In the beginning of the movie I could picture myself in that classroom full of aspiring lawyers being taught how to litigate and ultimately destroy the *Plessy v. Ferguson* ruling. I could remember the time I wanted to be a lawyer. After the graduation of nine out of thirty students from the Howard University Law School the true drama began. Seeing the southern school children and the places where they attended school made me hurt on the inside. I look at how I take my education and the people I learn with for granted. Even though I'm the only black person in this history class and stick out like a sore thumb it has its advantages. The movie almost made me cry twice. Once when the little boys and girls picked out the white dolls as being "good" and the black dolls as being "bad" with them being black children. The second time was when the final decision was made by the Supreme Court.

Public Monuments

As a follow-up activity designed to determine whether or not students can link time periods together and also to employ the power of public monuments, I share with students an interesting set of sculptures located on the state capitol grounds in Annapolis, Maryland. In 1881, a statue of Chief Justice Roger B. Taney was unveiled in front of the state capitol. In 1996, three years after his death, a monument to Thurgood Marshall by Antonio Mendez was dedicated. Marshall hailed from the Baltimore area. The Marshall memorial is on the opposite side of the State House. I juxtapose the slide images of both sculptures, reminding students of the respective roles of the men who are memorialized. The statue of Taney is a simple portrait sculpture showing him seated in his robes. The monument to Marshall is a bit more complex as it involves a grouping of several sculptures. In a plaza, the centerpiece sculpture depicts as he looked in 1954, and behind the statue seated on raised pillars is a frieze with the statement "Equal Justice Before The Law." Across the short plaza sits a two-group composition of a black school-age boy and girl seated looking at Marshall, and on the opposite side of the plaza is a solitary sculpture of Marshall as a young law student at Howard University gazing at the older Marshall. The whole sculptural arrangement works quite nicely. Students are asked to look at the slides and recall what they remember about each man. Spending more time on the memorial to Marshall, I ask students to tell me what they think the additional figures mean as part of the sculptural arrangement. Students are quick to point out that the school children represent Marshall's efforts to end segregation in public schools. They have a harder time determining the placement of the other sculpture, so I have to lead them to that discovery by asking them to focus carefully on the figure and what he looks like and what he is carrying. Once it is determined that the figure represents the young Marshall, all the pieces fall into place. Finally, I ask students to comment in their journals on the placement of the two statues on state capitol grounds, representing two different men who held two different positions on the place of blacks in American society. May wrote:

> The juxtaposition of these two sculptures at the Maryland State House seems to be a bit ironic when considering their history. Roger B. Taney as a Supreme Court Justice before the Civil War made the blatantly racist ruling in the *Dred Scott* case, however representative of that time, that blacks were not entitled to the rights guaranteed to all by the Constitution due to their inherent inferiority. Thurgood Marshall adamantly fought for these very rights in the famous *Brown* case. The two

men, equally prominent in their respective fields, had two essentially opposing ideas. The fact that there were commemorative sculptures made for these two figures then placed on the same grounds of the Maryland State House represents the complexity of the nation's history. I'm sure Justice Taney was a respectable man, but unfortunately unenlightened to equality, as were many of the nation's forefathers. I don't think that everyone who held racist beliefs should be forgotten and disrespected—racism was sadly, but undeniably a significant and accepted attribute of many prominent people. On the other hand, those like Thurgood Marshall who was a leading figure in a moral crusade must be remembered and honored. Therefore, we have Marshall and Taney on the same grounds—a reminder of our history and a reflection of the present. In some ways, the placement of these two figures is almost logical—they show the progression of the ever-present issue of race and equality.

Concluding this material with this lesson helps me to reach the objective of getting students to analyze the past within its context as well as to recognize the evolutionary process of what it means to be an American. By wrestling with issues such as this, students will develop critical and historical thinking skills that can assist them in contending with the often conflicting nature found in American history.

Crafting a Civil Rights Tree

One of the great aspects of our social studies department at West Springfield High School is our naturally collaborative nature. We talk at lunch or in the halls as we continue our own personal and professional growth as teachers. We often support each other by living out the phrase, "Imitation is the sincerest form of flattery." If we see something that works in a colleague's class, we try it in our own classrooms. When Laurie Fischer was trying to figure out how to cover a huge amount of material by the end of the year, she hit on an idea of combining material from Reconstruction with the Civil Rights movement a century later. She accomplished this by having students create a civil rights tree. When I saw the quality of work students produced for her classes, I decided to try it out on my own, with Laurie as my coach.

For the most part, I followed Laurie's lead and made few adjustments. First, I asked my students to write a journal about trees. They could write anything they wanted about trees. Their journals might simply consist of things about trees such as leaves, bark, the changing of color, providing shade, and so forth. This was simply to get them to focus on the idea of "trees." Next, I put the following quote by W. E. B. DuBois on the chalkboard, "The root of the trees rather than the leaves is the source of its life." I asked students to interpret this quote in their journals. Many students talked about the importance of having a firm foundation and being rooted in one's belief of self. Other students wrote that a tree could not have any leaves if it had no roots. Some students indicated that all life emanates from a single source, in this case roots. I was pleased that they were getting the picture.

Then I announced that we would be working on creating civil rights trees. Some of my students had friends in Laurie's classes so they were familiar with the project. In addition, Laurie had placed some of her best trees on display in the library. So I urged students to go check out these outstanding examples. On my handout explaining the assignment, I explained to students that as a result of this project they would be able to answer the following questions:

1. How did the movement evolve?
2. What made it peak?
3. Does the movement continue today?
4. Who was and is responsible for keeping the flame burning?
5. What people in society were instrumental in seeing justice achieved and civil rights addressed?
6. Were there downfalls?
7. What laws and legislations were passed?
8. What court decisions were involved?
9. Who paid the ultimate price for all of our freedom with their lives?

Students were next given a list of fifty vocabulary terms relative to the topic. This list consisted of the names of people, court cases, events, legislation, and organizations that played a role in this movement. The following is a list of some, but not all, of the terms.

1. Langston Hughes
2. Barbara Jordan
3. A. Philip Randolph
4. Jackie Robinson
5. lunch-counter sit-ins
6. Harlem Renaissance
7. Little Rock 9
8. nonviolent direct action
9. Freedom Riders
10. Bloody Sunday
11. Black Panthers
12. black power/pride
13. Heart of Atlanta Motel
14. Student Non-Violent Coordinating Committee

Working either individually or in groups of no more than four, students were to create these trees that measured the growth and patterns of the Civil Rights movement. Essentially, they were to construct a living timeline in the symbolic representation of a tree. Because there was a great deal of historical territory to cover, we agreed that the roots for these trees would be the Thirteenth, Fourteenth, and Fifteenth Amendments to the Constitution, all adopted during Reconstruction. This gave students a baseline from which to work. For assessment and evaluation purposes, there were ten categories that needed to be addressed, with each category being worth ten points for a total of one hundred points. The categories measured both academic knowledge and research/working skills. The requirements for the tree were as follows:

1. Build a minimum of a 5-foot tree. The design is up to the student(s). Trees may be three-dimensional or two-dimensional. A variety of material can be employed.

2. Each leaf, branch, fruit, etc., is to be labeled with a title, explanatory statement, in complete sentences, relative to chronological order. Because this is a timeline, there should be natural and logical historical progression of people and events.

3. Include a minimum of half of the vocabulary terms provided.

4. Include at least ten additional terms/people/events that are not found on the provided list.

5. Include at least ten visual images such as photos, graphs, and charts.

6. Give your tree a thoughtful title.

7. Be historically accurate.

8. Use proper grammar and sentence structure.

9. Exhibit creativity.

10. Submit a bibliography of no fewer than seven sources for individual trees and no fewer than ten sources for group efforts, of which only three may be from the Internet. Students may not cite standard encyclopedias in their sources.

Students were given six weeks to conduct their research and build their trees. I directed them to an entire list of appropriate Internet addresses and useful websites. *The History Highway 2000: A Guide to Internet Resources* (Trinkle and Merriman 2000) is an outstanding resource. In addition, I provided students with two of my favorite websites: The National Park Service's Civil Rights Sites at *www.cr.nps.gov/nr/travel/civilrights* and the National Voting Rights Museum at *www.votingrights.org*. Laurie also dropped in to visit my class and explained to my students

Figure 4–3
Civil Rights Trees

the kind of work her students submitted. She brought along some samples for demonstration and modeling.

When the completed trees were submitted for evaluation, I was pleased with the work of my students (see Figure 4–3). They had clearly followed the directions and had conducted extensive research. Some of the trees were made out of chicken wire and papier-mâché, others were constructed from PVC pipes, and some students used fabric and other craft material. It was a nice variety of trees reflecting all kinds of learning styles and differentiation. In addition, the assignment was academically rigorous requiring bonafide student research.

Using Rosa Parks Documents to Teach

When it can be worked into my curriculum, I like to use interesting primary-source material to complement my instruction. At the beginning of teaching the Civil Rights movement, if I ask students to brainstorm about who and what prior knowledge they have regarding this subject, I almost universally hear the name Rosa Parks. Most students are familiar with the name of this civil rights pioneer from what they learned in either elementary school or junior high. However, most are not that familiar with the real story of Parks and the subsequent Montgomery bus boycott. Using some documents from the National Archives collection that are related to the federal court case that emerged as the result of litigation against the bus company can help students to recognize additional legal implications about the Civil Rights movement as well as the historical place of race and racial perception in American history. Some of these documents are shown in Figures 4–4a, 4–4b, and 4–4c. These documents were published in the May/June 1999 issue of *Social Education* and the following lesson plan is based on their presentation in that professional journal. The documents used here are the actual arrest records of Rosa Parks for refusing to give up her seat to a white man. These documents became part of the federal case and were submitted as evidence in *Browder v. Gayle*. They help launch an explanation of the meaning of nonviolent direct action as was practiced by so many as part of a planned strategy to end segregation. If you teach students about this discipline, it is important to let them know that individuals were deliberately trained in a variety of ways to resist assault and abuse without striking back. While self-defense activity was not really a part of the 381-day Montgomery bus boycott, this event was nevertheless the beginning of nonviolent direct action and set the stage for future passive resistance such as the lunch-counter sit-ins and Freedom Rides. Nonviolent direct action was the bedrock of the early movement, and once underway, it was difficult to stop. You might want to have students recall what they learned about Thoreau or have them read passages from *On Civil Disobedience* before you proceed with this lesson. Once students understand the idea of nonviolent direct action, you can move on to using the documents.

Duplicate the documents, hand them out, and then generate a classroom conversation based on the following questions:

1. Who was arrested? Do you recognize the name?
2. Who arrested this person?
3. When and where was she arrested?
4. Who signed the warrant for her arrest?
5. What was the complaint?
6. Does anything surprise you about the arrest? The arrest records?
7. What else do you want to know about the arrest that the records don't tell you?

Once you have worked through those questions, brainstorm with students the definition of the word *nationality*. Then read to students

Figure 4–4a
Rosa Parks Documents (Montgomery, Alabama, Police Records)

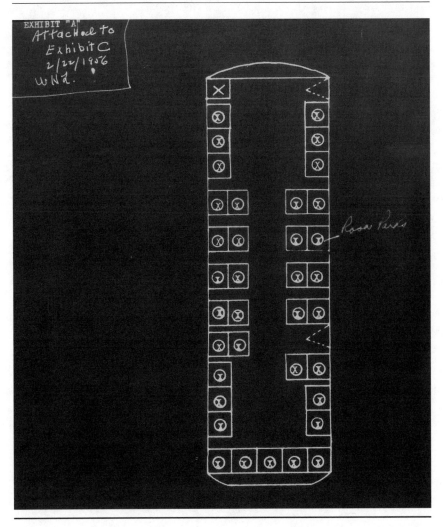

the dictionary definition of the word. Next, have students reread the police report and alert them to what was written about Rosa Parks' nationality. It's effective at this point to have students compare the dictionary definition with the response written on the police report. Follow up with the following questions:

1. How do the forms differ?

2. What might explain this difference?

3. What can you infer from this difference about the official view of black citizen's of Montgomery, Alabama, at the time of Rosa Parks' arrest?

To give additional meaning to this lesson, have one of your students obtain a blank police report from your local police department. Let stu-

Figure 4–4b
Rosa Parks Documents

Misc.

POLICE DEPARTMENT
CITY OF MONTGOMERY

Date 12-1-55   19

Complainant   J.F. Blake   (wm)

Address   27 No. Lewis St.   Phone No.

Offense   Misc.   Reported By Same as above

Address   Phone No.

Date and Time Offense Committed   12-1-55   6:06 pm

Place of Occurrence   In Front of Empire Theatre (On Montgomery Street)

Person or Property Attacked

How Attacked

Person Wanted

Value of Property Stolen   Value Recovered

Details of Complaint (list, describe and give value of property stolen)

We received a call upon arrival the bus operator said he had a colored female

sitting in the white section of the bus, and would not move back.

We (Day & Mixon) also saw her.

The bus operator signed a warrant for her. Rosa Parks, (cf) 634 Cleveland Court.

Rosa Parks (cf) was charged with chapter 6 section 11 of the Montgomery City Code.

Warrant #14254

THIS OFFENSE IS DECLARED: Officers J. D. Day
UNFOUNDED   □
CLEARED BY ARREST   □   D. W. Mixon
EXCEPTIONALLY CLEARED   □
INACTIVE (NOT CLEARED)   □
                                    Division   Patrol   Time 7:00 pm
10M—PARAGON PRESS—24501   12-1-55

Figure 4–4c
Rosa Parks Documents

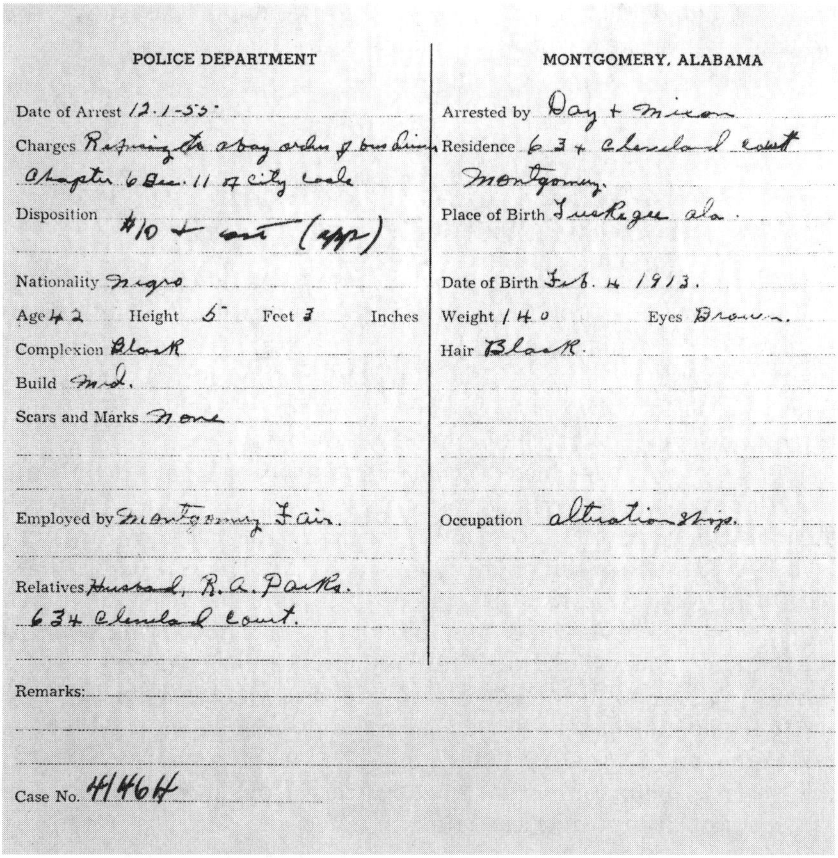

POLICE DEPARTMENT — MONTGOMERY, ALABAMA

Date of Arrest 12-1-55.
Charges Refusing to obey orders of bus driver. Chapter 6 Sec. 11 of City code
Disposition $10 + cost (app)
Nationality Negro
Age 42 Height 5 Feet 3 Inches
Complexion Black
Build Med.
Scars and Marks None
Employed by Montgomery Fair.
Relatives Husband, R. A. Parks. 634 Cleveland court.

Arrested by Day + Mixon
Residence 634 Cleveland court Montgomery.
Place of Birth Tuskegee Ala.
Date of Birth Feb. 4 1913.
Weight 140 Eyes Brown.
Hair Black.
Occupation altration shop.

Remarks:

Case No. 4/46H

dents compare and contrast the modern form with the one that was used in the arrest of Rosa Parks. Have your class consider why they think information about race and nationality are collected on these and other forms. Another tack you might take with students is to have them relate any experiences that they have had in refusing to obey authority. Encourage students who are willing to share their experiences to explain their motives for disobedience. A discussion of consequences might follow with a comparison to the consequences people in Montgomery and other southern communities had to suffer for their actions.

Any discussion or lesson related to nonviolent, passive resistance should also examine the role of authority during the Civil Rights movement. When I show *A Time for Justice,* I like to stop the film just prior to the scenes documenting the lunch-counter sit-ins and ask students to focus on who gets carried off to jail. This graphic footage documents the horrific assault on the demonstrators—one would think that the attackers would be the ones arrested, but this was not the case; it was the nonviolent protesters who were hauled off to jail.

What Can America Learn from the Civil Rights Movement?

Regardless of how I have taught these lessons over the years, I always end any coverage of the Civil Rights movement with student journal responses to the question, "What can America learn from the Civil Rights movement?" This critical thinking question forces students to reflect on all that they have learned about the movement and apply their knowledge in a meaningful and relevant way.

One of the things I have learned over the years when teaching the Civil Rights movement is that most students have little prior knowledge about the movement. But I am always struck by the fact that of any unit I teach, students take this one very much to heart. I have to admit, that's part of my objective. As a proponent of experiential teaching mixed with good, solid historical grounding, I hope that I am adding layers to the foundation of civil rights. Many students acknowledge how close in time we still are to the actual events. The visual images help to bridge the time gap, plus people like Rosa Parks and John Lewis are still alive and visible on the American landscape, so there is tangible meaning to the lessons. The material they have learned is not about abstractions. Tanisha, an African American student, noted in her journal, "Without this struggle I myself would not be here today."

May concluded the unit by sharing:

> The actual Civil Rights movement ended forty years ago—there are no more Freedom Riders, sit-ins, or marchers for voting rights. But I was living in downtown L.A. during the Rodney King riots; I watched the news last night debating whether or not the NAACP should boycott Virginia tourism for the governor's declaration of April as Confederate History Month—race is very much an issue in the mixing bowl of the United States. The Civil Rights Movement and the Civil War seem to be the two major times this nation tackled the controversial issue of color. Both events were scarred by violence and preceded with negligence and apathy. Nothing in this world can be ignored forever, every issue must be dealt with at its root. The Civil Rights Movement forced the nation to deal with its racism and refused to subside qui-

etly—those involved had the passion and persistence, and justice on their side, to achieve the goals. The Movement can teach that nothing left unjust is left quieted forever, and that when the cry for justice heard, it will be heard forcefully and powerfully.

One of my goals for this material, regardless of how I present it, is to have students come face-to-face with the idea that for two centuries in our history, we legalized exclusion. A whole group of people was excluded from all aspects of society, solely based on the color of their skin. Sometimes I ask students to think about what it means to be excluded. We all know what it feels like at some level, whether we were kept out of a play group as youngsters, or squeezed out of a clique at school, or marginalized at the workplace. In some ways, we are lucky how our nation has evolved. Despite our flaws as a nation, a vehicle was somehow created that allowed the oppressed to raise their voices and generate positive change. Martin Luther King, Jr., expressed it best when speaking in Montgomery during the bus boycott:

> We have known humiliation, we have known oppressive language, we have been plunged into the abyss of oppression. And we decided to raise up only with the weapon of protest. It is one of the greatest glories of America that we have the right of protest.

In some sense, this was a first in the history of the world. In turn, those who engendered the change helped America on the road of its journey of continual redefinition and renewal and, in the process, liberated blacks as well as whites.

There are many other ways that you can teach this important period in American history. I know teachers who use copies of Alabama and Mississippi literacy tests with their students. These teachers have their students take the tests and score them as they might have been scored in the 1960s. Activities such as this provide students with insight into the kind of obstacle many blacks in the South faced. Copies of such literacy tests can be found on the Internet or in many updated United States history textbooks.

Perhaps Dan summed up the power of positive collective action best in his journal when he wrote:

> We need to learn that we can initiate change when something is wrong. We can force politicians and the government to correct social injustices and right previous wrongs if people can organize and focus on their goals. I just participated in the Million Mom March which pushed for safer gun laws. It's too early to tell whether this protest has made any changes. But, being there and seeing thousands of people brought to tears by eyewitness accounts of the Columbine tragedy showed me

how they felt. Those people and millions across the country are unifying over issues like these and are starting to make change.

In many ways, Dan has been touched by the best legacy of the Civil Rights movement, a legacy that will forever be timeless in the American experience.

Resources

Books

Beales, Melba Pattillo. 1994. *Warriors Don't Cry.* New York: Washington Square Press.

Branch, Taylor. 1988. *Parting the Waters: America in the King Years, 1954–63.* New York: Simon and Schuster.

———. 1998. *Pillar of Fire: America in the King Years, 1963–65.* New York: Simon and Schuster.

Bullard, Sara. 1993. *Free At Last: A History of the Civil Rights Movement and Those Who Died in the Struggle.* New York: Oxford University Press.

Caigin, Seth, and Philip Dray. 1988. *We Are Not Afraid: The Story of Goodman, Schwerner, and Chaney and the Civil Rights Campaign for Mississippi.* New York: Macmillan.

Carson, Clayborne, ed. 1998. *The Autobiography of Martin Luther King, Jr.* New York: Warner Brothers.

Durham, Michael S. 1991. *Powerful Days: The Civil Rights Photography of Charles Moore.* New York: Stewart, Tabori, and Chang.

Dyson, Michael Eric. 2000. *I May Not Get There With You: The True Story of Martin Luther King, Jr.* New York: Free Press.

Garrow, David. 1978. *Protest at Selma.* New Haven: Yale University Press.

———. 1986. *Bearing the Cross: Martin Luther King, Jr. and the Southern Christian Leadership Conference.* New York: Random House.

———, ed. 1986. *The Walking City: The Montgomery Bus Boycott, 1955–56.* New York: Carlson Publishing.

Haley, Alex, and Betty Shabazz. 1965. *The Autobiography of Malcolm X.* New York: Grove Press.

Hampton, Henry, and Steve Fayer. 1990. *Voices of Freedom: An Oral History of the Civil Rights Movement from the 1950s Through the 1980s.* New York: Bantam.

Hennessey, Maureen Hart, and Anne Knutson. 1999. *Norman Rockwell: Pictures for the American People.* Atlanta, GA: High Museum of Art.

Kaiser, Steven. 1996. *The Civil Rights Movement: A Photographic History, 1954–68.* New York: Abbeville Press.

Kennedy, Stetson. 1990. *Jim Crow Guide: The Way It Was*. Boca Raton, FL: Florida Atlantic Press.

Kluger, Richard. 1977. *Simple Justice: The History of Brown v. Board of Education and Black America's Struggle for Equality*. New York: Random House.

Lewis, John. 1999. *Walking with the Wind: A Memoir of the Movement*. New York: Simon and Schuster.

Lincoln, C. Eric, and Lawrence H. Mamiya. 1990. *The Black Church in the African American Experience*. Durham, NC: Duke University Press.

McAdam, Doug. 1988. *Freedom Summer*. New York: Oxford University Press.

Moody, Anne. 1968. *Coming of Age in Mississippi*. New York: Doubleday.

Morris, Aldon D. 1984. *The Origins of the Civil Rights Movement: Black Communities Organizing for Change*. New York: Free Press.

Oates, Stephen B. 1982. *Let the Trumpet Sound: The Life of Martin Luther King, Jr.* New York: Harper and Row.

Powledge, Fred. 1991. *Free At Last? The Civil Rights Movement and the People Who Made It*. Boston: Little, Brown.

Robinson, Jo Ann. 1987. *The Montgomery Bus Boycott and the Women Who Started It*. Knoxville, TN: University of Tennessee Press.

Rogers, Mary Beth. 1998. *Barbara Jordan: American Hero*. New York: Bantam.

Siegel, Beatrice. 1993. *Murder on the Highway: The Viola Liuzzo Story*. New York: Four Winds Press.

Soos, Troy. 1999. *Hanging Curve*. New York: Kensington Books.

Stanton, Mary. 1998. *From Selma to Sorrow: The Life and Death of Viola Liuzzo*. Athens, GA: University of Georgia Press.

Tygiel, Jules. 1983. *Baseball's Great Experiment: Jackie Robinson and His Legacy*. New York: Random House.

Washington, James M., ed. 1986. *A Testament of Hope: The Essential Writings and Speeches of Martin Luther King, Jr.* San Francisco: HarperCollins.

Williams, Juan. 1987. *Eyes on the Prize: America's Civil Rights Years, 1954–65*. New York: Viking.

Witcover, Jules. 1997. *The Year the Dream Died: Revisiting 1968 in America*. New York: Warner Books.

Woodward, Comer Vann. 1989. *The Strange Career of Jim Crow*. New York: Oxford University Press.

Films/Videos

A Time for Justice: America's Civil Rights Movement. Producer: Charles Guggenheim. 38 minutes. Teaching Tolerance, 1992, videocassette.

Great American Political Speeches: 80 Years of Political Oratory. Producer: Parker Payson. 240 minutes. Pieri and Springs Production, 1995, videocassette.

Eyes on the Prize: America's Civil Rights Years, 1954–65. Producer: Henry Hampton, Jr. 840 minutes. Blackside, 1996, videocassette.

Martin Luther King Jr.: The Man and the Dream. Producer: Linda Gopaul. 60 minutes. Black Audio Films,1997, videocassette.

Malcolm X. Producer: Ron Steinman. 60 minutes. ABC News Productions, 1995, videocassette.

Simple Justice. Producer: Yanna Kroyt Brandt. 150 minutes. New Images Productions, 1993, videocassette.

Chapter Five

Gender and the American Past

Remember the ladies . . . For if you do not we are wont to foment a revolution of our own.

—Attributed to Abigail Adams

In 1848, the first Women's Rights Convention was held in the small town of Seneca Falls, New York. Contrary to popular belief, Susan B. Anthony was not the organizer, nor did she attend the meeting. The convention held in the Wesleyan Chapel was organized by Elizabeth Cady Stanton and Lucretia Mott, among others. The most significant contemporary of the day to attend was Frederick Douglass. The great black abolitionist and orator came because he believed that the issue of women's rights was tied to the issue of abolition of slavery. Three hundred people attended the convention. As a result of the convention, one hundred delegates, among whom were thirty-two men, drafted and signed the Declaration of Sentiments, an often overlooked document in American history. This particular declaration, modeled directly on the Declaration of Independence, incorporated the same language with the exception of a more inclusive tone by usage of the terms *men* and *women* throughout the document. The National Park Service maintains sites relative to that event and offers a solid and up-to-date interpretation of the convention as well as its long-standing implications in American history.

The Women's National Hall of Fame is just down the street from the Park Service's Visitor Center.

Although I include women in all areas of study in American history, I do want to spend some time here discussing a few specifics related to women, who have at times been marginalized or kept out on the fringes of enjoying the totality of our national life.

It's imperative that students understand that in 1776, when Thomas Jefferson and the Committee of Five penned the Declaration of Independence, their language was restricted to the term *men* because that is what they meant. In the thinking of the American Enlightenment, the term *men* was exclusive to white property owners over the age of twenty-one. Property owners were defined as men of means and substance: northern merchants, lawyers, artisans, and southern plantation owners. Neither Jefferson nor his companions could have foreseen just how their writing would be interpreted in the ensuing years. Historian Gordon Wood asserts that the phrase "We hold these truths to be self-evident, that all men are created equal and that they are endowed by their creator with certain inalienable rights among these are which life, liberty and the pursuit of happiness" became a somewhat permissive doctrine latched on to over succeeding years by all people and groups. Some scholars will even argue that by 1787 and the Constitutional Convention, the framers of the Constitution deliberately intended to limit the definition of "We the people . . ." in a much more narrow sense than had been outlined in the Declaration of Independence. To these delegates in Philadelphia, the most important function of government was to secure their rights and protection of their property. However, as a nation, we have ever since been debating what is meant by the phrase, "We the people." The debate and conflict generated by that single phrase continues to be played out in American life. A good source for more study on this topic is Eric Foner's *The Story of American Freedom* (1998).

Where To Begin

I like to begin instruction of early American history by looking at the definition of roles during colonial times. When teaching about Puritan New England, I like to use two devices for instruction. There is a very good segment from the video series *Profiles in Courage* on *Anne Hutchinson* (1966). This fifty-minute film provides me with ample material to explore the clear definition of roles between men and women and how those roles played themselves out in society. By examining the case of Anne Hutchinson, who was excommunicated from her church because of her particular interpretation of the Bible, students will easily recognize that she was in part treated the way she was by Puritan elders because she was a woman. It's very interesting showing this film and watching the reaction of my students as the drama unfolds. Most of my female students are put off by the attitude taken toward Hutchinson by the church elders. Post-film discussion always proves lively as many girls express their outrage at how Hutchinson was treated. Usually the boys in the classroom remain silent, perhaps not wanting to stir the pot further.

The Shadow of Hate (1995) video also has a section on women from New England. This film and accompanying magazine, *Us and Them*, look at the case of Mary Dyer, a Quaker who was executed by the Puritan leadership of Massachusetts Bay Colony for expression of her views. As is pointed out in the sidebar of the magazine, "Women in Massachusetts were not even allowed to discuss a sermon, much less voice their own ideas about religion." In the accompanying teacher's guide, there are questions that I can pose to my students after having them read the excerpt from *Us and Them* that include:

1. In what sense was Mary Dyer one of "us" who became one of "them"?
2. Why were the voices of women silenced in the Puritan Church?
3. People who are willing to sacrifice their lives for their beliefs are rare. Why do you believe Mary Dyer is not a well-known historical figure?

Again, these are thought-provoking questions that, when discussed among students, will provide further fertile ground for good dialogue. I remind students to keep in mind as they study these issues both historically and objectively that those of us living today should not use a twenty-first-century perspective to judge those individuals living in the past. In order to impart this maxim to my students, I like to use the following model as an example. Many people have been critical of America's seeming indifference toward the Holocaust during the 1930s and 1940s. In particular, criticism is leveled against American policy makers including President Franklin Roosevelt (though antisemitic) for not bombing the rail lines to the concentration camps during the Second World War. What we have to remember is that we now have more than a half-century of Holocaust memory that allows us to look back over time and see what happened in a greater totality. Sometimes having 20/20 vision can put historical analysis in a kind of perspective that is not fair to the participants who played out the drama. As historian David McCullough often points out, ". . . we know what happened. The people living then did not have the time and space to see how the story would turn out." In my classroom, this is a critical component of my instruction. It's a valuable lesson in historiography with which all of my students need to be familiar.

The Salem Witch Trials

Another area of the colonial experience and women's history to study is the infamous Salem witch trials of 1692–1693. There are plenty of outstanding resources that you can use to teach this fascinating episode. Background reading for preparation includes *The Devil in Massachusetts* by Marion Starkey (1949), *The Devil in the Shape of a Woman* by Carol Karlsen (1987), and *Entertaining Satan: Witchcraft and the Culture of Early New England* by John Putnam Demos (1982). Most US history textbooks offer extensive coverage of the Salem witch trials. Two good films that you can use to complement student reading are *The Witches of Salem: The Horror and the Hope* (1972), which is a half hour long and provides a condensed history of the causes and the subsequent outcomes of the trials; and the very moving *Three Sovereigns for Sarah* (1986), starring Vanessa Redgrave as Sarah Cloyce, which was produced for public television. *Three Sovereigns for Sarah* is two and a half hours long; the best way to use it is to show selected segments, pausing every now and then to provide some analysis and answer questions students may have.

Advanced students can handle James West Davidson's and Mark Hamilton Lytle's *After the Fact: The Art of Historical Detection* (1986). In Chapter 2, "The Visible and Invisible Worlds of Salem," students will explore this topic in a historiographical context using the skills of a professional historian to determine the cause of the hysteria that spread like wildfire throughout Massachusetts.

When I teach this material, I like to ask my students why they think only five of the nineteen people who were accused of witchcraft and executed were males. When students realize this, they begin to understand that women in colonial, Puritan New England were not really regarded as a vital part of the community beyond the realm of child rearing. For these students, it's hard to comprehend what by today's standards are seeming indignities.

Rounding out this material on the Salem witch trials, I like to show my slides of the Witch Trial Memorial located in Salem, Massachusetts, which today fashions itself as a community long tied to its infamous past. The Witch Trial Memorial, a collaborative design between architect James Cutler and artist Maggie Smith, was dedicated in 1992 on the occasion of the Salem Witch Trial Tercentenary. Speaking at the dedication were author and Holocaust survivor Elie Wiesel and playwright Arthur Miller, whose 1953 drama *The Crucible* chronicles the story of the witch trials. *The Crucible* was intended as a piece to reflect the injustices of McCarthyism and the 1950s "witch hunt" for communists in America. Many schools across the United States teach *The Crucible* either when teachers are teaching the colonial period in US history or when they are teaching the 1950s. Studying the Salem witch trials ensures that students have to wrestle with the issues of injustice and false accusation as are acted out in Miller's classic. I know of teachers who have successfully had the play acted out in class to make for more effective teaching.

The Witch Trial Memorial consists of a unique design. It is park-like and located adjacent to the colonial cemetery. A low stone wall borders three sides of the park and jutting out from the wall are nineteen bench-like structures that represent each victim. On each bench is the name and the execution date of the victim. In the center of the park are six black locust trees, the last trees to bloom and the first to lose their blooms. Black locusts may have also been the trees on Gallow's Hill, from which the accused were hanged. These trees symbolize the innocence of the victims. As you enter the park, you walk across pavement on which are inscribed the words of the victims asserting their innocence. This is a deliberate device used to trigger each visitor's emotion toward the indifference or perhaps the fear of association by the community toward the accused. In addition, the wall near the entrance is designed to block out the pleas of the victims. The memorial works quite well and serves as a place for reflection on what happened to these individuals, mostly women and their spouses, who were killed in a kind of Puritan feeding frenzy. The benches also serve as headstones of a sort because the victims were denied a Christian burial.

On first glance, students are attracted to the macabre nature of this episode. But as they learn more and more about the event and its causes and effects, they recognize that individuals paid a price simply for being who they were. It's a story that has been played out time and again in our history.

Foundations for the Women's Movement— Seneca Falls, 1848

Moving into more recent women's history, I like to have my students study the foundations of the Women's movement, in particular, the Seneca Falls Convention. For class instruction I rely on the following:

1. a copy of both the Declaration of Independence and the Declaration of Sentiments
2. slides that I have taken at the Women's Rights National Historical Park and the Women's National Hall of Fame

3. slides of the Women's Rights National Memorial sculpted by Adelaide Johnson

4. articles from the *Washington Post* concerning the 1997 controversy to move the Women's Rights National Memorial from the basement of the US Capitol to the Rotunda

By the time I introduce this topic to my classes, students are already familiar with the shifting viewpoints regarding women and their place in society. They are familiar with the place of defined roles in American history and with Abigail Adams' famous statement in a letter to her husband, John, that serves as the epigram for this chapter. The prior knowledge that students have regarding women's history in America is important in order for this lesson to make sense.

First, I have students review the Declaration of Independence. I ask them to count how many times they see the word *men* in the document. Next, we quickly review the intent and purpose of the Declaration of Independence. Once that is completed, I pass out to students copies of the Declaration of Sentiments. I obtained my copy during my visit to Women's Rights National Historical Park, but most updated American history textbooks have now included this document in their appendices. Students read the Declaration of Sentiments and compare and contrast it with the Declaration of Independence. I advise students to look for any similarities and or differences between the two documents. The similarity between the two documents is obvious to students. Once that point has been raised, we ponder the following questions:

1. In what ways are the documents similar?

2. Why do you think the authors of the Declaration of Sentiments modeled their statement on the Declaration of Independence? Do you think this was a deliberate action and if so, why?

3. What is the point of the Declaration of Sentiments?

4. Why do you think the delegates at the Seneca Falls Convention felt that they needed to issue such a statement?

5. How many people signed the Declaration of Sentiments? Of those names, whose do you recognize?

6. How many males signed the document and what can you infer from their names? To this question students should recognize that they are mostly married men whose wives attended the convention, so logically the next prompt is:

7. Why do you think these men signed the document and what might that say about these individuals, given the tenor of the times?

After we have discussed student responses to these questions I put up the slides I took during a visit to Seneca Falls and provide students with a brief background lecture to the conference. It's important to keep this conference within the context of the times. Students need to understand that this period of American history was marked by what I have heard referred to as "Freedom's Ferment"—the first true social reform era in America. By 1848 various issues of social justice and injustice were at the forefront of the minds of many Americans, particularly in the North. Connections made between the Women's movement and the Utopians, the Abolition movement, Horace Mann's call for public education, and Dorothea Dix's efforts on behalf of the imprisoned and insane must be seen all within the context of each other and the times. Part of my agenda is to have students understand why women took leadership roles during this age of reform. It's my intent that students clearly see that women had a vested interest in the success of these other movements, as victories there would further their cause, particularly in their quest for the right to vote. Once I am done with the slides of sites related to the convention, I show my slides of some of the displays in the National Women's Hall of Fame, which includes inductees such as Dr. Sally Ride, the first female astronaut; Abigail Adams; Eleanor Roosevelt; Margaret Sanger, advocate of the birth control movement; Clara Barton; painter Mary Cassatt; and activist Alice Paul, among many others. I like to use these images again to reflect the inclusive nature of our history and to demonstrate that many women of many diverse backgrounds and with different talents played a significant role in shaping our history. You can always make transparencies of photographs of these women from picture books and augment the images with a brief lecture. The *American History Videodisk* also includes images of many of these women.

One of the best resources available to teachers covering this period in American history is the 1999 video production of Ken Burns' and Paul Barnes' film, *Not for Ourselves Alone: The Story of Elizabeth Cady Stanton and Susan B. Anthony*. This lengthy documentary is best suited as a subtext to teaching. It covers a lengthy period of time in American history, the mid-nineteenth century to the passage of the Nineteenth Amendment to the Constitution in 1919. You can weave the film in and out of your instruction as you please while covering other aspects of American history. If you prefer, you can simply use segments of the film to complement your instruction. There is an outstanding faculty and teaching guide that accompanies the film, loaded with primary sources, political cartoons, and a timeline. Should you prefer only to use selected portions of the film, the guide is video indexed with time sequences listed to provide you easy access. This material is tied to excellent lesson plans that you can easily implement in your classroom. As a bonus, the guide lists additional resources for you to consider using for either personal investigation or classroom use. No social studies department or school library should be without this among their resource collection.

Teachers who really are energized by a particular topic will, over time, create interesting lesson plans based on their interests. However, I would encourage teachers who are new to the profession to look at the Center for Learning's reproducible lessons as contained in the four-volume series *US History*. In these volumes, arranged chronologically, teachers will find lessons that reflect a broad base of topics related to women in American history. For example, in Volume One, *America Creating the Dream: Beginnings to 1865* (Caliguire et al. 1991), there's a self-contained lesson on the Cult of Domesticity as well as a lesson on the Mill Girls who worked in Lowell, Massachusetts. I like to combine this lesson with the playing of the James Taylor song, "Millworker" found on his album, *Flag*. The lesson and the song make a nice fit and you can easily download the lyrics to the song off the Internet. The combination of the song with this lesson (that includes primary-source document evaluation consisting of The Lowell Manufacturing Company's Rules and Regulations, Women's House Rules, and an excerpt from *Loom and Spindle* by Harriet H. Robinson) brings the conditions that these women had to endure into stark reality.

Manchester, New Hampshire's Historic Association has produced (for a reasonable price) a very good set of lesson plans with fifteen over-sized photographs of Manchester's Amoskeag Mill—the largest mill in the world by 1912. These photographs and the lesson plans explore the Mill, daily life, and production. The teacher's guide includes questions to accompany each photograph that you can raise with students. You can also combine visual images found on the *American History Videodisk* to complement the lesson. These images, some lithograph drawings, and other photographs, provide visual documentation of what millwork was like. The power of combining all these components helps students to grasp the difficulty and monotony these women faced day in and day out. I also like to teach this material with a slide of the statue of the *Mill Girl* in Manchester, New Hampshire. Most of the public sculptures they have seen in class prior to this have been of military or political figures. By showing the *Mill Girl*, I can raise with students the question of why a community would honor someone from the working class, and we can explore the idea of the common person in the development of the United States.

For fun, you can use the five-minute clip from the motion picture *Hello Dolly*, in which the male employees of Horace Vandergelder's (Walter Matthau) business sing "It Takes a Woman." Have students watch the film clip and then ask them how the song reinforces the tenets of the Cult of Domesticity. You can have students compare and contrast how some things have changed while others have stayed the same over a period of over one hundred years. Skillful use of these lessons, taught within the total context of American history, will help your students to trace and track trends that seem to shift with the passage of time.

The National Women's Rights Memorial

One of the ways I like to pull together a variety of strands with teaching the Women's movement is to relate the continuing saga of the National Women's Rights Memorial that was sculpted by the feminist Adelaide Johnson and given to the people of the United States in 1921 by the National Women's Party. The memorial was meant to be a tribute to the passing of the Nineteenth Amendment and pay homage to three women who worked tirelessly to secure the right to vote for women. The marble sculpture consists of a portraiture grouping of three pioneers of the Women's movement, Elizabeth Cady Stanton, Lucretia Mott, and Susan B. Anthony. The women are depicted from about the chest up and appear to be incomplete. In fact, the sculpture has earned the dubious title of *Three Biddies in a Bathtub* because all you see encased in and protruding from a block of marble are the portraits. Behind the portrait of Stanton there is a shaft of irregular marble, partially carved. The incomplete nature of the sculpture was a deliberate choice on the part of Johnson, who wanted to demonstrate to the world and the male power structure of Congress and the nation that in her opinion the Women's movement was not yet completed and thus neither was her statuary tribute. When the piece was shipped from the artist's Italian studio, it stood for a short time in the Rotunda of the US Capitol, then members of Congress relegated it to the basement of the Capitol. Tourists to the Capitol could see the sculpture as part of the tour, but the fact remained that it was not enshrined in one of the most sacred spaces of America—the Rotunda of what has often been referred to as the "people's building." This did not sit well with the female members of Congress, who in April 1995, on the seventy-fifth anniversary of the passage of the Nineteenth Amendment, urged that the statue be returned to its rightful place of honor alongside the men who shaped the destiny of our country. Many opponents in Congress argued that the cost of $75,000 to move the statue was prohibitive and that the sculpture should stay where it was, in the Capitol crypt.

I cut the various articles out of the *Washington Post* that reported the saga. There was even a cover story article in the August 1997 issue of the *Organization of American Historians Newsletter.* These articles provided good grist for my lesson plan mill, and because I already had slide images of the piece, I knew I could dovetail together my images with the unfolding story. The tale got even more interesting when the National Political Congress of Black Women raised objections to the move, because in their estimation the sculpture did not represent the totality of the Suffragette movement, because the figure of Sojourner Truth was not included in the piece. To these women, Truth played just as much a role in the Women's movement as did Stanton, Mott, and Anthony. As I continued to follow the debate, I asked my students to read the various articles and to offer comments. The vast majority of the students agreed that the sculpture should be moved. They believed that the arguments raised by the opponents were flawed. Some members of the National Political Congress of Black Women wanted to solve the dilemma by having a contemporary sculptor "finish" the Johnson piece by adding a figure of Truth. To them the exclusion of Truth had negative racial overtones. None of my students objected to honoring Sojourner Truth, they simply felt it would have been an effrontery to Johnson to add to her sculpture. To my students' way of thinking, a separate statue to Truth should be commissioned and displayed. In the end, the National Women's Rights Memorial was moved back to the Rotunda, but there was no resolution as to the question of a suitable memorial to Sojourner Truth or other black women and activists like Ida B. Wells or Alice Paul.

Students enjoy this kind of reflective thinking activity tied to a visual with which they can relate. It made our discussion much more relevant and, once again, brought together the dynamics of how many issues and tensions converge together in our national past as well as in the present. Having students recognize this aspect of American life and history, and wrestle with its implications, is important if they are going to be participants in our ever-changing democracy. I take particular delight when a student reports to me that on a visit to the Capitol they have been certain to look at this uniquely American sculpture.

An interesting project might be to have your students design a fitting memorial for the Women's movement using some of the ideas presented here. To make this activity a true measure of assessment, have students link different specific milestones or landmarks to their memorial in the same manner that issues related to the Civil Rights movement play into the creation of the civil rights tree, as discussed in the previous chapter.

Working with Related Primary Sources

Several books available on the market address women's concerns and contain a variety of primary-source text documents that address all kinds of topics in American history. *Letters of a Nation,* edited by Andrew Carroll (1997), contains over one hundred letters written by Americans dealing with a host of issues. Many of these letters are personal and quite moving. *Eyewitness to America,* edited by David Colbert (1997), is another outstanding source covering five hundred years of American history, reporting how that history happened by people who experienced it firsthand. Finally, the two-volume series, *Soul of America,* edited by Robert Baron (1994a, 1994b), contains many different important documents related to all aspects of American life. Baron has compiled an outstanding collection of different documents, including key pieces of legislation, Supreme Court decisions, and other important documents, such as the Declaration of Sentiments. Within these three sources, you will find plenty of documents that relate to many of the issues pertinent to the Women's movement. For example, in Volume I of *Soul of America,* you might consider having students read the speech, "Ain't I a Woman," which Sojourner Truth delivered at a suffragettes rally in Ohio in 1851. You can augment this speech with the material on the debate over the National Women's Rights Memorial. By doing this, students will have additional information upon which to make an informed opinion about the role and interpretation of that statue. Combining instructional material in such a manner invigorates your curriculum. The more you have in your repertoire, the better chance you have of demonstrating the depth and breadth of history to your students.

In *Eyewitness to America,* you could direct students to the account by Pauline Cuoio Pepe of the Triangle Shirtwaist Company Fire of 1911. With this material, you can compare and contrast the conditions that led to this tragedy, which killed 146 people, mostly immigrant women, with the working conditions faced by the women who worked in the New England textile mills. In doing this, students can make judgments about how change took place or did not take place over time on a related issue.

In *Letters of a Nation,* there is an entire section devoted to "Letters of Social Concern, Struggle, and Contempt." Here students can read some of the correspondence of the Women's movement leadership such as a letter from Elizabeth Cady Stanton to Susan B. Anthony on "Establishing Woman on Her Rightful Throne" followed by Anthony's letter to Stanton on "Leaving the Battle to Another Generation of Women." These letters can be taught within context or, if you like, compared and contrasted to other letters in this section. If you choose the latter option, you can raise the following questions with your students:

1. Why do you think that these letters were written?

2. How are these letters similar in tone and sentiment?

3. What do letters like these say about the "progress" of America as well as the failure to deliver the "American dream" to a segment of the population?

Students often think that the history of the United States was one of linear progression from point A to point B. As teachers of history, we need to help students understand the fallacy of this notion. There have been points in our history when progress was not made by groups of people and, in some instances, there was a regression of progress. True, the period at the turn of the nineteenth and twentieth centuries is often referred to as the progressive period, but for some groups, like many immigrants and blacks, there was no progress. It's critical that students understand this if they are to have a balanced view of our past.

Another excellent primary resource to consider using is the *American Journey: History in Your Hands* CD-ROM, "Women in America." With this resource, you have over two hundred documents and five hundred illustrations consisting of the words and letters of writers, pacifists, rebels, pioneers, slaves, prominent leaders, and ordinary women who played their part in building America. Again, you can use this material to supplement your textbook, to compare and contrast women and their roles in different geographic regions, during different time periods, and in a multiple of settings. CD-ROM packages such as this offer teachers and students opportunities to design effective oral presentations or PowerPoint programs. If you prefer having your students work directly with the sources, then you can have these transcribed documents downloaded and printed out to be delivered directly to your students' hands.

"I Am Woman"

Another intriguing lesson uses contemporary documents including a song. Give students an excerpt from Betty Friedan's *The Feminine Mystique* (1963) and the lyrics to Helen Reddy's song, "I Am Woman." "The mystique," according to Freidan, "was the image of the woman as mother, as wife, living through her husband, through her children, giving up her own dreams for that." Freidan concluded, "The only way for a woman, as for a man, to find herself, to know herself as a person, is by creative work of her own." Again, many updated US history textbooks include excerpts from Friedan's landmark work. You can also find appropriate material to use on the web. Tell students that Friedan's book was published several years before the song. Have students read an excerpt from *The Feminine Mystique*. Depending on the excerpt you use, field any questions from students to clarify any issues or misunderstandings that they might have. Then play "I Am Woman." It might be interesting to relate to students the story of Reddy's 1972 Grammy Award acceptance speech when she said, "I'd like to thank God, because SHE makes everything possible." You can ask students how Reddy's comment reflects the tenor of the time and women. When the song is finished, ask students to compare and contrast the song to what Friedan wrote. Use the following prompts:

1. How are these two sources related? What links can you make between them?

2. Do any of the song lyrics reflect Freidan's attitudes? If so, which ones?

3. How do you think Friedan's book influenced Helen Reddy's song?

A lesson such as this will demonstrate the dynamic relation between the history of the period and pop culture, while tying together two related strands of the period. You can always raise the enduring question, "Does life imitate art or is it the other way around?" This is sure to generate a healthy discussion among students.

The Equal Rights Amendment

This is also a good place to discuss the Equal Rights Amendment and its failure to be ratified. For this you can use Lesson 33 in the Center for Learning's *US History: Seeking New Directions, 1960–1990* as a springboard to other activities. A copy of the ERA can also be found in most updated textbooks and on the web. You can have fun with this. Consider having your students do the following:

1. Hold a dialogue between Susan B. Anthony, Elizabeth Cady Stanton, or Sojourner Truth, among others, regarding the failure of the ERA to pass.

2. Assign a student to be a contemporary newspaper reporter whose job is to interview one of the women just listed and write an article about her reaction to the failure of the ERA to pass.

3. Have students role play a conversation among Betty Freidan, Helen Reddy, and one of the early women's rights supporters regarding the failure of the ERA to pass.

4. Have students role play and conduct a debate between Susan B. Anthony and Phyllis Schlafly.

When looking at the Equal Rights Amendment, be sure to inform students that it failed to pass only by a narrow margin—thirty-five of the fifty states ratified the amendment. Students can also learn the political lessons of the failure of the ERA to pass because those opposed to the amendment, including conservative Phyllis Schlafly, were able to redefine the debate. What was intended by supporters to merely extend rights lost focus among mainstream America and ended up going down to defeat because opponents shifted the debate to such things as women being drafted into the army and the possibility of unisex public restrooms.

Desert Sojourn

Debi Holmes-Binney has published a very good first-person account of her experience in the Great Salt Lake Desert. She went to the desert alone in 1994 for forty days to try and resolve some nagging self-doubts.

Her book, *Desert Sojourn* (2000) is an outstanding account of her trials, tribulations, doubts, and eventual triumph. As writing goes, Holmes-Binney's book models good journal-writing techniques. You can have students read passages from *Desert Sojourn* and then compare them with selected passages from *The Feminine Mystique*. Have students consider the similar goals of these women. Ask them if Holmes-Binney is the kind of woman that Freidan writes about and if so, how does she mirror the new woman? Or ask students what fears of Holmes-Binney seem to be rooted in attitudes held by women prior to the modern feminist movement? On another tack, you might want to compare Holmes-Binney's writing with Helen Reddy's song. Students might consider how *Desert Sojourn* measures up to Reddy's attitude in "I Am Woman." One way to use Holmes-Binney's work is to ask students to reflect on what Susan B. Anthony, Sojourner Truth, or others might think after reading *Desert Sojourn*. It would be interesting to note how many students would see the relationship between Sojourner Truth's name and Holmes-Binney's book title. You could also discuss how Holmes-Binney's writings reflect changing perceptions of women regarding themselves.

Women's Rights and the National Archives

I prefer to use original documents as often as possible—facsimile documents have, to me, a more authentic feel than a transcription. That's why I am a big proponent of the document lesson plans developed by the National Archives Education Office. Some of these lessons can be found online as well as in their classic teacher resource, *Teaching with Documents*, Volumes One and Two. In a number of their document-based teaching kits, you will find lessons that deal with women's history. Combined, these lessons reflect the panorama of issues in this arena, from important pieces of legislation to the life of an ordinary pioneer woman on the Great Plains. One lesson plan in particular that I find very useful with students is the lesson on the Nineteenth Amendment found in "The Progressive Years 1898–1917." This lesson is simple to use and brings to life such prosuffrage groups as the Women's Suffrage Party, the National American Women's Suffrage Association, and the National Women's Party. The two documents used in this lesson are a prosuffrage postcard that ridicules the antisuffrage position and the suffrage resolution introduced in Congress in 1919. In this lesson, students explore such questions as "Why in the early 1900s do you think some men *and* women objected to women's suffrage? This is a very good place to pause and launch in to a bit of history of women and voting in America. Granted, if you are teaching a survey course on American history, you will have covered some of these issues. Students should know that according to the Constitution, the states control the voting process and hence in the late nineteenth century such states as Wyoming and Montana permitted women to vote in elections long before the Nineteenth Amendment became law. For example, I relate the story of Jeanette Rankin, who was the first woman elected to Congress in 1914. I ask students how could it possibly be that a woman was elected to Congress before women had the right to vote. Once I clue them in about the progressive nature of the western states, they begin to see the full picture. Students are also surprised by the fact that some women were opposed to having the vote, to which I simply remind them that one's attitudes depends on where and when one was raised, so that it was not unusual for women couched in the Cult of Domesticity to oppose suffragettes and their cause. As an extension, after students complete this document, you can have them compare the arguments raised in the early twentieth century against the women's vote to those views held by critics of the Equal Rights Amendment. This will require that students poke around in the library or online to find a copy of the Equal Rights Amendment. Again, this is a strategy that links time periods and demonstrates once more the dynamics of ideas over time.

Who Built America?

Any discussion about resources on women's or social history can benefit from the wonderful CD-ROM program, *Who Built America: From the Centennial Celebration of 1876 to the Great War of 1914* (1993). This important tool was crafted by the American Social History Project, led by Roy Rosenzweig, Steve Brier, and Josh Brown. On this CD-ROM you will find close to five thousand pages of text, six hundred high-resolution images, fifty-five graphs and charts, four hours of audio, and forty-five minutes of film; a proverbial archive of many sources that you and your students can uncover. Highly diverse in scope and scale, this CD-ROM is very teacher and student friendly. I have found it most effective when working with students on outside research projects, for which students come in after school and we work together to locate information and develop ideas for either papers or presentations. Teachers can also employ this tool in large classroom setting or in a computer lab while working with a larger number of students. Another value of this technology is how it can help you to develop superior lesson plans by drawing on a host of primary sources. The CD-ROM package contains a teachers' guide that offers lesson plans matched to specific topics. What I have found most important with this program is that students clearly are able to see the relationship between a number of issues within the same time frame. For example, let's return to the Triangle Factory Fire. By using the extensive material on this tragedy, which includes grim photographs of the fire and its aftermath, political cartoons, and eyewitness audio recollections, students will come to recognize the links between the Labor movement and the issues that confronted women. Many students become outraged when they learn that the factory owners were acquitted of any charges of wrongdoing in the trial that followed. Students also come to understand that the Labor movement and the Women's movement needed to form political alliances at certain junctures in order to secure rights related to workers and women.

The program is easy to navigate, and you can build and develop lessons that merge all kinds of social, ethnic, racial, and gender issues. For teachers who like to include detailed examinations of daily life, you can get none better than this program.

In addition to covering the depth and expanse of this thirty-eight year time frame, you will find the resources to be well balanced. For example, in the subsection "Singing and Speaking for Suffrage: Women's Suffrage: For and Against," you will find six print documents and an audio recording that relates both sides of the suffrage debate, including, for example, Florence Kelley's discussion of "Strength in Numbers: On Women, Labor, and the Power of the Ballot." Some ideas about how to use this material include having students role play and act out the different aspects of the debates that were offered for and against women's rights, using the actual dialogue of the participants, or putting together archival photographic essays related to women's rights and working conditions, much in the same way the Jacob Riis did in his book, *How the Other Half Lives* (1890), which by the way is also a part of *Who Built America?* (1993). Another thought would be to have students use this as a resource to explore the similarity between women's working conditions in northern factories and sweat shops and the life of a female sharecropper in the deep South. Again, using this tool, you could have some students role play the parts while others act as journalists and report their findings to newspapers. Another thought would be to have someone research the work of Ida B. Wells and excerpts from her exposé *The Red Record* found on the CD-ROM and then investigate the impact that the lynching epidemic had on black women. However you choose to use the wealth of multimedia material, you will find it an excellent companion for you and students—well beyond that of being an electronic textbook.

Howard Zinn

Howard Zinn is an interesting historian to use when teaching women's history as well as the history of people who textbooks have too often neglected in the past. I encourage you to secure a copy of his book, *A People's History of the United States, 1492–Present* (1995, 1997a) and to use it as either a reference or as a teaching tool. Though a bit left of center and somewhat polemic, Zinn offers an alternative viewpoint that students will not find in most textbooks. His book is loaded with marvelous quotations that echo all manner of conflict that has taken place within the United States. These quotations are nicely offset from the text, making his book very teacher and student friendly. Additionally, his work is well written and a pleasure to read. Chapter 6, "The Intimately Oppressed," examines women's history in America. In this compact twenty-page chapter, you will encounter some of the women I have already discussed, such as Anne Hutchinson, Mary Dyer, and the women who organized the Seneca Falls Conference. You will also gain insight into the male power structure that held women in subservience for so many years. What makes Zinn work with teachers and students is his easy-to-understand and invigorating writing style. There is an excellent abridged teaching edition of Zinn's book that provides excellent questions for teachers to ask and for students to respond to at the back of each chapter. These are not your typical "end of the history book chapter questions," but rather thought-provoking queries into the heart of the issue. There is even an exercise comparing Zinn's work with standard US history textbooks on the market. What a great way to teach and learn—covering content as well as practicing historiography.

Women During War and in Military Service

I like to spend a little time dealing with the role of American women who either served in the armed forces or worked in factories and munitions plants as early as the Civil War. In the chapter on Vietnam, I explore the role of women in that conflict in specific detail, but here I'd like to talk about the other wars and the role that women played in them.

The American Revolution

During the American Revolution, there was a female Paul Revere, sixteen-year-old Sybl Ludington, who rode twice as far as Revere, harder, and in a driving rainstorm, warning the New York and Connecticut countryside about an impending British attack. Like Revere's ride, hers was a cry to get the local militia mustered. Unfortunately for Ludington, she did not have a press agent by the name of Longfellow to promote her exploits. Hence, we have no poem about this heroine. In 1961, the Daughters of the American Revolution commissioned a statue of Ludington, sculpted by Anna Hyatt Huntington, to be placed in Carmel, New York, near her home. I compare and contrast Ludington with Revere and ask students to speculate why they do not know about her, but they know about Revere. It is the poem by Longfellow.

There *are* two poems written about Ludington, but they were penned in the twentieth century, and I discovered them only while snooping around the Carmel Public Library. One of them, by George Noble, "How Tryon Was Driven Back," was written in 1913; the other, "On an April Night—1777," by Fred C. Warner, was penned later in the century. It is interesting to compare and contrast Longfellow's work with these two later pieces. I also can use slides I have of Cyrus Dallin's statue of Revere, located in Boston, to compare and contrast it with Huntington's Ludington. The Ludington statue is actually a better sculpture. One of my intentions in using this material on Ludington is to demonstrate that there were ordinary women who played a role in the War for Independence, not just the more notable personalities such as Abigail Adams or Martha Washington. Given that Ludington was a teenager, her exploits resonate well with my students.

The Civil War

During the Civil War, women also served on both sides of the Mason-Dixon Line. A number of them like Belle Boyd, were spies. Others, like Clara Barton, Mary Bickerdyke, and Dorothea Dix, helped on the battlefield. Women also worked in munitions factories. One of the little-known stories from the Civil War is that of the tragic explosion that took place at the Washington Arsenal on June 17, 1864. Over one hundred women had been at work in a shed making cartridges for small arms when the shed suddenly exploded. Some accounts indicate that gunpowder in casings left outside near the shed ignited from exposure to the sun. Many of the women were burned to death as their flammable hoop skirts erupted in flames. Of the many victims, only twenty-one could be positively identified. There was a city-wide outpouring of grief, and a large funeral followed by a procession was held on June 20 and attended by President Abraham Lincoln. Those who were killed were buried together in the Congressional Cemetery. A year later, a twenty-foot monument was erected over the grave topped by a grieving statue of a Victorian woman. Over the years, I have taken students out to the Congressional Cemetery. This is one of the graves we visit.

In recent years, there has been much scholarship as to the role women played disguised as men in the war effort. At least one hundred fifty women served in both the Union and Confederate armies in combat regiments. In many of these cases, fellow soldiers protected the identities of these women warriors. For many years, I have had students select and read from a list of diaries, letters, or memoirs of soldiers that were published as books. On the list were the titles *The Journal of Charlotte Forten* (Forten 1981) and *A Southern Woman's Story* by Phoebe Yates

Pember (1954). Both of these books deal with women who worked on the homefront. A few years ago, a new title appeared on the market, *An Uncommon Soldier* (1994), which are the Civil War letters of Sarah Rosetta Wakeman—alias Private Lyons Wakeman of the 153rd New York State Volunteers. This illuminating collection of letters is perfect to use for instruction when teaching the Civil War era. It only runs ninety-seven pages; it has an excellent Foreword by James M. McPherson and a solid Preface by the editor, Lauren Cook Burgess. To assess their reading, I have students write a journal entry that is a letter to the person whose accounts or letters they have read in their journal. Here's what Jessica wrote to Sarah Wakeman:

> Dear Sarah Wakeman:
> I have read your book and found it fascinating. Many thoughts have come to mind, too. First of all I think it was great of you to serve in the Civil War, not for yourself but to help out your family. I think it was very unselfish of you to decide to pay off your family's debt. If it were me I don't know if I would have done the same thing. I greatly admire you. You disguised yourself as a man, sent money to your parents and managed to write them as well. You did what a man did in the army and it shows your courage and strength. Your faith in God was also mentioned. I am curious as to why you chose to fight in the war. I am also amazed how your parents accepted what you did.
> Sincerely, Jessica

I think it is important for students to know about the various efforts and sacrifices women made during the Civil War, because eventually those efforts were recalled by suffragettes to justify why women should have the right to vote. Particularly in the North, many of the women who served for the war effort as clerks and nurses were at the forefront of the Women's Rights movement. It is therefore impossible to teach this material without a good lesson or two on the role of women during the Civil War. If you ever travel to Civil War battlefields, specifically those administered by the National Park Service, you will find in park bookstores a separate section on women's studies and the Civil War. There you will find numerous gems that you can share with your classes.

World War I

When I teach World War I and the role of women, I again use primary-source material made available in the National Archives Teaching Kit, *World War I—The Homefront*. There are twelve documents in this package, both textual as well as eight, 8 inch by 10 inch, easily reproducible,

black-and-white photographic images of women at work for the war effort. Some of the pictures show women rolling bandages for the Red
Cross, another documents women working in munitions plants, and
there's a photograph of women working on a farm growing crops for
the military. Generally, I make a class set of handouts of all the photographs. When the students receive their packets, I ask them to look
at each picture carefully to try to determine what is going on in the
photograph. Providing clues, I ask students to take into account dress,
location of job, expressions of patriotism, welfare of workers, sanitary
conditions, "modern" conveniences, as well as the possible purpose of
the photograph. Then, I have students compile a chart of what they see.
Next, I ask students to assess the kinds of experiences these women
had. To do this, I ask students to consider what these women might have
been doing had there been no war, in other words, to reflect on how
their daily life had changed. We then talk about the differences and
compare life for women before and during the war. If you like, you can
record these differences on the board or on an overhead transparency.
Another way to approach using these eight photographs, as suggested
by the National Archives lesson designers, is to break students into
eight small groups to evaluate the images. Each group should prepare
a written summary of the activities documented in the photograph.
Again, you can ask each group and then the class as a whole what these
photographs suggest about everyday life and the role of women in
1917. It is very easy to conclude this activity by using another photograph from the kit that depicts a woman suffragette picketing outside
the White House with a placard that reads, "Kaiser Wilson." I like to ask
students what they can infer from this photograph and how what they
see in this image compares to the images that they have studied. Most
students are quick to pick up the fact that women obviously played a
role in the war effort and felt by virtue of such behavior they deserved
the right to vote. Of course, the Nineteenth Amendment was passed
within two years of the end of World War I. This timely relationship
should not escape students.

World War II

When it comes to World War II and women, the amount of resources
available to teachers is extraordinary. There are films, songs, diary and
memoir accounts, and a plethora of secondary works to which you can
refer and use. One of the best films I have ever used in my teaching career is a film called, *The Life and Times of Rosie the Riveter* (1980). This film
is a sixty-minute look at the role of women who worked in the factories, munitions plants, and shipyards. Using oral history interviews as
well as contemporary and archival photographs, the film gives viewers
a glimpse into the life of five women, black and white, who made up

part of the industrial workforce during the Second World War. Included in this montage are clips of government-produced films that documented and publicized the role of women. Rounding out the film is a rare recording of the song, "Rosie the Riveter." Now and then we see photographs of these women working as young girls juxtaposed against images of them today. It's a bit sentimental, but works. The other advantage of this film is that it documents the lives of white and black women. It includes the stories of the problems black women had to endure on the jobsite. Once again, students see how pervasive racism has been in our society, even during a war that was waged to defeat tyrannical governments.

Another activity I like to teach is how "Rosie the Riveter" got her nickname. This derives from the cover illustration that Norman Rockwell painted for a 1943 issue of the *Saturday Evening Post*. Rockwell painted a female factory worker—based on Michelangelo's pose of the prophet Isaiah from the Sistine Chapel—taking a meal break from work. You can find this image in just about any oversize, coffee table book of Rockwell's work—have a color transparency made. Rosie wears blue overalls on which war-bond buttons are affixed. Across her lap rests a rivet gun. Cradled under her arm is a lunch box on which we see the name ROSIE. Though seated, Rosie's feet rest on a copy of Adolph Hitler's *Mein Kampf*. Rosie's visor is pushed back off her head and above it appears a halo. The backdrop is the American flag. This is Rockwell at his patriotic best. Each year I look forward to showing this image to my students and having them analyze what they see. A nice way to complement this image is to ask students to either recall what they saw in the film, *The Life and Times of Rosie the Riveter,* and compare it to what they see in Rockwell's image or to use other photographic evidence of women at work in factories, shipyards, and munitions plants for comparative purposes. Many of the sources I've mentioned will contain these photographs.

I feel it is necessary to point out to students that so much of the fabric of American social life changed as a result of World War II. The late twentieth century Women's movement would not have been possible had not millions of women participated in the industrial workforce during World War II. As a result, attitudes changed and barriers began to fall. It was out of this that activists such as Betty Freidan emerged and took up the clarion call for women that had been heralded by her political and social ancestors, Stanton and Anthony. From this would grow the National Organization for Women and the political and social agenda that they promote. The last thirty-five years of the twentieth century were marked by larger numbers of women entering the workforce— well beyond the "traditional" roles filled by women—namely teachers, nurses, and secretaries. New phrases emerged such as the "glass ceiling" as women sought higher levels of professional achievement. By the end

of the century, more women were in the workforce in a professional ca-
pacity than ever before. Along with all this emerged an increase in the
divorce rate and the number of single mothers. We continue to wrestle
as a society with the "rightful" place of women.

Recent Military Activity

For the past two decades, women have attended the national military
service academies. However, it has taken more than twenty years for
private or state supported military institutions, such as The Citadel or
Virginia Military Institute to accept women as part of their ranks—they
were forced to do so by court order. During Operation Just Cause, the
American invasion of Panama in 1989, and the subsequent Persian Gulf
War, women played critical combat roles for the first time in American
history. A popular movie, though fictitious, *Courage Under Fire* (1996),
starring Meg Ryan and Denzel Washington, speculated on the first possible female recipient of the Congressional Medal of Honor during the
Persian Gulf War. In 1997, at the Ceremonial Entrance to Arlington National Cemetery, The National Women in Military Service for America
Memorial was dedicated. Part memorial and part museum, the foundation that administers the perpetuity of the memorial explains that visitors will "experience the collective history of women in the military
along with the individual stories of registered servicewomen." The five
points of their mission statement state the purpose of the memorial: To
recognize all women who have served in the armed forces; to document the experiences of women and tell their stories of service, sacrifice, and achievement; to make these contributions a visible part of our
history; to illustrate their partnership with men in defense of our nation; and to serve as an inspiration for others. As with many of our new
national memorials, the Women in Military Service for America Memorial has an education division that organizes teacher inservice and outreach programs. The education program is a multifaceted resource for
teachers and students both in and outside of the classroom. Jennifer Fin-
stein, education specialist, explains that the purpose of the education
program is "to increase awareness about the roles that women have
played in the defense of the United States." Many of their programs
serve not only local school districts in the immediate Washington, DC,
metro area, but they also have excellent outreach material including a
national speakers bureau of women who are willing to speak with students, biographical material relative to servicewomen in the various geographic locales of the country, era-specific education kits that can be
sent to you, related Women's History Month articles that can be downloaded from their website, Women's History Month material that is tied
to the specific and different yearly themes of each Women's History
Month, and many other activities that you will find of value to your

students. These programs are designed in part to help teachers meet national and local history standards. Additionally, they sponsor student writing contests, on-site scavenger hunts, and living history programs for children and adults. On their website at *www.womensmemorial.org* you can access all kinds of information relative to women who served in our armed forces from the Revolution to the present, as well as access the educational programs.

Other Thoughts Regarding Women in American History

There are certainly plenty of other topics related to women's history that could be explored and taught. Why not consider using Willa Cather's classics *O Pioneers!* (1992) or *My Antonia* (1994), if not in whole then in part, when you discuss the Westward movement and settlement of the Great Plains. The characters in her novels are strong and positive, and her plots offer an excellent look at daily life. If you like using films, I recommend *Norma Rae* (1979), or the documentary PBS film *New York* (1999), where you will find all manner of issues over time related to the Big Apple and women. The twenty-five minute segment on the Triangle Factory Fire alone is most compelling and moving. Another excellent documentary from which you can pull good instructional material ranging from flappers and vamps, to Rosie the Riveter, to the significance of the Women's movement of the 1960s and 1970s is *The Century: America's Time* (1999) jointly produced by ABC News and the History Channel. The episode on the 1920s and women is particularly good. As with anything in the teaching of history, the possibilities are endless. One of my favorite females in American history is Eleanor Roosevelt. The Teaching with Historic Places Program has a lesson plan devoted solely to Roosevelt and her home, Val-Kill Cottage, located on the grounds of Hyde Park, her husband Franklin's home.

My purpose was to expose you to what I have found to be successful. If you have a particular interest in broadening your base, I recommend that you contact your local college or university and ask faculty members who work with women's studies about their ideas. Again, for advanced placement or honors students, Davidson and Lytle's (1995), *After the Fact,* has a chapter, "From Rosie To Lucy: The Mass Media and Images of Women in the 1950s." Here you and your students can explore stereotyping and mythmaking as it relates to gender.

If you remain open to your own learning process, you will find that not only will you be more personally and professionally fulfilled, but your students will reap the rewards of your benefit. No one can ask for a better teaching and learning experience than that.

Resources

Books

Bacon, Margaret Hope. 1999. *Valiant Friend: The Life of Lucretia Mott.* Philadelphia: Friends General Conference.

Battle, Kemp. 1997. *Hearts of Fire: Great Women of American Lore and Beyond.* New York: Harmony Books.

Bernhardt, Virginia, and Elizabeth Fox-Genovese. 1995. *The Birth of American Feminism: The Seneca Falls Convention of 1848.* Maplecrest, PA: Brandywine Press.

Black, Allida, M., ed. 1995. *What I Hope to Leave Behind: The Essential Essays of Eleanor Roosevelt.* New York: Carlson Publishing.

Brodie, Laura Fairchild. 2000. *Breaking Out: VMI and the Coming of Women.* New York: Pantheon.

Burgess, Lauren Cook, ed. 1995. *Uncommon Soldier: The Civil War Letters of Sarah Rosetta Wakeman, Alias Pvt. Lyons Wakeman, 153rd Regiment, New York State Volunteers, 1862–1864.* New York: Oxford University Press.

Butterfield, L. H., et al., eds. 1975. *The Book of John and Abigail Adams: Selected Letters of the Adams Family, 1762–1784.* Cambridge: Harvard University Press.

Caliguire, Augustine, Allan J. Keller, Roberta J. Leach, and James A. Wasowski. 1991. *America Creating the Dream: Beginnings to 1865.* Vol. 1. Rocky River, OH: The Center for Learning.

Cather, Willa. 1992. *O Pioneers!* New York: Vintage Classic Editions.

———. 1994. *My Antonia.* New York: Vintage Classics Edition.

Colman, Penny. 1995. *Rosie the Riveter: Women Working on the Homefront in World War II.* New York: Crown.

Cook, Blanche Wiesen. 1992. *Eleanor Roosevelt: Volume 1, 1884–1935.* New York: Viking.

———. 1995. *Eleanor Roosevelt: Volume 2, 1933–1938.* New York: Viking.

Dash, Jean. 1996. *We Shall Not Be Moved: The Women Factory Strike of 1909.* New York: Scholastic Press.

Davidson, James West, and Mark Hamilton Lytle. 1995. *After the Fact: The Art of Historical Detection.* New York: Knopf.

Demos, John Putnam. 1982. *Entertaining Satan: Witchcraft and the Culture of Early New England.* New York: Oxford University Press.

Dunwell, Steve. 1978. *The Run of the Mill.* Boston: David R. Godine.

Evans, Sara M. 1989. *Born for Liberty: A History of Women in America.* New York: Free Press.

Forten, Charlotte. 1981. *The Journal of Charlotte Forten.* Edited with an Introduction by Ray Allen Billington. New York: Norton.

Freidan, Betty. 1963. *The Feminine Mystique.* New York: W. W. Norton.

———. 2000. *Life So Far.* New York: Simon and Schuster.

Griffith, Elizabeth. 1984. *In Her Own Right: The Life of Elizabeth Cady Stanton.* New York: Oxford University Press.

Gurko, Miriam. 1974. *The Ladies of Seneca Falls: Birth of the Women's Rights Movement.* New York: Macmillan.

Hareven, Tamara K., and Randolph Langebach. 1978. *Amoskeag: Life and Work in an American Factory City.* New York: Pantheon.

———. 1982. *Family Time and Industrial Time.* Cambridge: Cambridge University Press.

Hartmann, Susan M. 1982. *The Homefront and Beyond: American Women in the 1940s.* Boston: Twayne Publishers.

Holm, Jeanne M. 1992. *Women in the Military: An Unfinished Revolution.* Novato, CA: Presidio Press.

———. 1998. *In Defense of a Nation: Servicewomen in World War II.* Arlington, VA: Vandamere Press.

Holmes-Binney, Debi. 2000. *Desert Sojourn: A Woman's Forty Days and Nights Alone.* Seattle: Seal Press.

Karlsen, Carol. 1987. *The Devil in the Shape of a Woman.* New York: Norton.

Keetley, Dawn, and John Pettigrew, eds. 2000. *Public Women, Public Words: A Documentary History of American Feminism: Beginnings to 1900.* Madison, WI: Madison House Publishing.

Kent, Zachary. 1989. *The Story of the Triangle Factory Fire.* Chicago: Children's Press.

Kerber, Linda K. 1998. *No Constitutional Right to Be Ladies.* New York: Hill and Wang.

Kerber, Linda K., et al. 1995. *U.S. History as Women's History: New Feminist Essays.* Chapel Hill, NC: The University of North Carolina Press.

Langley, Winston E., and Vivian C. Fox. 1998. *Women's Rights in the United States: A Documentary History.* Westport, CT: Greenwood Publishing.

Lash, Joseph P. 1972. *Eleanor Roosevelt: The Years Alone.* New York: Norton.

Leonard, Elizabeth. 1999. *All the Daring of the Soldiers: Women of the Civil War.* New York: Norton.

Lunardini, Christine. 1997. *What Every American Should Know About Women's History.* Holbrook, MA: Adams Media Corporation.

Manegold, Catherine S. 1999. *In Glory's Shadow: Shannon Faulkner, The Citadel, and a Changing America.* New York: Knopf.

Mankiller, Wilma, et al., eds. 1998. *The Readers Companion to US Women's History.* Boston: Houghton Mifflin.

Miller, Arthur. 1996. *The Crucible.* Edited by Harold Bloom, New York: Chelsea House.

Norman, Elizabeth M. 1999. *We Band of Angels: The Untold Story of American Nurses Trapped on Bataan by the Japanese.* New York: Random House.

Painter, Nell Irvin. 1996. *Sojourner Truth: A Life, a Symbol.* New York: Norton.

Pember, Phoebe Yates. 1954. *A Southern Woman's Story: Life in Confederate Richmond*. Edited by Bell I. Wiley. Marietta, GA: Mockingbird Books.

Poulos, Paula Nassen, ed. 1996. *A Women's War Too: US Women in the Military in World War II*. Washington: National Archives.

Robinson, Harriet H. 1976. *Loom and Spindle, or Life Among the Early Mill Girls*. Kailua, HI: Press Pacifica.

Roosevelt, Eleanor. 1949. *This I Remember*. New York: Harper and Brothers.

———. 1961. *The Autobiography of Eleanor Roosevelt*. New York: HarperCollins.

Rose, Phyllis, ed. 1993. *The Norton Book of Women's Lives*. New York: Norton.

Ruiz, Vicki L., and Ellen Carol Dubois. 2000. *Unequal Sisters: A Multicultural Reader in Women's History*. New York: Routledge.

Schneir, Miriam, ed. 1992. *Feminism: The Essential Historical Writings*. New York: Vintage.

Sherr, Lynn. 1995. *Failure Is Impossible: Susan B. Anthony in Her Own Words*. New York: Random House.

Sherr, Lynn, and Juarte Kazickas. 1994. *Susan B. Anthony Slept Here: A Guide to American Women's Landmarks*. New York: Time Books.

Stalcup, Brenda, ed. 1996. *The Women's Rights Movement: Opposing Viewpoints*. San Diego: Greenhaven Press.

Stanley, Sandra C. 1993. *Women in the Military*. New York: Messner.

Starkey, Marion C. 1949. *The Devil in Massachusetts*. New York: Knopf.

Stein, Leon. 1977. *Out of the Sweatshop: The Struggle for Industrial Democracy*. New York: Quadrangle Press.

Steinem, Gloria. 1994. *Moving Beyond Words*. New York: Simon and Schuster.

Wakeman, Sarah Rosetta. 1994. *An Uncommon Soldier: The Civil War Letters of Sarah Rosetta Wakeman, alias Private Lyons Wakeman, 153rd Regiment, New York State Volunteers*. Lauren Cook Burgess, ed. Pasadena, MD: The Minerva Center.

Ward, Geoffrey C., and Ken Burns. 1992. *Not for Ourselves Alone: The Story of Elizabeth Cady Stanton and Susan B. Anthony*. New York: Knopf.

Washington, Margaret, ed. 1993. *The Narrative of Sojourner Truth*. New York: Vintage.

Weatherford, Doris. 1990. *American Women and World War II*. New York: Facts on File.

Wheeler, Marjorie, ed. 1995. *One Woman, One Vote: Rediscovering the Women's Suffrage Movement*. Troutdale, OR: New Sage Press.

Zeinert, Karen. 1994. *Those Incredible Women of World War II*. Brookfield, CT: Millbrook Press.

Videos/Films

Anne Hutchinson, Profiles in Courage video series. Producers: Gordon Oliver and Robert Saudek; Director: Cyril Ritchard. 50 minutes. Robert Saudek Associates, 1966, videocassette.

Courage Under Fire. Producer: Joseph M. Singer; Director: Edward Zwick. 100 minutes. Fox, 1996, videocassette.

Dreams of Equality. Producers: Allen Mondell and Cynthia Salzman Mondell. 28 minutes. A Media Projects, Inc., Production, 1993, videocasette.

Eleanor Roosevelt. Producers: Kathryn Dietz and Sue Williams. 150 minutes. Ambrica Productions, 2000, videocasette.

Hello Dolly. Producer: Ernest Lehman; Director: Gene Kelly. 129 minutes. Fox, 1969, videocassette.

New York: A Documentary Film. Producer: Ric Burns. 600 minutes. Steeplechase Films, 1999, videocasette.

Norma Rae. Producers: Tamara Asseyev and Alex Rose; Director: Martin Ritt. 110 minutes. Fox, 1979, videocasette.

Not for Ourselves Alone: The Story of Elizabeth Cady Stanton and Susan B. Anthony. Producers: Ken Burns and Paul Barnes. 120 minutes. Florentine Films, 1999, videocasette.

The Life and Times of Rosie the Riveter. Producer: Connie Field. 65 minutes. Direct Cinema, 1980, videocasette.

The Shadow of Hate: A History of Intolerance in America. Producer: Charles Guggenheim. 40 minutes. Teaching of Tolerance, 1995, videocassette.

The Witches of Salem: The Horror and the Hope. Producer: Dennis Azzarella; Director: Dennis Azzarella. 28 minutes. Azzarella Unlimited Productions, 1972, videocasette.

Three Sovereigns for Sarah. Producer: Victor Pisano; Director: Philip Leacock. 152 minutes. Night Owl Productions, 1986, videocasette.

Electronic Resources

American History Videodisk. 1999. Annapolis, MD: Instructional Resources Corporation.

Who Built America? From the Centennial Celebration of 1876 to the Great War of 1914. CD-ROM. 1993. American Social History Productions. New York: Voyager.

Chapter Six

Remembering Vietnam

We had done nothing more than endure. We had survived, and that was our only victory.

—Philip Caputo, *A Rumor of War*

Some call it the Vietnam Veterans Memorial, others call it the Wall. Located on the Mall in Washington, DC, it is the most visited memorial in the nation's capital. When you look at it, you can see your reflection. That was the artist's intent, to have your reflection stir within you a sense of recognition of your mortality measured against the lives of those whose names are etched on the black granite. It's hard to imagine 58,281 names as anything but an abstraction, but when you see them etched neatly in row after row, the reality of the number strikes you like a hammer blow. The simplicity of its design and nickname belies the fact that the men and women whose names are recorded on the memorial died in one of the most complex and complicated conflicts in American history—the Vietnam War.

Jan Scruggs is the Vietnam Veteran who spearheaded the memorial project by organizing the Vietnam Veterans Memorial Fund. The organization raised private money to create and erect the memorial on the national Mall in Washington, DC. Almost from the outset, controversies arose. Many Americans simply wanted to forget the war and what it did to the United States. To them, a memorial would only open old wounds. To counter that argument, Scruggs believed that the memorial, as he envisioned it, would generate a much needed healing process for the nation. There were people who felt that a memorial of sorts was appropriate but not on the national Mall, which was intended only for imposing national icons, such as George Washington, Thomas Jefferson, and Abraham Lincoln. The skeptics abounded. But through Scruggs' personal effort, the memorial was approved by Congress and a site was reserved on the Mall near the Lincoln Memorial. Following this was a national design competition. The national debate continued in the aftermath of the selection of the design by Maya Ying-lin, then a twenty-one-year-old architecture student attending Yale University. The debate over the design mirrored the difficulty of establishing consensus over the direction of the war. To many, the debate about the memorial's design re-opened old wounds. At some points, it turned nasty and the whole project was in jeopardy. According to some, the Wall was more like a black gash of shame or too abstract for their suiting. It seemed to many that the Wall did not embody the kind of traditional memorials placed on the Mall. There were individuals who would have been more comfortable with a figurative, academic sculpture of sorts. In the end, a compromise was struck and it was agreed that two years after the dedication of the Wall, a freestanding figurative sculpture and a flag would be added to the memorial.

I did not lose anyone I knew in America's longest war. Nor did I know any real war protesters. But Vietnam was part of my life day in and day out, as it was for all of America during its tenure. Each night on the *CBS Evening News* with Walter Cronkite, I remember watching the military action and the other assorted reports that filtered out of that far-off, foreign country. And during every Friday night broadcast, Cronkite would announce the casualty figures for the week. Sometimes I got scared, thinking that the war would last forever and that I would get drafted and be killed. I remember where I was, in a barber shop, in Maynard, Massachusetts, waiting to get a haircut, when the radio reports came in about the Kent State shootings. I was twelve. From eighth grade until the Paris Peace Accords were signed in 1973, when I was a sophomore in high school, I remember students wearing activist buttons against the war, or wrist bracelets for those missing in action, and classmates refusing to stand or turning their backs to the flag during the "Pledge of Allegiance." As a senior, in the spring of 1975, the sudden collapse of South Vietnam was a topic of discussion in social studies classes and among students in general. To a nation that had built its self-image, in part, on the confidence of its military legacy of previous wars aligned with a tradition of fair play, the war wasn't supposed to end the way it did, but that's how it indeed ended. And as the last members of our embassy in Saigon lifted off the roof of that building in a helicopter, the debate began as to why the United States lost the war in Vietnam and who was to blame. Some even asserted that we didn't lose the war, we just didn't win.

When I started teaching at West Springfield High School in 1980, I could ask my students the question, "How many of you had fathers who served in Vietnam?" Many hands would go up. Twenty years later, fewer hands go up, and of those that do, a number belong to students whose grandfathers, not fathers, served in Vietnam.

As the most divisive issue to face America since the Civil War, the Vietnam War tore at the moral fiber of the United States. Those tumultuous years profoundly changed America. A kind of innocence was lost by everyone who experienced those years. Students studying the war today have no sense of immediacy or recognition that the world in which they lived was shaped by those events of the second half of the twentieth century and the Cold War, just as my generation lacked a sense of immediacy about World War II. Students are far less politically active or aware than students of my generation were, but these students have never faced the possibility of being drafted and shipped off to Southeast Asia to wage war against the Viet Cong. Today's students are oblivious to this kind of reality, through no fault of their own.

As we move into the twenty-first century, the lessons of Vietnam can instruct teachers and students in a variety of ways. In teaching about the American experience in Vietnam, teachers can offer students excellent lessons that develop and promote historical and critical thinking. We need to impart to our students that somehow the United States must learn a myriad of lessons in order not to repeat the tragic pitfalls of Vietnam in an increasingly complex world that calls out for American leadership. Beirut, Panama, the Gulf War, Somalia, Bosnia, and Kosovo are all military actions that have been fought in the shadow of the legacy of Vietnam. Needless to say, there will be future conflicts in which America will be embroiled, and our students, the leaders of tomorrow, must be prepared to respond to such struggles in a historical context and framework that offers the best kind of thinking and analysis possible. If we are to learn anything from Vietnam, it is this simple lesson: there are indeed lessons to be learned.

As a teacher, you have a great deal of sources from which to draw. In this chapter, I will demonstrate to you the kinds of things I have done in my classroom to impart these important lessons about Vietnam to my students. As with all of my advice, you are free to pick and choose, develop what works for you and your students. Regardless of your approach, you will find that time well spent building your Vietnam curriculum will enhance not only your knowledge of this significant event, but also that of your students.

Where to Begin

Echoes from the Wall

I suggest that you first scout around your social studies/history department to see if your school ever received a free copy of the curriculum package developed by the Vietnam Veterans Memorial Fund, "Echoes from the Wall." This outstanding teaching product was sent free to every high school in the United States. If you have not previously taught the Vietnam War or have limited resources at your hands, this is the place to start. "Echoes from the Wall" is well balanced and contains highly relevant and useful lesson plans and necessary historical background. The kit includes an extensive teacher's guide with reproducible handouts, a timeline poster, a videotape on Vietnam from the CNN *Cold War* series, *Vietnam: 1954–1968* (1999) and two books written by Jan Scruggs, founder and president of the Vietnam Veterans Memorial Fund, *Why Vietnam Still Matters* (1996) and *Voices from the Wall* (1998). You'll also find an excerpt from Stanley Karnow's seminal work, *Vietnam: A History* (1997), which provides critical background information. The lesson plans include material that can be taught in individual segments or as part of team and cooperative learning exercises. These lessons are appropriate for 7–12 teaching as well as for college instruction. The beauty of this curriculum package is that, for such a divisive event, it is apolitical. All aspects and perspectives of the war are presented through the voices of the combatants of all ranks: the soldiers, sailors, and airmen, the pro-war activists, the anti-war dissidents, and the Vietnamese people. Some of the lessons explore the music of the period, others examine the place of American prisoners of war. There are interesting lessons about government policy making and its related complexity, and intriguing lessons about GIs who fought the war on the front lines and their experiences once they came home. Tips are also provided for incorporating the use of Vietnam Veteran Oral History panels into your curriculum. Proponents of multiple intelligences, cooperative learning, and alternative assessment will find "Echoes from the Wall" in line with their philosophies because the activities presented were created with them in mind. The lessons are crafted in such a way that they reach divergent learning styles and offer differentiated activities. In addition, "Echoes" is aligned to meet the national and assorted state history standards. In addition to the excellent teaching materials, a comprehensive resource guide assists you with follow-up planning and learning. In a nutshell, "Echoes from the Wall" provides you with everything and more that you need to get started in teaching about Vietnam. If your school did not receive "Echoes from the Wall," you can contact the Vietnam Veterans Memorial Fund in Washington, DC, and they will send you a kit.

Brainstorming and Three Films

One of the best ways to begin instruction about the Vietnam War is to ask students to brainstorm what they already know about it. Students whose parents are veterans may have a better understanding of terminology than others. But I have also discovered that even students whose parents are veterans have limited knowledge because their father or mother rarely speaks about the war. Many students have had their understanding of the war shaped by the media, specifically Hollywood and the myriad of interpretations presented by the entertainment industry. Once you get this activity started, you can write on either the chalkboard or on newsprint the terms or ideas offered by your students. This will give both you and your students some confidence in approaching the topic because you will have a visual record of what your class already knows about the war. Once this is complete, you can move on to a much more detailed approach to teaching the war.

I have been teaching the Vietnam War in my classes for about fifteen years, long before "Echoes from the Wall" was available. My point here is to provide you with additional information, material, and approaches that I or my colleagues have used with success in teaching this topic. Because the history of Vietnam is so complex and so fraught with issues that are centuries old, the best method I have discovered is to provide students with a background lecture and ancillary support material, including a handout of a timeline of the history of Vietnam from the eighteenth century to the present. Timelines such as these can be found in many updated American history textbooks or are located in the front of many historical narratives written about the war. It is essential that students understand the background to American participation in Vietnam. Without the proper historical context, students will get lost and nothing will make sense. Next I pass out a map of Vietnam. Again, there are good maps to be found in recent US history textbooks. The map I use comes from the book *The Eyewitness History of the Vietnam War, 1961–1975* by George Esper and the Associated Press (1983). I make an overhead transparency of the map and have students locate on their copies of the maps the important places I want them to know. An understanding of the geography is crucial when studying this or any other war so that learners can understand how terrain and location of bodies of water and cities play into the narrative of the history.

Next, I generally have students review the timeline handout and ask them if there are any terms or events they recognize. You can then compare this to the list that they have previously compiled. This helps the process of continually building links from one element of instruction to the next.

Finally, I pass out a list of twenty things about the Vietnam War that they should know or recognize at the end of our study. This is a great assessment tool that need not be graded. Students can keep it in their notebooks and you can refer to it time and again when you are covering specific topics of the war. The list can be found in Appendix D.

There are two good films I like to use in my introduction to Vietnam. One is called *The Vietnam War: A Case Study for Critical Thinking* (1987), and runs about fifty minutes. The producers of this film created two different overlays of narration with the same video footage. The first twenty minutes presents a liberal historical interpretation of the war and the second twenty minutes a conservative approach. Appropriate background information to American participation in Vietnam is provided in each segment, though within the context of its presented viewpoint. The film comes with a reproducible handout that you can use with students to analyze both perspectives. This film effectively provides students with a window into the differing interpretations of the war. Students can hear different attitudes, narrated within the same historical context, and come to see how different conclusions can be reached when the same basic data are offered for analysis and interpretation. *The Vietnam War: A Case Study for Critical Thinking* is perfect to use either for classes that are taught in the block or the standard fifty-minute segment. Both formats offer teachers and students the opportunity to discuss the content of the film. For the block, you could either show the film in its totality and then discuss the points at its conclusion, or you can stop the video after each segment and discuss each segment separately to ensure that students learned the critical information. If you teach in the standard fifty-minute format, I suggest that you use the latter approach and split showing and discussing the film over two days. The beauty of this film is the way it sets up the conclusions reached by different historians and then allows students and teachers to pick apart those interpretations. Neither interpretation is given credence over the other. The film concludes in an open-ended fashion, leaving the viewer to make his or her own judgment. It's an outstanding exercise in developing the kinds of lifetime skills that history can teach to students.

The second film I like to use is *Vietnam: Chronicle of a War* (1981), produced by CBS News. Using television news footage and assorted sound bites from the CBS News archives, this film puts in historical sequence the major events of the war starting with good background information on the French colonial era, through the gradual buildup of US ground forces, the escalation in 1965 and 1966, the turning point of the Tet Offensive on 1968, Vietnamization, the 1973 cease fire, and the subsequent collapse of the South Vietnamese government in 1975. The narration is provided by a number of CBS News reporters such as Walter Cronkite, Dan Rather, Charles Collingswood, and others. While trying to be objective in providing a detailed history, it does have a slant that tends to lean toward the perspective that we never should have been involved in the conflict. Seeing the same news footage that was shown night after night on television has a great impact on students. They can easily come to understand the impact the television had on the war because the footage and the tone are very grim. When showing this film, I use a handout that was generated by one of my colleagues, Ron Maggiano. It is a series of questions that chronicles the film and assists students in picking out the salient points. After the film is finished, I go over the questions in class to make sure students have gotten the right information. You can find the film questions in Appendix D. *Vietnam: Chronicle of a War* is a little less than ninety minutes long and works well in a block split over two days. A technique I am coming to rely on more and more when showing longer documentary type films, such as this one, is to pause the film and add my own analysis or editorial comments at certain places. For example, just when the film reaches the part about the Tet Offensive, I pause and direct students to pay careful attention to this segment of the film as it is significant in the narrative of the story. Students like *Vietnam: Chronicle of a War* because it follows an easy-to-understand story line and provides a frame of reference from which they can understand the significance of the military and political implications of the conflict.

Once the film is over, I go back to using the map so that students can identify more clearly the places discussed in the film. We locate places such as Saigon, Hanoi, the Mekong River, and the Tonkin Gulf. All of this helps to reinforce learning.

Using Primary Sources

Keeping in line with the philosophy of my friends in the Education Office of the National Archives, I like to use facsimiles of documents when I teach with primary-source material. I find the following three documents found in the National Archives helpful when teaching about Vietnam: the February 1946 cable from Ho Chi Minh to President Harry Truman, the Tonkin Gulf Resolution of August 1964, and the 1973 War Powers Act. I provide students with copies of the documents and use them within them within the chronological sequence of my teaching.

The Ho Chi Minh Cable

Students in particular find the Ho Chi Minh document, shown in Figure 6–1, to be the most fascinating. Because students have already seen

Figure 6–1
Ho Chi Minh Diplomatic Cable

VIỆT-NAM DÂN CHỦ CỘNG HÒA

CHÍNH PHỦ LÂM THỜI

BO NGOAI GIAO
    *

HANOI FEBRUARY 28 1946

TELEGRAM

PRESIDENT HOCHIMINH VIETNAM DEMOCRATIC REPUBLIC HANOI

TO THE PRESIDENT OF THE UNITED STATES OF AMERICA WASHINGTON D.C.

ON BEHALF OF VIETNAM GOVERNMENT AND PEOPLE I BEG TO INFORM YOU

THAT IN COURSE OF CONVERSATIONS BETWEEN VIETNAM GOVERNMENT AND FRENCH

REPRESENTATIVES THE LATTER REQUIRE THE SECESSION OF COCHINCHINA AND THE

RETURN OF FRENCH TROOPS IN HANOI STOP MEANWHILE FRENCH POPULATION AND

TROOPS ARE MAKING ACTIVE PREPARATIONS FOR A COUP DE MAIN IN HANOI AND

FOR MILLTARY AGGRESSION STOP I THEREFORE MOST EARNESTLY APPEAL TO YOU

PERSONALLY AND TO THE AMERICAN PEOPLE TO INTERFERE URGENTLY IN SUPPORT

OF OUR INDEPENDENCE AND HELP MAKING THE NEGOTIATIONS MORE IN KEEPING WITH

THE PRINCIPLES OF THE ATLANTIC AND SAN FRANCISCO CHARTERS

    RESPECTFULLY

                        HOCHIMINH

---

one of the two films previously discussed, they can draw some conclusions from an initial survey of the document. For example, they can identify key items or players, such as who is Ho Chi Minh and what country is trying to reassert its authority over what was then, in 1946 Indochina—France. Having already studied World War II, students will be able to tap into prior knowledge by identifying the Atlantic and San Francisco Charters. But again, some additional important background information is needed to put the document in better historical context. I tell students to look at the date and ask them who was the president of the United States in 1946. Once we have identified Truman, I then tell students that history may have taken a different track had Franklin Roosevelt not died in 1945. Roosevelt was committed to national self-determination of former colonial dominions at the end of

World War II. Although it may be an exercise in futility to raise the "what if?" question, it helps students to put these events in context.

After I give students my five-minute background lecture, I ask the following questions. "Why would Ho have raised the Declaration of Independence with American officials?" "Why would Ho admire Washington and Jefferson?" These two questions force students to draw on prior knowledge about America's struggle for independence and make connections between our struggle and the struggle of the Vietnamese to resist colonial occupation. Students are quick to compare Ho to Washington as one who was able to keep an army in the field and secure a victory over superior forces.

My next question is, "What do you think was Truman's response to the 1946 cable?" Students acknowledge that there probably was little or no response given what they have already learned about Vietnam. Their assessment is correct.

Finally, I tell students that the 1946 cable was declassified in 1986. I then ask them to consider that date and determine how many years this was after the fall of South Vietnam. I ask students to consider why the United States government waited until 1986 to declassify the document. Most reply that to have revealed to the American public this document at an earlier date could have been embarrassing given the direction that the war took. Additionally, in Ho's cable was a request for assistance, rejected by the United States, that asked the government of the United States to live up to its share of the Atlantic Charter and the mission of the United Nations in the San Francisco Charter. Using Ho's cable with students lays additional groundwork for students to see just how complex the seeds of our involvement in Vietnam was and presents them with some frame of reference as to why certain choices were made by the United States.

From here you can reinforce ideas from the films you have shown as to the eventual defeat of the French in 1954 and the partitioning of Indochina into North and South Vietnam along the seventeenth parallel in 1955, with North Vietnam being communist and South Vietnam being established as a democratic republic, thereby setting the stage for the eventual conflict.

The Tonkin Gulf Resolution

I use the Tonkin Gulf Resolution when we begin looking at the escalation of the war in the mid-1960s. With this document, you can launch into issues with students as to why Vietnam was never an officially declared war and why Congress would essentially hand over to the president an unlimited use of military power. Because students have prior knowledge, you can prompt them into speculating why President Lyndon Johnson asked for such sweeping power and why what he asked for was granted by Congress. By now, students should be able to point to the Cold War competition between the United States and the Soviet Union, the Domino Theory, and to the fact that Johnson, a Democrat, was sensitive to the fact that China fell to the Communists on the watch of a Democratic president, Truman, and that South Korea almost fell into communist hands, also under Truman. Again, this piece of legislation was a child of the policy of "containment." One of the issues I want students to consider is whether or not, in their opinion, the Tonkin Gulf incident justified such a massive use of force.

The War Powers Act of 1973

As we begin to put closure on the study of Vietnam, I provide students with a copy of the 1973 War Powers Act, which was a congressional reaction to the Vietnam War. I ask students to review the document and pick out the important details. In particular, I am looking to see if they can detect how this document regulates the power of the presidency to commit troops to combat within the guise of congressional legislation. My questions to students again have to do with justifications: "Was Congress justified in passing the War Powers Act?" "If so, why?" "What historical reasoning can they offer?" I also want students to consider how this act might pose problems for the president when trying to prosecute an armed conflict against an aggressor. Here I like to point out that in 1991, when President George Bush put together the coalition of forces to drive Saddam Hussein out of Kuwait, he went to Congress to ask for a vote of confidence. It is interesting to compare Johnson and Bush and their approaches to Congress. You can postulate with students why Bush approached Congress the way he did and ask them to determine how the War Powers Act played into this military action. Either way, students should take away from the War Powers Act a better understanding of the nature of checks and balances in our governmental structure and a historical reference point that continues to play a role today—all out of the legacy of Vietnam. Copies of the Tonkin Gulf Resolution and related lesson plans can be found in Volume One of *Teaching with Documents from the National Archives*. Copies of the War Powers Act can be found in any good source about the end of the Vietnam War or the Nixon administration. Even some of the better American history and government textbooks now include a copy of this congressional legislation.

A Blend of Histories

The history of Vietnam is a blend of politics, military planning, and personal grief. To teach this blend using the three documents just described, you can clearly trace the political aspects of the war. When used effectively with the films suggested, students can come to grips with the political dimensions of the war. Foreign policy and decision making no longer are concepts but rather become reality with the documents in student hands. The films trace the political and military machinery, based on containment, which sometimes got in the way of each other, during the course of the war.

To provide students with a more microscopic look at the political realities of the war, I like to use an eighteen-minute segment from tape two of the *American Experience* production of *LBJ* (1991). The segment I show students is the clip about early 1968 and the Tet Offensive. In this short clip, students see an embattled Lyndon Johnson and Secretary of Defense Robert McNamara. They learn of Johnson's dilemma of escalation and the growing frustration with the war at home, and they see Walter Cronkite's important news editorial that changed the direction of the war and led Johnson to make the apocryphal statement, "If I've lost Cronkite, I've lost middle America." Finally, they witness Johnson's speech to the nation in which he told Americans and the world that he would "not seek, nor accept the nomination of my party for another term as your president."

Beyond the politics, there are the stories of the ordinary Americans who carried out military and political policy in Vietnam. For this there are numerous resources you can use with your students. Two books that I like to use are *Dear America: Letters Home from Vietnam,* edited by Bernard Edelman (1985) and *Shrapnel in the Heart* (1987), an anthology of letters left behind at the Wall, edited by Laura Palmer. Both books are quite moving and resonate well with young people. You can assign the entire book for reading followed by an assessment activity, or read excerpts to your classes. I think the latter of the two makes for more powerful reading. It can become quite emotional when I share these readings with students. Sometimes tears have been shed. Students find a connection in these books because many of the writers are young people, not much older than themselves.

Related to this is the Home Box Office film, *Dear America* (1987). Over the years, students have told me that this was the most meaningful film that I showed while they were in my class. *Dear America* is a wonderful film that combines dramatic readings of some of the letters found in the book of the same name. Hollywood personalities such as Robert DiNiro, Robin Williams, Michael J. Fox, and Kathleen Turner read the letters matched to music of the Vietnam era, still photographs taken by servicemen and women in Vietnam, and film footage of the war, (some of it being home movies shot by people serving in Southeast Asia). The film runs almost ninety minutes, and I always have students respond to the film in the their journals. May wrote:

> I don't know if it's right to say I loved a war movie, but I really did love
> watching *Dear America.* I think it's great that they found and collected

all those letters and accompanying pictures of *all* those soldiers. They were *all* so young and good-looking . . . I can't imagine the teenagers of today being able to handle such situations, but listening to the letters of the young soldiers in Vietnam, I think the boys became more brave and more sensitive in the face of war. How did they bear to see their friends, partners in pain, crying, dying? I couldn't help but wish that they get to come home, even though the Vietnamese were faced with the threat of communism. I wish they would win over communism, but I wish they wouldn't have to lose their lives, their friends. . . . all I can say is . . . I hate war—I just hate it.

Elizabeth responded:

Perhaps the most touching segment of the film was the end, in which the mother's letter to her dead son was read. This was an appropriate way of reminding viewers that, yes, the soldiers told a large part of the Vietnam story, but they couldn't create the ending. It is the people left behind who must write their own conclusion, and as the video illustrated, some have still not been able to do that.

I always share with students the titles of other books that they might want to consider reading on their own. Usually I bring in and show students the different books I've read. The book, *Bloods: An Oral History of the Vietnam War by Black Veterans* (1989) is a classic book of the period whose stories are compiled by journalist Wallace Terry. Language and descriptions in this book are graphic however, as are most accounts of the Vietnam War, so be sure to review it carefully before introducing it to your classes. One year, I was showing them *Bloods*, and David, my lone African American student in my fifth-period class, immediately put his hand out indicating he wanted to see the book. So I handed it to him. As I proceeded to tell the class the other titles I had with me, David flipped through the pages, then stopped me and asked if he could read an excerpt to the class (see Figure 6–2). I was more than happy to consent. What David read was an evocative piece about what a black GI experienced in the aftermath of an intense firefight. Having David read this aloud to the class was powerful. Teachable moments like these should never be passed up by instructors. I find that sometimes that is the best way to get a student engaged in his or her learning, when there's a real, personal connection to be made.

Other books you might want to share with your students or have them read include *A Piece of My Heart: Oral Histories of Twenty-Six Women Who Served in Vietnam,* by Keith Walker (1991); *A Rumor of War,* by Philip Caputo (1977); *The Things They Carried,* by Tim O'Brien (1990); and *Home Before Morning: The Story of an Army Nurse in Vietnam* (1983), by Lynda Van Devanter. All of these titles, among plenty of others, offer first-rate extended and personal primary source reading.

Figure 6–2
David Reading an Excerpt from *Bloods*

Period Music and Photography

I like to use music to help instruct about Vietnam. Generally, I have a CD or tape playing vintage music as students enter the room. The thing about this music as compared to the music I play for the American Revolution, the Civil War, or the Labor movement is that many of the stu-

dents' parents (and their teachers) listen(ed) to this music. The best way
to use music for academic instruction is to have students analyze the
songs and their meanings. With the lyrics in hand, students can follow
the words and it helps them to clarify the meaning of the song. Songs I
like to use are Peter, Paul, and Mary's "Where Have All the Flowers
Gone," Barry Sadler's "The Ballad of the Green Berets," Marvin Gaye's
"What's Goin On," and Tom Paxton's version of the Phil Ochs song
"Letter from LBJ/Lyndon Johnson Told the Nation." Other songs you
might want to consider using are Edwin Starr's "War," and "American
Woman," sung by the Guess Who. There is no one single compiled CD
or tape with Vietnam-era music. You're going to have to build a collection culling songs from different albums. Some songs are easier to find
than others. One suggestion I have would be to contact the education
and outreach office of the Rock and Roll Hall of Fame in Cleveland,
Ohio. After I play each song, we discuss the lyrics and, as a quick measure of student learning, I ask them what different parts of the song
mean. For example, I'll ask, "What's the metaphor of flowers in 'Where
Have All the Flowers Gone'?" Or, "To what letter does Paxton refer in
'Letter from LBJ'?" Another, question might be, "How are these songs
related to the Anti-war movement?" This quick review helps to keep
students on their toes and reinforces the entire strand of learning by
connecting different lessons together.

Much of the music from the Vietnam era is linked to the Anti-war
movement, so you can use it to talk about this aspect of the conflict.
You can easily dovetail the music with some of the anti-war excerpts
found in "Echoes from the Wall."

One way to focus on the Anti-war movement is to spend some time
with students exploring the tragic affair at Kent State University in Ohio
on May 4, 1970. Again, you will have to provide background information as to why President Richard Nixon ordered 31,000 American soldiers into Cambodia, which many on college campuses around the nation took to be a signal of further escalation of the war. Students should
also be told the reasons why the Ohio National Guard was called out by
the governor to help quell several days of disturbances on the Kent State
campus and the subsequent tragic firing by the guard into the crowd,
leaving four students dead and nine wounded. After I have placed this
event within the context of the war and homefront activities, I use the
same technique that I use for the provocative photograph activity outlined in Chapter 4. In this case, I use the Pulitzer Prize–winning photograph taken by John Filo that shows a screaming Mary Ann Vecchio
kneeling next to the body of one of the four dead students, Jeff Miller.
Once again, I suggest that you turn to the book, *Moments: The Pulitzer
Prize Photographs* (Leekley 1978) for specific details to share with your
students and to find the image that can be turned into an overhead
transparency. Unlike the photograph discussed in Chapter 4, most

students need very little prompting to recognize this picture; they have seen it in either books or films. But while many of them can readily identify the photograph, their sense of the history about Kent State and the origin of the photograph is somewhat limited. As the teacher, you will need to clarify the story.

This photograph can also be used in conjunction with the Crosby, Stills, Nash, and Young song "Ohio." I like to keep the image up on the screen and play the song. Then we discuss the implications of this event and how the death of four students raised more attention in America than the deaths of Americans fighting in Southeast Asia. This is also a good place to examine the role of colleges in the Anti-war movement as well as to explore why so many young Americans were opposed to that conflict.

The Hessian

One of the most intriguing teaching activities I ever designed pertaining to Vietnam came from a book that, though set during the waning days of the American Revolution, really is a reflection of how many Americans had come to feel about war in general by the time the book was published in 1972. Howard Fast's *The Hessian* is a powerful historical novel in which the "dirty business of war" is examined in light of conflicting values and ethical considerations.

The Hessian deals with a fictitious incident near Ridgefield, Connecticut, in 1780. A patrol party of the German mercenaries is on a reconnaissance mission and, during their foray, they execute a retarded man who they presume is a spy. The execution is discovered and the local gentry and militia of the Fairfield County community set a trap and ambush the Hessians, killing all but one of them—their sixteen-year-old drummer boy, Hans Pohl, who escapes and is harbored for a short time by a local Quaker family. His whereabouts are discovered, and he is tried by a kind of kangaroo military tribunal that is bent on carrying out one last act of retribution. All calls by various members of Ridgefield to spare the boy's life fall on deaf ears and Pohl is hanged. Like all of Fast's good novels, this one resonates with much action, a genuine sympathy for the oppressed, hated, or misunderstood and a moral. To link the book to Vietnam, I give my students a historical head activity, but this time it has a twist. On their assignment sheet, they have to look up the dictionary definition of the word *ethics* and record what they find. Two of the ten images in the historical head template must somehow link the book and the Vietnam War. Students read the book as study the war, so they are, by virtue of this activity, in essence comparing the eighteenth and twentieth centuries. In addition, I share with students a detailed, three-page handout that I put together about the My Lai massacre. This handout includes an eyewitness-excerpt from the book *Eyewitness to America*

(Colbert 1997) and *The Eyewitness History of the Vietnam War, 1961–1975* by George Esper and the Associated Press (1983). There is also a condensed discussion of this controversial episode in the film *Vietnam: Chronicle of a War* (1981), which includes a fairly detailed examination of the My Lai massacre.

As with the day we discussed *Freedom Road* and *The Last Frontier*, I arrange the desks in a circle so that students can share their historical heads and so that we can hold a solid conversation. Before students share their historical heads, we talk about the definition of the word *ethics*. I ask each student to give me the dictionary definition of the word followed by their own definition. Then I ask students to discuss their thoughts on the book. These conversations are generally lively and some of the most engaging I have ever held with students. Students prove able to make the best kind of intellectual and emotional leap, as is my objective. As part of their learning, they come to see how warfare, regardless of its time period, is ruthless and complex. Often there are gray areas that can be defined differently by different people based on their experiences. Values are often spit into the wind whether it's the American Revolution or Vietnam. In concluding this activity, I read to students this excerpt from Philip Caputo's classic, *A Rumor of War* (1977):

> Everything rotted and corroded quickly over there: bodies, boot leather, canvas, metal, morals. Scorched by the sun, wracked by the wind and rain of the monsoon, fighting in alien swamps and jungles, our humanity rubbed off of us as the protective bluing rubbed off the barrels of our rifles. We were fighting in the cruelest kind of conflict, a people's war. It was no orderly campaign, as in Europe, but a war for survival waged in a wilderness without rules or laws; a war in which each soldier fought for his own life and the lives of the men beside him, not caring who he killed in that personal cause or how many or in what manner and feeling only contempt for those who sought to impose on his savage struggle the mincing distinctions of civilized warfare—that code of battlefield ethics that attempted to humanize an essentially inhuman war. According to those "rules of engagement," it was morally right to shoot an unarmed Vietnamese who was running, but wrong to shoot one who was standing or walking; it was wrong to shoot an enemy prisoner at close range, but right for a sniper at long range to kill an enemy soldier who was no more able than a prisoner to defend himself; it was wrong for infantrymen to destroy a village with white-phosphorus grenades, but right for a fighter pilot to drop napalm on it. Ethics seemed to be a matter of distance and technology. You could never go wrong if you killed people at long range with sophisticated weapons. And then there was that inspiring order issued by General Greene: kill VC. In the patriotic fervor of the Kennedy years, we had asked, "What can we do for our country?" and our country answered, "Kill VC." That was the strategy, the best our best military minds could come up with: organized butchery. But organized or not,

butchery was butchery, so who was to speak of rules and ethics in a war that had none? (299–30)

Using the Virtual Wall

In November 1999, the Vietnam Veterans Memorial Fund unveiled the Virtual Wall. This online database includes every one of the 58,281 names on the Vietnam Veterans Memorial in Washington, DC. Much like the Wall in Washington, where people constantly leave remembrances, the same holds true for the Virtual Wall (see Figure 6–3). Family members, relatives, and friends can leave online remembrances to loved ones via the Internet. You can find scanned photos, letters, comments, and audio remembrances on the Virtual Wall. The purpose of the Virtual Wall is to continue the ongoing educational mission of the Vietnam Veterans Memorial Fund as well as to provide individuals who have not visited the Wall in Washington to do so vicariously through the Internet.

The Virtual Wall is also intended to be a tool for use in the schools. Teachers using the Virtual Wall can bring the Vietnam Veterans Memorial right into their schools and use its resources as an adjunct to instruction. I have found use of the Virtual Wall in combination with the Wall in Washington to be a very effective teaching tool.

I decided to cull off the Virtual Wall the names of Americans from Virginia, West Virginia, Maryland, and Washington, DC, who had been killed during the war and who also had had remembrances left on the Virtual Wall. I printed out the names, one for each of my 130 students, and then cut them into slips of paper. As I walked through the room having students pick names from a Vietnam-era US Army helmet, Peter, Paul, and Mary's "Where Have All the Flowers Gone" was playing in the background. I also placed inside the helmet the names of several of the eight women who lost their lives during the war. Some students requested to do specific names of friends of their families. I found it very appropriate to have those students research the requested individual.

Once each student had a name, I then dispatched them to both the Wall in Washington, DC, and the Virtual Wall. Obviously, students who do not live near Washington, DC can use the Virtual Wall for this exercise. At the actual memorial, students were to locate the name of their soldier and complete a name rubbing. Volunteers and National Park Service personnel provide paper and special pencils at the memorial to use for rubbings. Once students secured their rubbing, they were to then cross-reference that name on the Virtual Wall to find out as much as they could about their individual. On the day that their name rubbings and journal entries about their learning experience were due, I had students affix to the wall outside my classroom the rubbings that they

Figure 6–3
Lexie Researching on the Virtual Wall

had collected. Students using only the Virtual Wall can download and print out their information for display. The assignment worked far better than I had imagined. By working through this moving activity, students were able to make a personal connection with an ordinary American who perished during America's longest war. Deanna wrote,

My visit to both the real Wall and the Virtual Wall were moving. I feel like I have "adopted" a Vietnam veteran; mine is Harold Kenneth Rapport.

Although his name was rather high up on the actual Wall, when I went to visit it and observe it I felt connected with just one of the many men who gave his life for our country. Harold Kenneth Rappaport died for the United States; he died for independence, freedom, democracy; he died for me. Going to visit one specific person put a name and personality to all those who died. Vietnam is no longer a statistic to me. Vietnam is a man, it is Harold K. Rappaport.

Mike recorded,

Two weeks ago, my Dad and I visited the Vietnam Veterans Memorial in Washington. I think that the Wall is one of the most impressive memorials in Washington simply because of its tremendous size.

Upon arriving at the memorial, I made a rubbing of the name James Westbrook. At the time, that is all it was—a name. But when I returned home and visited the Virtual Wall, the name changed into an individual as I learned about his life. Westbrook was a black captain from Memphis, Tennessee who served in the Army Reserve. He arrived in Vietnam on July 11, 1967, and a little more than a year later, on August 25, 1968, he was gunned down during a small scuffle in the South Vietnamese province of Tay Ninh. Westbrook, who was just 26 at the time of his death, left behind a wife in the United States.

I recognize that I have a unique opportunity living so close to Washington and the assorted memorials on the national Mall, but there are plenty of ways to create immediacy in your own classroom. I suggest that you create your own Vietnam Veterans Memorial based on the Virtual Wall. Try locating the names of individuals from your state or community. To do so, simply click on *Reflections,* click on *Generalized Search* and fill in the name of your state. Have students conduct some research about your school during the Vietnam War, and see if any alumni have names on both Walls. An extension of this might be to have your school dedicate a plaque in honor of those alumni who lost their lives. Not every name on the Virtual Wall has had a remembrance left behind. One project you might consider is having students use those names to collect oral histories about those individuals who graduated from your school and then post them on the Virtual Wall.

There are also four Traveling Walls that tour the country. These are reduced walls that replicate the Wall in Washington. Contact the Vietnam Veterans Memorial Fund to find out when a Traveling Wall will be in or near your community and use that resource as a means to make the Vietnam War meaningful to your students.

Be sure to access the Virtual Wall yourself. It is an outstanding resource that can be used in many effective ways in your classroom. Let your own creative juices flow to see what you can develop for both you and your students.

Discussing the Additions to the Wall

In 1984, sculptor Frederick Hart's *Three Servicemen* was unveiled a short distance from the Wall. This ensemble depicts three American GIs, one white, one black, and one Hispanic. All three are facing the Wall and are physically connected to one another through Hart's skillful placing of their hands. Art critics were satisfied with the choice and it seemed that the furor was over. However, shortly after the *Three Servicemen* was unveiled, groups representing women's interests in Vietnam clamored for a memorial. There was more discussion with Congress and the National Capitol Commission on Fine Arts and in 1993 the Women's Memorial by sculptor Glenna Goodacre was dedicated.

By the time this third memorial was placed by the Wall, I had been using memorials as part of my teaching repertoire. We followed the story with interest in my classes. I provided students with copies of articles related to the women's memorial when they appeared in the *Washington Post.* Students read the articles and then we held discussions. There was, among concerned parties, a fear that the Vietnam Veterans Memorial was going to be drowned in a sea of "additions." In fact, shortly after the women started the process for a memorial, proponents of a memorial to dogs who had lost their lives raised their issue. After the women's memorial was unveiled, Congress agreed that no more additions to the Vietnam Veterans Memorial would take place. However, recently Congress did vote to add another memorial, this one to victims of Agent Orange and to individuals who have committed suicide as a result of suffering Post Traumatic Stress Disorder.

Teaching about the saga of the National Vietnam Veterans Memorial makes for a particularly good lesson in civic pride, consensus, and the legacy of a shadow of an event that is still close to us. I have always been able to incorporate these themes into my classes whenever the issue emerges. Talking about the debate over this particular memorial is a great way for students to examine the idea of consensus because that was such a critical element of the war. It's an excellent paradox comparing the war to the memorial.

No matter how you choose to use the Vietnam Veterans Memorial in class, you can generate discussions with your students over their particular impressions of the assorted memorials. You can find photographic images of the memorials on the web. Show them to your students or have them conduct their own research. Then raise questions such as the following about the design:

1. Should this memorial be on the national Mall? Why or why not?
2. Do they think it's appropriate? Why or why not?
3. How in their opinion does the Wall and memorial additions serve as healing devices?
4. How do they, if at all, see a relationship between the Wall and the war?
5. What does all of the controversy surrounding all of the memorials say about the war and how we view the war and its participants? Does this say anything about us, and if so, what?

There are a number of very good classroom-appropriate videotapes that document the history of the memorial and its impact on Vietnam Veterans, those who lost a loved one during the war, and the nation in general. Video titles include, *The Wall That Heals* (1997) and *All the Unsung Heroes* (1990).

As a wrap-up, intriguing questions that you can pose to your students are:

1. In one hundred years, what do you think the Vietnam Veterans Memorial will mean to people?
2. What factors might impact how the memorial is viewed in one hundred years?

Using Other Vietnam Veterans Memorials

I like to photograph different Vietnam Veterans memorials across the country. In the wake of the dedication of the national memorial, scores of states, communities, and municipalities began erecting monuments to the men and women who served in Vietnam. I have assembled quite a collection of slide images of these monuments and use them as part of my instruction. As part of my lecture and subsequent discussion, I ask students to consider if these memorials are, in their opinion, more successful than the one located in Washington. Many of these memorials were erected after the national memorial, and it is clear that the designing architects and sculptors took lessons from the near debacle in Washington. Many of them include men and women and blacks, whites, and Hispanics. Some of them, such as the one New York City dedicated to its Vietnam Veterans Memorial, are abstract in nature but incorporate segments from veterans' letters into the design; others, such as the one in Wilmington, Delaware, by Charles Parks, remain true to the figurative academic tradition depicting a black GI carrying a wounded white GI to receive medical attention.

Other monuments whose images I use include:

1. *The Westchester County, New York Memorial* located in Somers, New York, by Julia Evans Cohen
2. *The Tennessee Vietnam Veterans Memorial* on the state capitol grounds in Nashville by Alan LeQuire
3. *Hill 881 South* in San Antonio, Texas, by Austin Deuel
4. *The New York City Vietnam Veterans Memorial* designed by architects Peter Wormser and William Fellows
5. *The Fairfield Connecticut Vietnam Veterans Memorial,* in Danbury, Connecticut, by George Koras among others

When students look at these memorials, I ask them to draw comparisons with the one in Washington by prompting them with questions such as:

1. Which one, if any, do you like? Why?
2. Do you think any of them are more successful than the national memorial? If so, why? If not, why not?
3. What elements or themes from the Vietnam War are present in these memorials?
4. How did these artists or designers appear to learn lessons about commemorating the Vietnam War from the controversy over the national memorial?

As an extension activity, you might want to have your students design a Vietnam Veterans memorial. This activity can be effectively used as a means of final assessment on what students have learned about the Vietnam War while tapping into different learning styles and effectively using differentiation. Here are the criteria I use for student-designed memorials:

- The final memorial and or design must be drawn on paper, no smaller than 8½ by 11 inches, or students may submit a three-dimensional model. On a separate sheet of paper, they must include the following:
  - a statement explaining the design and its reflection of the Vietnam War
  - an indication of the materials out of which the memorial is made, i.e. bronze, marble, etc.
  - the specific location where they intend to erect this memorial with an explanation of the choice of site

If you approach this assignment from this perspective, students will have a great deal of latitude from which to work. Some students may submit freestanding statues; others might design a memorial park or garden. Leave the choice up to them. This is a great way to pull all components of teaching about Vietnam together in a student-centered package.

The Classroom and Vietnam Veterans

Without a doubt, one of the best resources we have are the numbers of Vietnam Veterans who live in our communities. It is estimated that three million American men and women served in Southeast Asia. Increasingly, Vietnam Veterans are willing to share not only their experiences, but their views on the war with people who are interested.

Beginning in the mid-1980s, I began having Vietnam Veterans and other people connected to the time period, such as anti-war protesters and psychologists who worked with veterans suffering from Post Traumatic Stress Disorder, speak to my classes. Some of the veterans were still on active duty. Several of them had brought cameras to Vietnam and taken slides. Not only are my students afforded firsthand accounts, but they also can witness these personal visuals. When I first began inviting speakers, I had different people come in on different days, but in today's climate of block scheduling, I have moved, along with my colleagues on the US History team, to arrange a speakers panel. More will be discussed later in this chapter about how to set up a speakers panel.

In some cases, feelings are still raw regarding the war, not so much with the veterans, but with some of my students. One year in the mid-1980s, it was almost as if the war were taking place in my classroom. Some students whose fathers had served in Vietnam thought that the different speakers represented a more liberal view of the conflict. A number of them were not pleased with the comments or attitudes of the anti-war protester. Even though I had laid out some fairly simple and clear ground rules about listening to our guests, the fact that a number of the speakers kept using the phrase "we lost the war" bothered some students. One student, whose dad was a Vietnam Veteran, got so upset at what he thought was an unreasonable argument about America's role that he angrily stalked out of class. Talk about "living history." What ended up happening in my classroom twelve years after the fall of Saigon was nothing short of the kinds of heated exchanges that took place between the "Hawks" and the "Doves" of the period. Today, students don't react with the same kind of fervor; they tend to be more open and balanced in their approach to learning. Then again, we're a number of years farther down the road from Vietnam.

In order to secure speakers for your classes, first find out if any of your students had parents or grandparents serve in Vietnam. Next, check among your faculty to ascertain whether a colleague or two might be Vietnam Veterans. If so, ask if they would be willing to speak with you and your students. If not, contact your local chapters of the Veterans of Foreign Wars or the American Legion. In many cases, these two organizations have a list of people who are willing to speak with school groups. Seek a balanced presentation. Look for individuals who can reflect the range of issues from the Vietnam War—bring in soldiers, sailors, pilots, nurses, protesters, and policy makers; if possible, perhaps a former prisoner of war. Try to have people who represent the races speak—Vietnam was fought by a multicultural force. Consider locating someone in your community who is Vietnamese and maybe fled the country in 1975 or came here as a boat person in the years following the collapse of South Vietnam. The better rounded your panel can be, the more of a true learning experience it will be for your students.

When you have speakers, set clear guidelines and rules for your students to follow. Make sure that the students recognize and understand that these people are freely giving of their time and that they are deserving of respect. To prepare my students for guest speakers, I provide them each with an index card on which they are to write a question that they would like to have answered. This helps students to focus. Part of this technique is to have students tap into prior learning about Vietnam so as to raise reflective questions.

"Echoes from the Wall" also includes excellent suggestions for you to follow when working with Vietnam Veterans, including comprehensive guides and resources for teacher and veterans prepared by the Veterans Education Project (VEP), an organization in Amherst, Massachusetts. VEP trains veterans from their area to share personal stories of military service in social studies classes, after-school programs, and assemblies. Their vets have made tremendous inroads with marginalized learners who are in schools that are often wracked with violence. VEP's program seeks to assist students in these environments to turn away from violence by listening to the words and experiences of men and women who were exposed to the horror of war during their tours of duty in Vietnam's jungles, firebases, and evacuation hospitals. VEP—whose work has won local acclaim from Massachusetts educators, as well as national recognition from the National Council on Crime and Delinquency and the Congressional Black Caucus of the US Congress—has proven that veterans from the community can use the legacy of the Vietnam War to make a difference in the lives of young people and to address some significant contemporary issues. "Teachers have told us that some of their difficult students, who are turned off to textbooks, have been completely engaged by a veterans' stories," reported Rob

Wilson, a former teacher who is VEP's director. "Not only do these stories bring history to life, they can de-glorify the glorious Hollywood depictions of war that so many kids are exposed to and communicate important messages about decision making and responsible citizenship." If you are reluctant about working with Vietnam Veterans, for whatever reasons, I suggest you look at the Module Three Appendix in the Echoes curriculum and Teacher's Guide or visit the Vietnam Veterans' Memorial Fund (VVMF) curriculum website at *www.teachvietnam.com* and go to the *Resources* section. Here you will find useful information to help you create a first-rate learning experience for your students. VEP also trains veterans to work effectively in school environments to ensure a positive experience for both students and speakers. There also appears to be some residual healing effects for the veterans themselves. Stephen Sossaman, a Vietnam Veteran who not only works closely with VEP but also writes war-related poetry that can be found in "Echoes from the Wall," claims that "By speaking in classrooms, a veteran can transform a sometimes painful and confusing experience into a positive contribution toward young people's understanding. Speaker training with other veterans helps speakers better understand their experiences, select stories which complement schools' curricular and citizenship goals, and present these stories in powerful and memorable ways."

A Gay Vietnam Veteran

One of the graves in Washington, DC's, Congressional Cemetery that I like to take students to visit during our field trip to that historic cemetery is the grave of Leonard Matlovich. Matlovich, a decorated, two-tour Vietnam Veteran, was the first person in the United States military to openly admit his sexual preference. Despite his stellar military and combat record, he was discharged from the United States Air Force based on the grounds of his sexual preference. As a result of his "less than honorable discharge," in 1975, he was the first gay person to legally challenge the military's gay/lesbian policy. Matlovich's efforts raised consciousness across the country as to the status of gays in the military. Though reinstated in the Air Force, Matlovich chose to become involved in the Gay movement. In 1987, Matlovich was diagnosed with AIDS. He died a year later in June 1988. Matlovich's tombstone is described by his biographer, Mike Hippler: "The memorial is a simple slab of black granite inset with two pink granite triangles at the top. The triangle at the left, identical to the triangles which gay people were forced to wear in the concentration camps of Nazi Germany, points downward. In military symbolism, this is a sign of defeat. The triangle at the right points upward, a sign of victory. Beneath the two triangles are chiseled the phrases, 'Never Again' and 'Never Forget.' There is no name on the tombstone—simply the words, 'A Gay Vietnam Veteran.' This is followed by a statement: 'When I was in the military they gave me a medal for killing two men and a discharge for loving one.'"

When Matlovich's headstone was placed in the cemetery, prior to his death, he made arrangements for his name to be left off the marker. It was done anonymously to honor those who served in Vietnam. Matlovich said, "I really didn't want to be seen as self-serving. Had I died in Vietnam when I hit the mine, I would have been just another dead Vietnam vet, you see. I would not have been a specifically *gay* Vietnam veteran who died for his country. I knew there were thousands of gay veterans like me who would be proud to be remembered not only for their sacrifice but also for their sense of self-worth as gay people. I wanted it to be their monument as well as my own."

Matlovich was buried with military honors. His grave, which now includes his name and a Presidential Citation given to all American veterans, has become a kind of shrine for the gay community. When we visit his grave, I always tell my students Matlovich's story, much as I do for other notable people buried in the Congressional Cemetery. My students always are moved by our visit to Matlovich's final resting place. I think some of them can identify with being on the outside trying to break in to the mainstream, even if it's not a result of their sexual preference, but simply teenagers trying to fit in. Almost universally, their journal entries about our visit to the Congressional Cemetery mention Matlovich's grave. Over the years of our visit, I have often thought that this moment is one of significant consciousness raising.

A Junior Class Unit

One of the major reasons I enjoy working at my school and in my particular social studies department is because of the naturally professional and collegial atmosphere that prevails among department members. The US history team at West Springfield High School works well as a group and we are always sharing lesson plans and teaching ideas. Eleventh graders take the advanced placement exams and the Virginia Standards of Learning Tests in early May. One year when it came time to figure out what to teach in the remaining month of school following these exams, we decided to pool resources and develop a month-long intensive academic program on the Vietnam War. It was a great deal of work, but at the same time fun, and in the end, our students learned more about Vietnam than previous classes.

As a team, we decided that we would coordinate common activities with each other, specifically a two-day after-school Vietnam Film Festival, culminating with a two-day round-robin speakers panel of Vietnam Veterans. Each teacher would teach independent lessons on Vietnam within his or her class.

We began our planning early in the second semester. Each member of the US history team assumed various tasks related to the unit; one of us secured the films, one contacted veterans and veterans organizations to get speakers for the panel, and I put together the letter home to parents, including a guide to each of the selected films. All of the activities, including our independent teaching, were planned for the two weeks prior to the Memorial Day holiday.

We knew that the film festival would be the most controversial part of our plans, given the language and sexuality that are part of many films about Vietnam. Dr. Smith, our principal, assured us that he would support our project if we gave students the option to see a film that was not R-rated. We did require to have students stay after school on one of the two assigned film days, so a letter needed to be sent home to parents explaining the scope and purpose of the unit including the aforementioned film synopsis sheet. Both the letter and synopsis sheet can be found in the Appendix D.

We had permission from our other colleagues in the department to use their classrooms on the two days of the film festival. Each classroom had a sign on the door designating which films would be showing there. Each student received from his or her teacher a review sheet to use while watching the film. This video guide was based on the guide you can find on the web at *www.teachmovies.org*. We were committed to making sure that this was more than an entertaining exercise.

It was a task processing close to five hundred students through the two-day program, but it was quite evident to all of us as we filtered from classroom to classroom that students were transfixed by the films. We showed ten films, such as *Platoon* (1986), *Good Morning Vietnam* (1987), *The Green Berets* (1969), and *Hanoi Hilton* (1987), among others. It was our intention that, for classroom debriefing and post-film discussion, each film be watched by some students from each class. Thus, students did not have a choice of the film they could watch. They had to select a film by pulling a title from a hat, or in my class's case, a helmet. We told students that they were more than welcome to come and watch a second film if they wanted to on the other film day. For students who pulled an R-rated film from the list but who wanted to opt out of that film, we directed them to one of the G, PG, or PG-13 films. Part of our plan was to pique student curiosity so that if they really wanted to see a particular film, they would take the initiative and watch it on their own time.

After the film festival was over, each teacher held class discussions with his or her students so that all of the students would be exposed to the content and issues of the different films. As part of the review sheet each student had, they were to write a movie review and rate it on a scale of one to five stars. I simply had my students record their reviews in their journals.

The following week we held our speakers panel during every class period, again over two days, in the school's multipurpose room. Because no more than three classes at a time interacted with our guests, sessions with the different veterans were fairly intimate. There were five to six veterans on each panel. These were powerful sessions that put a real personal face on the war. What took the students by complete surprise was the fact that several faculty members were on the panel. You could hear remarks like, "Gee, I didn't know that Mr. Harpman or Mr. Deeney were Vietnam Veterans." When students encounter such vestiges from the recent past in their midst, it forces a kind of paradigm shift in their thinking. No longer is the event, in this case Vietnam, really that far removed from their existence.

The veterans sat in front of television monitors with maps of Vietnam showing above their heads. It was an effective touch because during their comments the veterans could point to the different places where they had served in Vietnam.

The way the panel agreed to speak was to have each individual get up and tell his story, and then when all of the veterans were finished with their tales, they would field questions from the students. Some of the stories they told about their experiences were harrowing. Some were humorous. All of the veterans agreed that there was no one single Vietnam experience. As they explained, each of them experienced Vietnam in a different and unique way. John Dibble, who lived with Vietnamese villagers below the Mekong River, said that not all of their memories are necessarily bad, countering a kind of stereotype that dogs Vietnam Veterans. Dibble said that in many cases he has fond memories of bonding and comradeship with other veterans. You could see the nodding of heads by other members of the panel affirming Dibble's remarks. Glen Lane, a former Green Beret, talked about serving with the Montagnard people up near the Cambodian border and eating monkey brains as part of a tribal meal ceremony. Tony Pizzo, who is short, talked about his dubious honor of being selected (because of his size) to be a tunnel rat, to flush out Viet Cong soldiers from the different tunnels that they burrowed in the country. Dibble also stated, when asked what he most remembered, that there is no real way to re-create the feelings he felt in Vietnam because it was a year of adrenaline rush on top of adrenaline rush. A number of the veterans mentioned that for them it was a period of time when they lost their innocence because their lives were at risk and that thoughts of death and dying ran through their heads on a daily basis. When Dibble said that being in a war zone you saw the best in people as well as the worst in people, once again there was a universal bobbing of the other veterans' heads.

The students had good questions. What helped this was that they had the necessary background from which to develop good questions that were relevant and in a historical context. When asked about their experiences after the war when they returned home, Matt's Dad, Tony Nelson, explained that when he came home from the war as a nineteen-year-old, his former babysitter asked him how many babies he had killed. Dibble said that he had a hard time adjusting to some of the nuances of American life that he had not been exposed to during his tour of duty. For example, he said that when he came home he had no idea what was meant by the term *ripped off*, to which he attributed a whole year of being out of contact with what veterans came to call "the world"; that is, the United States. Some students were eager to know the veterans' opinions regarding Jane Fonda, to which most veterans concurred that what she did by going to visit North Vietnam was wrong and exploitive.

One of the moving moments of the presentations was when Lane held up a back issue of *LIFE* magazine from June 27, 1969, that was lying on a table in the room. This was a special issue that had a photographic essay consisting of one photo of each of the 242 Americans who had died in Vietnam during one week that spring. Near tears, Lane held the magazine up to show students the page after page of portraits of young men, not much older than the students in the room, who died. Watching the students faces and their eyes told the whole story. They were touched and shocked at the same time.

A number of the questions posed by the students related to how these men felt about American policy in Vietnam. This proved to be a rather conservative panel—they all said that they felt that the motive and cause for which they were fighting was good. There was consensus among the veterans that part of the reason we lost the war was because it was micro-managed by civilian leaders and that it was waged as a limited war. The veterans' response, when asked about what lessons the United States could learn from this war, was a unanimous, "if a country is going to fight a war, then it must commit itself to total victory, much like the Allied effort to defeat Germany and Japan during World War II." For the veterans, there were too many gray areas during Vietnam and confining rules of engagement. There was unanimous agreement that the reason we won the Persian Gulf War was because of the lessons we learned in Vietnam, known as the [Colin] Powell Doctrine, which is to not gradually build up forces but to hit early and hard and foster national consensus on the part of the American government and public. In other words, have clear goals and objectives in mind.

Students also asked about the veterans' attitudes toward the films that they had watched, and most said that there is no real way, no matter how hard Hollywood tries, to capture combat on film. Lane said that in his opinion, *Platoon* was "crap" and that he thinks it is unfortunate that most Americans think Oliver Stone's portrayal of Vietnam is the whole war. Most of the veterans agreed that the best combat film about Vietnam is the film *Go Tell the Spartans* (1978), which was one of the films in the festival. Regarding student queries into the role of the press, there was again a consensus that the press and television played a role in turning public opinion in the United States against the war.

Having a living/oral history panel was an excellent way to provide meaning to the students. They could see and hear players from a place and time in American history. In my students' journals, they expressed gratitude as well as respect and reverence for these men and what they had experienced. Again, the face-to-face reality with the past made Vietnam no longer an abstraction, but a living and breathing reality.

During our special unit I continued to teach lessons—many of which have been described earlier in the chapter. On these days, the students were lively and eager to absorb more information. At one point, Matt shared with us his father's photo album from the war and told us that he learned things from hearing his dad speak as a member of the panel that he had never known about his dad. As a culminating activity and an authentic means of garnering students' synthesis and assessment of the material they had learned, I asked my students to create, based on everything they had learned, a political cartoon about Vietnam. In order to do this, I had to do some digging around in the library to find examples I could share with my students. There is no one book available that offers a collection of Vietnam-era cartoons, so I had to make copies from a number of different sources. There is a web site for the *Philadelphia Inquirer's* cartoonist Tony Auth's Vietnam cartoons at *www.philly.com/specials/2000/vietnam/auth*, which I also encourage you to explore. I spent half a period with students going over the different kinds of cartoons that were drawn during the period. I made copies for them as well as used the overhead projector to display the examples. One of Doug Marlette's cartoons included a drawing of the Pulitzer Prize–winning photo by Nick Ut that shows nine-year-old Phan Thi Kim Phuc running toward the camera having had her clothes shred off her body during a napalm attack. Again using the book, *Moments: The Pulitzer Prize Photographs* (Leekley 1978), I was able to make an overhead transparency of the photograph and show it to my students. I then had them look at Marlette's cartoon, which included the superimposed drawing of the photograph in which an adult is admonishing an anti-war protester for picketing American participation in Vietnam by saying, "You peace-nicks burn me up." I wanted to use this to demonstrate the power of photographs and how they shape our collective memory of events. It's important that students recognize the relationship between all aspects of the war and how many of these aspects played off each other, much of them showing up in political cartoons. The cartoon project results that students created were amazing. Student work reflected all the elements of the war: combat, politics, hawks versus doves, reaction on college campuses, and the homefront. I have included one here as an illustration (see Figure 6–4). It reflects the age of American GIs going off to serve in Vietnam. It did not matter to me for evaluation purposes whether or not students could draw, so I gave them the option of using clip art or images from the Internet. What mattered most to me was how effectively they were able to capture a particular sentiment of the war. I was looking for synthesis. They had indeed succeeded.

Lessons and Legacy of the War

As a final wrap-up to the unit, I explore with students the lessons and the legacy of the war. I think that this is a very important component of my instruction. These students are the leaders of tomorrow, and they need to be able to think through the issues that got us into our role in fighting in Vietnam—it's a true exercise in critical or historical thinking. There are several activities I use for closure. First, I use a question that my colleague Ron Maggiano developed for his students on a handout he prepared as a critical thinking activity. It reads:

> A "just war," as identified by Thomas Aquinas, must have three conditions—public authority, just cause, and the right motive. Based on all that you have learned about the Vietnam War, in your opinion, was it a "just war?" Why? Why Not?

I pose this question to my my students, give them time to think about it, and then launch into a class discussion. Students offer many different viewpoints. Many students believe that the war was based on a right motive and just cause, namely the containment of communism, but did not have public authority. Some students argue that it was in no way a just war given the fact that the government of South Vietnam was corrupt. Others raise the point that the United States had no business meddling in the affairs of foreign countries—in this case a civil war in Southeast Asia. A few students claim that if Truman had taken Ho

Figure 6–4
Student-Created Vietnam-Era Political Cartoon

" Child's Play"

Chi Minh's telegram more seriously, we might have avoided the political and military situation that eventually developed.

When we finish the discussion, I direct students to answer the following in their Journals: "What lessons can the United States learn from our experience in Vietnam?" This journal entry is arranged a bit differently than others because I incorporate a technique known as the Q-3-2-1. I ask students to answer the first question as they have done in all of their other entries, but at the end I want them to write out separately their responses to the following;

1. What are three things that you learned about the Vietnam War?
2. What are two things about which you would like to know more?
3. What is the one most important thing that you learned?

As with the question about whether or not Vietnam was a "just war," the answers in their journal entries vary. Andy and others felt that the media had too much access to information and then reported that information with a negative slant. These students argued that in future wars the media should be more tightly controlled, a lesson that the military did employ during the Persian Gulf War.

Casey wrote that Americans can learn the following from our Vietnam experiences:

> Not every country's ambitions are the same as ours. We saw the Vietnamese as present-day incarnations of our Revolutionary War soldiers fighting against oppression. This was not so—we misjudged the political forces within the country. Sometimes there are no immediate solutions for problems. We expected to go into the situation [in Vietnam] and solve everything, but there proved to be no panacea for the situation. Modern weaponry and scores of men don't amount to much when up against people ready to die for what they believe in. The Viet Cong had a common ideal that motivated them—we had resentful and embittered GI's counting the days until their tour of duty was finished.

Many other students pointed out in a similar vein that the Viet Cong were not unlike our War for Independence patriots who were seeking to oust a foreign power, Great Britain.

Caitlin wrote:

> I believe America is still learning lessons from Vietnam. For many, Vietnam was a mistake and a waste of US resources. For others, it was a fight for freedom in which others needed our assistance. We learned that we shouldn't under estimate the power of smaller countries and that being bigger doesn't mean that you will always win. We've learned a great deal about America, too. People became very angry and hostile toward the government, they set up rallies and protests. America had never seen people behave like this. We also learned what values our people hold. Many lied to get out of the draft, many hurt their own people during protests, four students were killed at Kent State—and they called it a "peace" rally. The population became divided—anti-

war and pro-war. But it wasn't so clear —the division—in America we had no 17th parallel.

In response to the Q-3-2-1 exercise she wrote:

> Three things I learned: (a) the United States was in Vietnam trying to contain communism, (b) 58,281 men and women died in the war, (c) there was dissension at home including tragedies like Kent State. Two things about which I would like to know more are: (a) the draft dodging and (b) Vietnamese accounts of the war. The most important thing I took away from this unit is that the United States did not succeed because we were so sure of ourselves and did not put control of the war into the right hands.

Many journals echoed similar sentiments to those of both Casey and Caitlin. The consensus among students was that if we are going to get into a war, we can't fight that war in a limited fashion and that support of the people of the United States is vital to any measure of success.

Elizabeth concluded her journal entry by saying, "Because of the Vietnam War, I believe that America is now less likely to get involved in foreign conflicts without seriously considering the consequences."

Students also wanted to learn more about the American prisoners of war and the use of Agent Orange. There were students who wanted more specific information about Post Traumatic Stress Disorder. Some students wanted to know about other battles besides the Tet Offensive. Even with the extended time we had devoted to this topic, it was hard to cover everything.

Summing it all up, May wrote:

> The Vietnam War truly seems to be one of those lessons where the more I learn, the more I realize what I don't know. I realized that during this unit, aside from the dated events, is that the controversial war encompasses more opposing, different perspectives than I can comprehend. Every time we watched a film or listened to a speaker, a different view of the war was presented. Some members of the speakers panel a very "democratic" attitude in which their mission and purpose seemed very defined. The powerful movie, *Dear America,* on the other hand, showed young boys at war wanting also to promote democracy, but more returning to their loved ones after counting their 365-day tour of duty. If there was another thing that we could have studied further, I would have liked to have learned more about the Vietnamese perspective. I know that there was some resentment, some friendships . . . but the war was only thirty years ago. How do they feel about us now?

Recently, a good friend of mine from high school, who works for a major multinational company that now conducts business in Vietnam, told me about a visit of his to Ho Chi Minh City, formerly Saigon. He said the Vietnamese people call the war the "American War" and that until recently the old US Embassy compound was known as the American War Crimes Museum. In an effort to draw more American capital into the country, the name of the museum has been softened a bit. I related this story to my students because many of them wanted to know about our current relations with Vietnam. Now that we have established diplomatic ties with Hanoi, I am certain that teachers in the coming years will be more readily able to answer that question than I am.

Final Thoughts

I have only scratched the surface of this event in American history. There is certainly room to include more. An entire year could be devoted to the Vietnam War. The list of potential lesson plans about the Vietnam War are endless. What is important is to provide enough students with a balanced presentation of information and material so that they can generate informed opinions.

When teaching about Vietnam, you are going to run into controversial issues such as appropriate use of photographs. As one of the most photographed events of the twentieth century, it is critical to use these images as part of your instruction. The photographs that I have used and discussed using in this chapter not only are important records of American history, but also made history by influencing public opinion around the world. Some of these images, as I've discussed, are stark and brutal. I believe that searing photographs such as these made up an important element of the conflict and to leave them out would not do justice to the historiography of the war. But you need to make your own choices about the photographs you choose.

You may confront strong language in some of the material about Vietnam. I suggest that you take the time to review all potential material. If necessary, talk amongst your colleagues. Discuss your plans with your principal or district social studies coordinator. Vietnam was not a "clean" war in the sense that World War II was. This war is harder to teach than World War II, which seems to be sanitized by history. Just compare the Hollywood films about both events. In many ways, with Vietnam Hollywood films, you can say that art imitated life.

There are plenty of other resources available that can assist you in teaching the Vietnam War. For advanced or honors students, you might want to use James West Davidson and Mark Hamilton Lytle's, *After the Fact: The Art of Historical Detection* (1995). In this book of historiography case studies, there is a chapter devoted to an extensive examination the Vietnam War. Primary Source Media also has a first-rate primary-source CD-ROM kit that contains extensive documents related to all aspects of the war. The Center for Learning's Book Four in its *US History Series* includes four excellent reproducible lesson plans, one of which is centered on a number of powerful excerpts from *Dear America*. These resources, in addition to "Echoes from the Wall," should be part of your arsenal for teaching about Vietnam. They are all quite affordable and will successfully augment your instruction.

In Appendix D, you will find copies of material that we use at West Springfield High School with great success. Feel free to use these resources as you wish. Each of us brings to our teaching of history a different kind of perspective, so generate lessons that you deem useful and appropriate for your students.

Teaching about the Vietnam War as part of our recent history is important if we are to understand where we have been and what we as a nation have become as the result of the most recent generation of our history. It is a war with a long shadow whose legacy will be felt for many years to come.

Resources

Books

Atkinson, Rick: 1989. *The Long Gray Line*. Boston: Houghton Mifflin.

Baritz, Loren. 1985. *Backfire*. New York: William Morrow.

Caputo, Philip. 1977. *A Rumor of War*. New York: Henry Holt.

Chong, Denise: 2000. *The Girl in the Picture: The Story of Kim Phuc and the Photograph That Changed the Course of the Vietnam War*. New York: Viking.

Colbert, David, ed. 1998. *Eyewitness to America*. New York: Vintage.

Cronkite, Walter. 1996. *A Reporter's Life*. New York: Knopf.

Davidson, James West, and Mark Hamilton Lytle. 1995. *After the Fact: The Art of Historical Detection*. New York: Knopf.

Doyle, Robert. 1994. *Voices from Captivity: Interpreting the American POW Narrative*. Lawrence, KS: University of Kansas Press.

Edelman, Bernard, ed. 1985. *Dear America: Letters Home from Vietnam*. New York: William Morrow.

Esper, George, and the Associated Press. 1983. *The Eyewitness History of the Vietnam War, 1961–1975*. New York: Ballantine.

Fast, Howard. 1996. *The Hessian*. Armonk, NY: M. E. Sharpe.

Gettleman, Marvin E., et. al., eds. 1995. *Vietnam and America*. New York: Grove Press.

Gitlin, Todd. 1993. *The Sixties: Years of Hope, Days of Rage*. New York: Bantam.

Gottlieb, Sherry Gershon. 1991. *Hell No We Won't Go*. New York: Viking.

Haig, Alexander M., Jr. 1994. *Inner Circles: How America Changed the World; A Memoir.* New York: Warner Books.

Hammond, William. 1998. *Reporting Vietnam.* Lawrence, KS: University of Kansas Press.

Herr, Michael. 1978. *Dispatches.* New York: Knopf.

Herring, George C. 1996. *LBJ and Vietnam: A Different Kind of War.* Austin, TX: University of Texas Press.

Hess, Stephen, and Sandy Northrop. 1996. *Drawn and Quartered: The History of American Political Cartoons.* Montgomery, AL: Elliott and Clark.

Hippler, Mike. 1989. *Matlovich: The Good Soldier.* Boston: Alyson Publications.

Kaiser, David. 2000. *American Tragedy: Kennedy, Johnson and the Origins of the Vietnam War.* Cambridge: Belknap.

Karnow, Stanley. 1997. *Vietnam: A History.* New York: Penguin Books.

Leekley, Sheryle and John. 1978. *Moments: The Pulitzer Prize Photographs.* New York: Crown.

Library of America. 1998. *Reporting Vietnam: 1959–1975.* New York: Library of America.

McCloud, Bill. 1989. *What Should We Tell Our Children About Vietnam.* Norman, OK: University of Oklahoma Press.

McMaster, H. R. 1997. *Dereliction of Duty: Lyndon Johnson, Robert McNamara, and the Joint Chiefs of Staff, and the Lies That Led to Vietnam.* New York: Harper-Collins.

McNamara, Robert. 1995. *In Retrospect: The Tragedy and Lessons of Vietnam.* New York: Time Books.

McNamara, Robert, et al. 1999. *Argument Without End: In Search of Answers to the Vietnam Tragedy.* New York: Public Affairs Press.

McPherson, Maya, ed. 1984. *Long Time Passing.* New York: Doubleday.

McGrath, John. 1975. *Prisoner of War: Six Years in Hanoi.* Annapolis, MD: US Naval Institute Press.

Mahoney, Phillip, ed. 1998. *From Both Sides Now: The Poetry of the Vietnam War and Its Aftermath.* New York: Scribner Poetry.

Marlette, Doug. 1980. *Drawing Blood: Political Cartoons by Marlette.* Washington, DC: Graphic Press.

O'Brien, Tim. 1979. *Going After Cacciato.* Boston: Houghton Mifflin.

———. 1990. *The Things They Carried.* Boston: Houghton Mifflin.

———. 1992. *If I Die in a Combat Zone: Box Me Up and Ship Me Home.* New York: Dell.

O'Nan, Stewart, ed. 1998. *The Vietnam Reader.* New York: Anchor Books.

Palmer, Laura. 1987. *Shrapnel in the Heart: Letters and Remembrances from the Vietnam Veterans Memorial.* New York: Random House.

Puller, Lewis B. 1991. *Fortunate Son: An Autobiography, The Healing of a Vietnam Vet.* New York: Grove Press.

Safer, Morely. 1990. *Flashbacks on Returning to Vietnam*. New York: Random House.

Santoli, Al, ed. 1988. *Everything We Had*. New York: Ballantine.

Scruggs, Jan. 1996. *Why Vietnam Still Matters*. Washington, DC: Vietnam Veterans Memorial Fund.

———. 1998. *Voices from the Wall*. Washington, DC: Vietnam Veterans Memorial Fund.

Scruggs, Jan, and Joel Swerdlow. 1992. *To Heal a Nation: The Vietnam Veterans Memorial*. New York: Harper Perennial.

Sheehan, Neil. 1989. *A Bright Shining Lie*. New York: Vintage Books.

Shilts, Randy. 1993. *Conduct Unbecoming: Gays and Lesbians in the US Military*. New York: St. Martin's Press.

Steinman, Ron. 2000. *Women in Vietnam: The Oral History*. New York: TV Books.

Terry, Wallace. 1989. *Bloods: An Oral History of the Vietnam War by Black Veterans*. New York: Ballantine.

Tollefson, James W. 1993. *The Strength Not to Fight: An Oral History of the Conscientious Objector*. New York: Little, Brown.

Tucker, Spencer C. 2000. *The Encyclopedia of the Vietnam War: A Political, Social, and Military History*. Santa Barbara, CA: ABC-CLIO Publishing.

Van Devanter, Lynda. 1983. *Home Before Morning: The Story of an Army Nurse in Vietnam*. New York: Beaufort Books.

The Wall: Images and Offerings from the Vietnam Veterans Memorial. 1987. New York: Collins.

Walker, Keith. 1991. *A Piece of My Heart: Oral Histories of Twenty-Six Women Who Served in Vietnam*. Novato, CA: Presidio Press.

Videos/Films

All the Unsung Heroes: The Story of the Vietnam Veterans Memorial. Producer: Roger Peterson. 20 minutes. The Friends of the Vietnam Veterans Memorial and the Vietnam Veterans Memorial Fund, 1990, videocasette.

Dear America: Letters Home from Vietnam. Producer: Bill Couturie; Directors: Bill Couturie and Thomas Bird. 85 minutes. The Couturie Company, Inc., 1987, videocasette.

The Fall of Saigon. Producer: George Carey. 90 minutes. Barraclough-Carey Productions, 1995, videocasette.

LBJ. Producer: David Grubin. 240 minutes. David Grubin Productions, 1991, videocasette.

Ordinary Americans: The Vietnam War. Producer: Joe Geraghty. 35 minutes. Close Up Television, 1998, videocasette.

Return with Honor. Producers: Freida Lee Mock and Terry Sanders. 102 minutes. Sanders and Mock/American Film Foundation Production, 1998, videocasette.

Vietnam: 1954–1968. Producers: Richard Melman and Neil Cameron. 46 minutes. Turner Original Productions, 1999, videocasette.

The Vietnam War: A Case Study for Critical Thinking. Producer: Education Audio Visual Company. 48 minutes. 1987, videocasette.

Vietnam: Chronicle of a War. Producer: CBS News Productions. 86 minutes. 1981, videocasette.

Vietnam: A Television History. Producer: Judith Vecchione. 780 minutes. WGBH-Boston, Central Independent Television/UK, Antenne-2 France in association with LRE Productions, 1983, videocasette

The Wall That Heals. Producer: John Hamilton. 49 minutes. Sitmar Entertainment, 1997, videocasette.

Epilogue

We must accept finite disappointment, but we must never lose infinite hope.

—Martin Luther King, Jr.

"Riding up the winding road of Saint Agnes Cemetery in the back of the rattling old truck, Francis Phelan became aware that the dead, even more than the living, settled down in neighborhoods." So opens William Kennedy's novel, *Ironweed* (1983). I find cemeteries fascinating places. They offer people all kinds of lessons, if one takes the time to stop and reflect on what they see and how the cemetery is arranged. There are many ironies to be found in American cemeteries. One I mention in this book is Barbara Jordan's grave in the Texas State Cemetery, situated on Patriot's Hill near several defenders of the Confederacy. In Sleepy Hollow Cemetery in Tarrytown, New York, you can find not far apart the graves of Andrew Carnegie, captain of industry and robber baron, and Samuel Gompers, a champion of labor. Andersonville National Cemetery at the site of the infamous Civil War prison in Andersonville, Georgia, contains the graves of the close to 13,000 Union soldiers who perished there between 1864 and 1865. Here you will find white soldiers buried side by side with black soldiers. Chances are, had these men died at home, they would not be buried side by side but rather in segregated cemeteries. Sometimes cemeteries mark the final episode of a particular conflict for the departed individual. I think it is that way in most national cemeteries, like Andersonville or the Punch Bowl in Hawaii.

One time, while taking some students down to Andersonville for Memorial Day weekend to decorate the graves with American flags, I happened upon on a grave with a framed poem resting against the headstone. It was the grave of Union soldier Herman Kolenbrander and the poem was written by Jennifer Bosveld, the wife of one of his descendants. She titled the poem *memoralis benedicto* and noted that in many ethnic traditions (American Indian, Irish, Welsh, African, and others) the restating of a person's name gives ever-strengthening honor to that person and etches his place in memory. I found the poem moving. It reads:

> We have come here looking for great Uncle Herman Kolenbrander
>   who fought in the Civil War and died in Andersonville prison.
> We have come here looking for great Uncle Herman Kolenbrander
>   who was one of thousands who died here.
> We have come here looking for great Uncle Herman Kolenbrander
>   who mattered as much as The President.
> We have come here looking for great Uncle Herman Kolenbrander
>   who came here from the Netherlands in 1856.
> We have come here looking for great Uncle Herman Kolenbrander
>   who must have suffered more than anyone should have to.
> We have come here looking for great Uncle Herman Kolenbrander
>   who spent innumerable days perhaps weeks or months hungry.
> We have come here looking for great Uncle Herman Kolenbrander
>   who would be ashamed of our petty wants and needs today.
> We have come here looking for great Uncle Herman Kolenbrander
>   who was the brother of Jim's Mom's Grandma Vander Linden.
> We have come here looking for great Uncle Herman Kolenbrander
>   who left us with a tintype photo of himself in a Yankee
>   uniform.
> We have come here looking for great Uncle Herman Kolenbrander
>   who is framed in gold and labeled so we remember.
> We have come here looking for great Uncle Herman Kolenbrander
>   who we pray had days of joy before the brutality of war.
> We have come here looking for great Uncle Herman Kolenbrander
>   who combed his hair for the photo and posed.
> We have come here looking for great Uncle Herman Kolenbrander
>   who did not know that his great grandnephew would
>   value him.
> We have come here looking for great Uncle Herman Kolenbrander
>   who did not know that his great grandnephew's wife
>   would too.
> We have come here looking for great Uncle Herman Kolenbrander
>   whose spirit lives in Jim Vander Linden Skalekamp Bosveld.
> We have come here looking for great Uncle Herman Kolenbrander
>   whose life was not the Andersonville prison.
> We have come here looking for great Uncle Herman Kolenbrander
>   who was about other dreams he was not able to fulfill.
> We have come here looking for great Uncle Herman Kolenbrander
>   who died wondering if anyone would remember what
>   happened here.
> We have come here looking for great Uncle Herman Kolenbrander
>   who we owe a great debt.

We have come here looking for great Uncle Herman Kolenbrander
    who had a family who grieved for him and still does.
We have come here looking for great Uncle Herman Kolenbrander
    who understood the importance of a great cause.
We have come here looking for great Uncle Herman Kolenbrander
    who was Dutch and possibly motivated by trade and market
    needs.
We have come here looking for great Uncle Herman Kolenbrander
    who allowed us to work beside our black brothers and sisters.
We have come here looking for great Uncle Herman Kolenbrander
    who might not be happy to see what we've let this country
    become.
We have come here looking for great Uncle Herman Kolenbrander
    who we might or might not have likes if we knew him, but
We have come here looking for great Uncle Herman Kolenbrander
    who we wish we could know that
We have come here looking for great Uncle Herman Kolenbrander
    who fought in the Civil War and died in Andersonville Prison.

All of us have been touched by conflict to some degree. Periodically, I have used this poem when I teach the Civil War to make a link between the past and the present and to demonstrate that conflicts, even those before our lifetimes, have long-standing implications—both personal as well as national.

When you teach about conflict in your classroom, keep in mind a few points. Remember that all of your students do not share the same collective memory. How you present material will be interpreted from each person's construct or worldview. Develop a classroom climate in which respect for others and divergent opinions are hallmarks of your instruction. Be certain to keep your teaching within a historical context, utilizing personal or student experiences to heighten your instruction. Remain sensitive to each individual in your classroom as well as to historical memory. Prepare students, and if need be school administrators and parents, for any controversial issues you may encounter, particularly with regard to language, word usage, and visual imagery. Have clear goals and objectives established with means of authentic assessment readily available to measure student learning and understanding. Keep an open mind for new ideas and teaching strategies that you may want to employ, be creative and don't be afraid to push the envelope.

There's a very compelling scene in the motion picture *Glory* (1989). Colonel Robert Gould Shaw (played by Matthew Broderick) and Tripp, a runaway slave and a private in the Massachusetts Fifty-Fourth Volunteer Infantry (portrayed by Denzel Washington) are engaged in a conversation about service, duty, and cause. Their conversation has racial overtones with both men trying to reconcile their differences within the larger context of slavery, injustice, and civil war. When Shaw remarks, "It's a real mess I suppose." Tripp responds, "Sure is and everybody's caught up in it." To which Shaw replies, "What are we going to do about it?" Tripp responds, "We ante up and kick in." That's how I feel about teaching about conflict. It's part of the human condition, something that we have to acknowledge; something to work through and with in order to present to our students the possibilities for tomorrow. I believe that the bottom line for any teaching about conflict should be to guide your students to a place where the ode of the ancient Greeks becomes a goal to which you and your students can aspire and that is to "tame the savageness of man and make gentle the life of this world."

Resources

Books

Kennedy, William. 1983. *Ironweed: A Novel.* New York: Viking Press.

Videos/Films

Glory. Producer: Freddie Fields; Director: Edward Zwick. 120 minutes. Tri-Star Pictures, 1989, videocassette.

Appendix A: The West

The West: Myth & Reality

A Mr. Percoco Film and Analysis Festival
Film Worksheet

Title of film _____

Director of film _____

Major stars of the film _____

Production company _____

Year film was released _____

Discussion Questions:

1. Was there something you didn't understand about the movie?

2. What did you like best about the movie? Why?

3. Why did [pick a character] do [select action]? What motivated him or her?

4. Is there something you would change about the plot? If so, what is it? Why would you make that change?

5. Who was your favorite character in the movie? Why?

The West: Myth & Reality

A Mr. Percoco Film and Analysis Festival
Film Synopses

Cheyenne Autumn. **Producer: Bernard Smith; Director: John Ford.**
    120 minutes. Warner Brothers, 1964, videocasette.
A sprawling and entertaining film about the Cheyenne Indian tribe and
its eventful journey back to original settlement after being relocated by
the government. Long before *Dances with Wolves,* Ford dramatized the
plight of the Indians much more realistically when it was not PC to do so.

Fort Apache. **Producer/Director: John Ford. 127 minutes.**
    RKO Pictures, 1948, videocasette.
In John Ford's somber exploration of Custer's "Last Stand" and the
mythologizing of American heroes, he slowly reveals the character of
Owen Thursday, who sees his new posting to the desolate Fort Apache
as a chance to claim the military honor he believes is rightfully his. Ar-
rogant, obsessed with military form, and ultimately self-destructive,
Thursday attempts to destroy the Indian warrior Cochise after luring
him across the border from Mexico.

How the West Was Won. **Producer/Director: John Ford. 165 minutes.**
    MGM, 1962, videocasette.
The history of Western Expansion as told by the story of one pioneer
family's history. Zebulon Prescott takes his family from New York, head-
ing west in the early 1800s. His children and grandchildren eventually
reach the western shores after years of hardship, war, and struggle.

I Will Fight No More Forever. **Producer: Stan Margulies; Director:**
    Richard T. Heffren. 105 minutes. Wolper Productions, 1976,
    videocasette.
This moving film is based on the historical story of the flight of the Nez
Perce Indians. The film chronicles the attempt by the US government to
place the Nez Perce on reservations and the subsequent attempt of the
Nez Perce to elude capture. Issues raised by the film include the ambiva-
lence of General Oliver Otis Howard and his mixed feelings of friendship
toward the Indians while bound by his duty as a soldier to obey orders.

The Plainsman. Producer: Cecil B. DeMille; Director: Cecil B. DeMille.
113 minutes. Paramount Pictures, 1937, videocassette.

Wild Bill Hickok attempts to stop an Indian uprising that was started by white gun-runners. A big, outlandish Western involving Buffalo Bill, Calamity Jane, George Custer, Wild Bill Hickok, and Abraham Lincoln.

The Searchers. Producer: Merian Cooper; Director: John Ford.
119 minutes. Warner Brothers, 1956, videocassette.

Ethan Edwards is an ex-Confederate soldier who returns home from the war three years later in 1868. Shortly after his return, his brother's family is massacred and his niece is captured by the Comanches. Ethan vows to bring his niece back and seek revenge for his brother's and his family's deaths. Edwards is joined by his nephew, Martin Pawley. The problem is that Pawley is half-Indian, and there's nothing more in the world that Edwards hates than Indians. The search will take five years and in the climax Edwards will be forced to examine his own humanity.

She Wore A Yellow Ribbon. Producers: John Ford and Merian Cooper;
Director: John Ford. 120 minutes. RKO Pictures, 1949,
videocassette.

Custer is dead, the Indians rise all over the West. Captain Brittles, who will retire in a few days, is ordered to bring the daughter of his major to the next Poststation. He dislikes the order, but he carries it out. Indians are attacking all over, and when he reaches the station he finds it destroyed, and the people who have lived there are dead. Back at his fort, he has to serve only one day. He rides to the Indians to persuade them to keep the peace, but his friend the old Chief is no longer Chief. Now there is a younger Chief who wants to fight. This mission brought nothing. The man who'll take Brittles command is also willing to fight. Brittles manages to make an attack on the Indian horses, driving them away with no casualties. Now out of service, Brittles decides to ride west. New orders arrive before he leaves and he is promoted to a command in the Scouts.

Stagecoach. Producer: Walter Wagner; Director: John Ford.
96 minutes. Warner Brothers, 1939, videocassette.

A simple stagecoach trip is complicated by the fact that Geronimo is on the warpath in the area. The passengers on the coach include a drunken doctor, a pregnant woman, a bank manager who has taken off with his client's money, and the famous Ringo Kid, among others. One of the great American films and a landmark in the maturing of the Western, balancing character study and solid action.

Appendix B: Custer/
Battle of the Little Bighorn

Hollywood Film Synopses

Custer of the West. **Producers: Philip Yordan and Louis Dolivet;**
Director: Robert Siodmak. 143 minutes. Security/Cinerama,
1968, videocassette.
A 1968 epic bust. Filmed in Spain, Cinerama tried to cash in on a big
sweeping western drama, but by the time the film was released audiences
and their movie interests had changed. Robert Shaw portrays Custer.

Fort Apache. **Producer: John Ford; Director: John Ford. 127 minutes.**
RKO Pictures, 1948, videocassette.
A post-World War II film, set in the Southwest, in which a Custer-like
character, Lieutenant Colonel Owen Thursday, a martinet, leads his regiment to their fate. Fort Apache's subtext addresses the need for sacrifice
to a nation that has lost thousands of men fighting a worthy cause. Henry
Fonda portrays Thursday. John Wayne stars as Captain Kirby York, who
despite knowing Thursday's flaws recognizes that a soldier must follow his duty. Shirley Temple rounds out the cast as Thursday's daughter,
Philadelphia.

Little Big Man. **Producer: Stuart Miller; Director: Arthur Penn.**
147 minutes. 20th Century Fox, 1970, videocassette.
Arthur Penn's morality play is not so much about Custer and the Little
Bighorn as it is a cinematic indictment regarding America's foreign pol-
icy in Vietnam. The West and the government treatment of the Plains
Indians serves as a metaphor for the United States' role in Southeast
Asia. Stars Dustin Hoffman as "Little Big Man," a white youth captured
and raised by the Cheyenne.

The Plainsman. **Producer: Cecil B. DeMille; Director: Cecil B. DeMille.**
   113 minutes. Paramount Pictures, 1937, videocassette.
A sprawling western, loaded with a fair share of hokum. The plot concerns the relationship amongst a montage of characters from western history besides Custer, including Wild Bill Hickok, Calamity Jane, and Buffalo Bill and their dealings with the Plains Indians. Stars Gary Cooper and Jean Arthur.

Sitting Bull. **Producer: W. R. Frank; Director: Sidney Salkow.**
   105 minutes. United Artists, 1956, videocassette.
A film that is in no way a reflection of any kind of historical reality. The Battle of the Little Bighorn is depicted as taking place in a wooded glen, not on the plains.

Son of the Morning Star. **Producers: Preston Fischer and Cyrus Yavneh;**
   Director: Mike Robe. 183 minutes. Republic Pictures, 1991,
   videocassette.
A television miniseries based on the best-selling book of the same name by Evan S. Connell. Gary Cole portrays Custer and Rosanna Arquette is his devoted wife, Libbie. Viewers witness the story of Custer and his wife, who after his death promoted the "legacy" of her husband. One of the best staged renditions of Custer's Last Stand.

They Died with Their Boots On. **Producer: Hal B. Wallis; Director: Raoul**
   Walsh. 140 minutes. Warner Brothers, 1941, videocassette.
Production on *They Died with Their Boots On* ended on the eve of American entry into World War II. Errol Flynn's portrayal of the doomed Custer borders on hero worship of which Libbie Custer would be proud. This film's subtext was intended to prepare the United States for its subsequent role in the Second World War. A patriotic bombast.

Video Guide

Last Stand at the Little Bighorn
Produced by Paul Stekler and James Welsh
Production Company: Midnight Films
copyright 1992

Objectives: At the end of watching this film students will:

- recognize why George Armstrong Custer was regarded as a hero in his time
- compare the two viewpoints examined by the film: that of the native peoples and that of the white settlers
- examine how history is recorded and by whom

Directions: Please answer the following questions based on having watched this film.

1. Did the defeat of Custer lead to the ultimate destruction of the way of life of the native peoples? Explain.

2. From your own point of view, who are the heroes of the Battle of the Little Bighorn and why?

3. Would the battle of the Little Bighorn have been recorded differently if reporters had covered Custer's actions in the same way that reporters cover war stories today?

4. Why do you think that Sitting Bull was reported to be a white man who was trained in military tactics?

5. Do you think that the ethnic background of a filmmaker makes a difference in the point of view presented in a film?

Video Guide

George Armstrong Custer: America's Golden Cavalier
Produced by Arthur Drooker
Production Company: Greystone Communications
copyright 1997

Directions: Please answer the following questions based on your having watched this A & E Biography film.

1. What were some influences in the early life of George Armstrong Custer?

2. How would you describe Custer's years at West Point?

3. How would you describe Custer's Civil War experiences? What accounted for Custer's meteoric rise in the Union Army? Who was his most important patron? Why?

4. How would you describe the marriage of George and Libbie Custer? Provide some specifics!

5. How did fighting American Indians on the Plains differ from fighting the Confederates?

6. What were some struggles the Custers had to make in adjusting to military life in the West?

7. What was significant about the Battle of the Washita? How did this battle shape Custer's style of fighting American Indians?

8. What was the "Royal Family"? Who were some members?

9. Who was Frederick Benteen? Who was Marcus Reno? How are both men tied to the story of Custer?

10. What were some things beyond Custer's control that contributed to his defeat at the Little Bighorn?

11. What were some things that *might* have been in Custer's control that contributed to his defeat at the Little Bighorn?

12. Why is it that Custer always made "good copy" for the press? How do you think this fact may have contributed to post-Battle of the Little Bighorn interpretations?

13. Why do various historians hold such divergent views about Custer? What might contribute to their interpretations?

14. Summarize the analysis of the following historians relevant to Custer's legacy:

- Jeffery D. Wert

- Paul Andrew Hutton

- Brian Pohanka

- Shirley Leckie

- Louise Barnett

- Robert Utley

Appendix C: Civil Rights Movement

Film Synopses

Crisis at Central High. Producer: Paul Levinson, et al.; Director:
Lamont Johnson. 120 minutes. CBS Entertainment Productions,
1981, videocassette.
The story of the 1957 integration of Little Rock Central High School,
where units of the 101st Airborne Division were ordered in to Little
Rock by President Eisenhower to protect the "Little Rock Nine." Starring Joanne Woodward.

Ghosts of Mississippi. Producer: Rob Reiner; Director: Rob Reiner.
131 minutes. Columbia Pictures, 1996, videocassette.
Dramatic account of the murder of NAACP worker Medgar Evers in
1963 and the quest to bring the killer to justice. Starring Whoopie Goldberg, Alec Baldwin, and James Woods.

The Jackie Robinson Story. Producer: Mort Briskin; Director: Alfred E.
Green. 76 minutes. Eagle Lion Films, 1950, videocassette.
Docudrama about the life of Jackie Robinson and his break into Major
League Baseball in 1947. Starring Jackie Robinson as himself and Ruby
Dee as his wife, Nancy.

The Long Walk Home. Producer: Howard W. Kotch, Jr.; Director:
Richard Pearce. 97 minutes. Miramax, 1990, videocassette.
A fictionalized account of the 1955 Montgomery Bus Boycott starring
Whoopie Goldberg and Sissey Spacek.

Simple Justice. Producer: Yanna Kroyt Brandt; Director: Helaine Head.
160 minutes. New Images Productions, 1993, videocassette.
Docudrama of the Howard University Law School and the NAACP's le-
gal fight to end segregation culminating in the 1954 *Brown v. Board of
Education, Topeka, Kansas,* decision. Starring James Avery, Peter Francis
James, and Andre Braugher.

Appendix D: Vietnam Material

Letter to Parents

May 1, 2000

Dear Parent/Guardian:

We would like to take this opportunity to advise you of a project that the US/VA history team will be working on with students enrolled in our classes. In an effort to educate with some depth the history of the Vietnam Era, we have assembled multifaceted learning activities for implementation after the Virginia Standards of Learning Exam. These activities will include an oral history panel discussion from a number of people who served in Vietnam or who participated in peace protests or demonstrations at home. On Friday, May 26, there will be an all junior class assembly to hear a presentation by Jan Scruggs, founder and president of the Vietnam Veterans Memorial Fund. Individual team members will also be conducting extensive classroom lessons dovetailed to all components of the learning activities. As an extension of the classroom lessons and the speakers, we are holding an after-school Vietnam Era Film Festival, which students should attend to broaden their understanding of the time period within a historical and cultural context. The same set of films will be offered on Wednesday, May 17, and Thursday, May 18. The film festival will be held over a two-day period so that all students can participate. As you may well be aware, some of the Hollywood interpretations of Vietnam are often violent in nature, filled with strong language, and carry an R rating. The films we selected represent a wide range of film interpretation. Participating students will select their films by pulling the title from a hat. We want to spread the students out among all the films so that once the activity is completed, students will be able to discuss with each other, via teacher-led dialogues, their reactions to the films they watched as well as to be able to compare and contrast all of the films. Students will be monitored by teachers during the after-school viewing. The films we have jointly agreed to show are:

The Green Berets (G)	*Coming Home* (R)
Flight of the Intruder (PG-13)	*Good Morning Vietnam* (R)
Go Tell the Spartans (R)	*The Deer Hunter* (R)
Platoon (R)	*To Heal a Nation* (PG)
Hanoi Hilton (R)	*Bat-21* (R)

If you prefer to have your son or daughter watch a film that does not carry an R rating, then please have him or her talk to his or her teacher so that the appropriate match can be facilitated. We want to ensure that all students receive the maximum benefit from this activity, while at the same time being comfortable with what they watch and see. Attached to this letter is a synopsis of each film.

If you have any questions, please don't hesitate to contact your child's teacher. For students who opt out of the film aspect of the unit, an equally relevant learning activity will be provided. You are more than welcome to participate in any of the activities outlined above.

Thank you for your time and consideration.

Sincerely,

The US/VA history team

Hollywood and Vietnam: Film Synopses

Bat-21. **Producer: Peter Markle; Director: Peter Markle.**
   105 minutes. Tri-Star Pictures, 1988, videocassette.
A story about the most successful air rescue mission of the war in 1972. Lt. Col. Iceal Hambleton, an electronics and missile expert, bails out when his surveillance plane is hit by a SAM missile over heavily infested enemy territory. He is forced to evade capture for a week and is finally rescued through an ingenious plan engineered through his commander and an old golfing pal. Strong language. (R)

Coming Home. **Producer: Jerome Hellman; Director: Hal Ashby.**
   126 minutes. United Artists, 1977, videocassette.
Jane Fonda and Jon Voight turn in Academy Award–winning performances in this look at life at home after the war. *Coming Home* explores the issues that faced veterans and their families in the months and years following service in Vietnam. This film contains strong language, partial nudity, and sexuality. (R)

The Deer Hunter. **Producers: Barry Spikings, Michael Deeley,**
   Michael Cimino, and John Peverall; Director: Michael Cimino.
   183 minutes. Universal Films, 1978, videocassette.
An epic film that follows the lives of three men from their jobs in Pennsylvania steel mills through combat in Vietnam and its aftermath. Combat sequences, strong language, and sexuality are part of director Michael Cimino's fabric. (R)

The Flight of the Intruder. **Producers: Marc Neufeld and Robert**
   Rehme; Director: John Milius. 113 minutes. Paramount, 1991,
   videocassette.
A film that chronicles the missions of pilots who flew the A6 Intruder during the war, which at its best is a clinic on A6 capabilities and tactics. This motion picture offers extensive coverage of the carrier-based air war fought against North Vietnam. There is a PG-13 romantic subplot. (PG-13)

Go Tell the Spartans. **Producers: Alan F. Bodoh and Michael Cannold;**
   Director: Ted Post. 114 minutes. Spartan Productions/Mar Vista
   Productions, 1978, videocassette.
An HBO original movie starring Burt Lancaster that is considered by many combat veterans to be the best film produced about the complexities of the land war and the issues that faced American infantrymen. Set in Vietnam in 1964, it explores the conflicting elements Americans faced before the big buildup of American troops. One scene of a death by

machete is the only graphic violence, but the film incorporates strong language. (R)

Good Morning Vietnam. **Producers: Mark Johnson and Larry Brezner; Director: Barry Levinson. 121 minutes. Touchstone, 1987, videocassette.**
A look at the war through the eyes and experiences of Armed Forces Radio DJ Adrian Cronauer as portrayed by Robin Williams. While at times irreverent, *Good Morning Vietnam* captures an interesting aspect of the war, life in Saigon and on a US urban military base. Strong language makes up part of the dialogue. (R)

The Green Berets. **Producer: Michael Wayne; Directors: John Wayne and Ray Kellogg. 141 minutes. Warner Brothers, 1969, videocassette.**
A set film piece directed by and starring John Wayne. This motion picture was made in 1965 in the years prior to the raging dissent generated by American participation in the Vietnam War. It is a patriotic and conservative view of America's role in Southeast Asia. (G)

Hanoi Hilton. **Producers: Menahem Golan and Yoram Globus; Director: Lionel Chetwynd. 130 minutes. Golan-Globus Productions, 1987, videocassette.**
Of this film President Ronald Reagan said, "Every American should see this powerful and moving film as a tribute to our POWs." Writer/director Lionel Chetwynd's fact-based account chronicles life inside the most notorious of all North Vietnamese prison camps, Hoa Lo Prison. Strong language, partial nudity, and grim prison sequences are depicted. (R)

Platoon. **Producer: Arnold Kopelson; Director: Oliver Stone. 120 minutes. Orion Pictures, 1986, videocassette.**
The Oliver Stone Academy Award–winning film that depicts the one-year tour of an infantry platoon. The film is highly politicized and an argument can be made that it was a film produced as a personal and political statement of Stone's. Graphic combat scenes and strong language. (R)

To Heal a Nation. **Producer: Robert M. Sertner; Director: Michael Pressman. 100 minutes. Von Zerneck-Samuels Productions, 1989, videocassette.**
Made for TV docudrama about Jan Scruggs and his struggle to secure a national memorial for Vietnam Veterans on the Mall in Washington, DC. (PG)

Vietnam War Worksheets

Worksheet A: Twenty Things
You Need to Know About Vietnam

1. Dien Bien Phu

2. Ho Chi Minh

3. Viet Cong

4. Lyndon Baines Johnson

5. General William Westmoreland

6. Robert McNamara

7. *U.S.S. Maddox*

8. Tonkin Gulf Resolution

9. Operation Rolling Thunder

10. "Search and Destroy"

11. Pacification

12. Agent Orange

13. "Free Fire Zones"

15. My Lai Massacre

16. Vietnamization

17. Cambodian Invasion

18. Kent State

19. Paris Peace Accords

20. War Powers Act

Worksheet B: Video Guide

Vietnam: Chronicle of a War

These questions correspond with the sequence of the film.

1. In what way was the Vietnam War unique?

2. When and how did American involvement in Vietnam begin?

3. Who was the leader of communist forces in Vietnam?

4. What happened at Dien Bien Phu in 1954?

5. Why and how was Vietnam divided? What was the dividing line between North and South Vietnam?

6. What minor incident in 1964 led to increased American military involvement in Vietnam?

7. What conditions and factors made the war so dangerous for American ground forces?

8. Who burned the Vietnamese village of Cam Ne? Why?

9. How many Americans were killed in 1966? How did the war change that year?

10. What was the goal of the "pacification" program?

11. Why did American aid programs designed to help the Vietnamese often fail?

12. How many Americans were serving in Vietnam at the end of 1967?

13. Why and how did American forces destroy jungle foliage?

14. How did the government of South Vietnam treat protesters and reporters?

15. What was the "sanitation" problem during the war? How was this solved?

16. When did the Tet Offensive begin? Why do some consider it the turning point of the war?

17. When and where did negotiations begin to end the war?

18. When did President Nixon begin the withdrawal of American troops? What was the purpose of Nixon's policy of "Vietnamization"?

19. What decision was made by President Nixon in the spring of 1970?

20. What happened at Kent State? Why?

21. What "unique event" happened to Charlie Company?

22. What was "Ralph"? What was "fragging"?
23. What action was secretly taken by Henry Kissinger in 1971?
24. What happened at My Lai 4? Who was responsible?
25. How many Vietnamese were disabled during the war?
26. When was the Paris Peace Agreement finally signed? What was the result?
27. How many Americans were listed as Missing In Action (MIA)?
28. When did the North Vietnamese offensive begin?
29. What was the most "heartbreaking tragedy" of the war?
30. What announcement was made by President Ford in 1975?

Critical Thinking

1. A "just war," as identified by Thomas Aquinas, must have three conditions—public authority, just cause, and the right motive. In your opinion, was the war in Vietnam a "just war"? Why? Why not?

2. What lessons should America learn from the Vietnam War?

Appendix E: Historical Head Template

Appendix F: Rubric Reference Page

The following guide sheet will provide you with important information as to how various activities are evaluated. I provide students with these rubrics when I initially give an assignment. The rubric for each different assignment is copied on a different colored sheet of paper.

Journals

$\sqrt{+}$ The grade of $\sqrt{+}$ is given when journals are neatly written in pen, in blue or black ink, and are one full page in length or more of substantive writing. The question assigned must be answered completely and demonstrate student reflection on the topic or question. Proper use of grammar and rules of writing are evident.

A $\sqrt{+}$ = 100

$\sqrt{}$ The grade of $\sqrt{}$ is given when journals are neatly written in pen, blue or black ink, or in readable pencil. Responses must be close to being a full page and should demonstrate a serious attempt on the part of the writer to deal with the question or topic assigned, with some evidence of student reflection. Proper use of grammar and rules of writing are evident.

A $\sqrt{}$ = 89

$\sqrt{-}$ The grade of $\sqrt{-}$ is given when journals are somewhat shallow in response and reflect a rushed attempt to answer the question. Grammar may be inconsistent and there may be spelling errors. Responses are far less than one full page and demonstrate little effort to address the question or topic assigned.

A $\sqrt{-}$ = 75

N.C.   A grade of No Credit is given when work is completed in a sloppy or haphazard manner. Very little attempt is made on the part of the writer to seriously address the question. Handwriting is sloppy and demonstrates a lack of care for the product or work. Students may opt to complete this activity again until it is completed in a satisfactory manner, otherwise the student will take a zero for the grade.

Historical Heads

A = 94–100   This grade is assigned when work is superior. All instructions for the activity have been followed, and the student demonstrates mastery of the person or event being studied. The historical head template is in color or the student has provided images from Clip Art, or some other such software package, or has downloaded images off the Net. The statements on the back of the page are either typed or written neatly in blue or black ink and consist of several complete sentences. Rules of grammar and spelling have been followed. If the assignment is related to a book, the corresponding page numbers are indicated at the end of the identifying statements.

B+ = 90–93   This grade is assigned when work is excellent. All instructions for the activity have been followed, and the student demonstrates substantial understanding of the person or event being studied. The historical head template is in color or the student has provided images from Clip Art, or some other such software package, or has downloaded images off the Net. The statements on the back are written neatly in blue or black ink and consist of several sentences. Proper use of grammar and spelling are evident. If the assignment is related to a book or reading, the corresponding page numbers are indicated at the end of identifying statements.

B = 84–89   This grade is assigned when work is good. Most instructions for the activity have been followed and the student demonstrates understanding of the person or event being studied. The historical head template is in color and images reflect the event or person. The statements on the back are written neatly in blue or black ink, or in legible pencil. Grammar and spelling are good, though there may be an occasional mistake. If the assignment is related to a book or reading, the corresponding page numbers are indicated at the end of identifying statements.

C+ = 80–83   This grade is assigned when the work is just above average. Instructions for the activity have not been totally completed. The product demonstrates a shallow interpretation of the person or event. The historical head template is only partly in color. Images are not animated or lively. The statements on the back are of limited reflection. Grammar and spelling mistakes are evident. If the assignment is related to a book or reading, some of the corresponding pages numbers may be missing.

C = 74–79   This grade is assigned when the work is average. Instructions for the activity have not been totally completed. The product demonstrates a weak interpretation of the person or event. The historical head template is in pencil. Images are not lively or animated. The statements on the back reflect little imagination or substance. They may be only one sentence. Grammar and spelling mistakes are evident. If the assignment is related to a book or reading, some of the corresponding page numbers may be missing.

D+ = 70–73   This grade is assigned when work is of poor or limited quality. Instructions have not been followed. The product demonstrates little interpretation of the person or event. The historical head template is sloppy or messy. The statements on the back are insubstantial. They may be only one or incomplete sentences. Grammar and spelling mistakes are evident. If the assignment is related to a book or reading, numerous corresponding page numbers are missing.

D = 64–69   This grade is assigned when work is very poor. Instructions have not been followed. The product demonstrates little thought, reflection, or imagination. The historical head template is sloppy, messy, or poorly conceived. Statements on the back are limited and in some cases may not even be present. Corresponding page numbers, if needed, are not evident.

F= Do You Really Want To Know??

Bumper Stickers

A = 94–100   This grade is assigned when work is superior. All instructions for the activity have been followed and the student demonstrates mastery of the person or event being studied. The bumper sticker is neatly produced and in color or the student has used images from Clip Art, or some other such software package, or has downloaded images off the Net. The phrase or statement on the bumper sticker clearly is related to the topic in a proper historical context.

B+ = 90–93   This grade is assigned when work is excellent. All instructions for the activity have been followed and the student demonstrates substantial understanding of the person or event being studied. The bumper sticker is neatly produced and in color or the student has provided images from Clip Art, or some other such software package, or has downloaded images off the Net. The phrase or statement on the bumper sticker clearly relates to the topic in a proper historical context.

B = 84–89   This grade is assigned when work is good. Most instructions for the activity have been followed and the student demonstrates understanding of the person or event being studied. The bumper sticker is neatly produced and in color. The phrase or statement on the bumper sticker clearly relates to the topic in a proper historical context.

C+ = 80–83   This grade is assigned when the work is just above average. Instructions for the activity have not been totally completed. The product demonstrates a shallow interpretation of the person or event. The bumper sticker is neat, but reflects little imagination. The phrase or statement on the bumper sticker somewhat relates to the topic.

C = 74–79   This grade is assigned when the work is average. Instructions for the activity have not been totally completed. The product demonstrates a weak interpretation of the person or event. The bumper sticker is in pencil. Little imagination is evident and the product represents a laissez-faire approach to the assignment.

D+ = 70–73   This grade is assigned when work is of poor or limited quality. Instructions have not been followed. The product demonstrates little interpretation of the person or event. The bumper sticker is sloppy or messy. The statement or phrase on the bumper sticker is insubstantial. Little effort or thought has been given to the activity.

D = 64–69   This grade is assigned when work is very poor. Instructions have not been followed. The product demonstrates little thought, reflection, or imagination. The bumper sticker is sloppy, messy, or poorly conceived.

F= Do You Really Want To Know??

Historical Scrapbooks

A = 94–100   This grade is assigned when work is superior. An obvious effort has been made to go beyond the criteria of the assignment. The finished product reflects solid, historical, academic scholarship. All aspects of the assignment have been followed. Chronology is evident. Historical context is evident. The work is neat and orderly. All images are appropriate to the time period. All written work is legible and spelling is correct. The summary sheet is typed and well written. The finished product reflects pride on the part of the creator. The bibliography is completed according to the WSHS Style Manual.

B+ = 90–93   This grade is assigned when work is excellent. A fine effort has been made to go beyond the criteria of the assignment. The finished product reflects solid, historical, academic scholarship. All aspects of the assignment have been followed. Chronology is evident. Historical context is evident. The work is neat and orderly. All images are appropriate to the time period. All written work is legible and spelling is correct. The summary sheet is typed and well written. The finished product reflects pride on the part of the creator. The bibliography is typed and completed according to the WSHS Style Manual.

B = 84–89   This grade is assigned when the work is good. The finished product reflects good historical and academic scholarship. Most aspects of the assignment have been followed. Chronology is good. The work is neat and orderly. All images are appropriate to the time period. All written work is legible but there may be some spelling errors. The summary sheet is well written in blue or black ink. The finished product reflects pride on the part of the creator. The bibliography is neatly handwritten and completed according to the WSHS Style Manual.

C+ = 80–83   This grade is assigned when the work is just above average. The finished product reflects an attempt to keep the topic within a historical context. Some parts of the directions have not been followed. Chronology is evident, but may be weak. Some images may be historically inappropriate. Written work may be difficult to read and there are obvious spelling errors. The finished product may be a bit lacking in pride of ownership. The summary sheet may be a bit brief and lacking depth. The bibliography is limited, but follows the WSHS Style Manual.

C = 74–79   This grade is assigned when the work is average. The finished product reflects an attempt to keep the topic within a historical context. A significant number of the directions have not been followed. Chronology is weak. Some images are historically inappropriate. Written work may be lacking in substance and is difficult to read. Spelling errors are obvious. The finished product is lacking in pride of ownership. The summary sheet is brief and lacks depth. The bibliography is limited in scope and format.

D+ = 70–73   This grade is assigned when work is of poor or limited quality. Instructions have not been followed. The product demonstrates little effort on the part of the creators. The finished product is sloppy or messy. Little effort or thought has been given to the activity. Parts of the product are missing.

D = 64–69   This grade is assigned when work is very poor. Instructions have not been followed. The product demonstrates little thought, reflection, or imagination. There are major gaps in the directions. The work is sloppy, messy, or poorly conceived. Significant parts of the product are missing.

F = Do You Really Want To Know??

Western Movie Poster/Film Plot Summary

A = 94–100   This grade is assigned when work is superior. All instructions for the activity have been followed and the student demonstrates a mastery of the time period being studied. The Poster is neatly produced and in color. The Film Plot Summary clearly matches the standards and objectives that have been taught.

B+ = 90–93   This grade is assigned when work is excellent. All instructions for the activity have been followed and the student demonstrates substantial understanding of the time period being studied. The Poster is neatly produced and in color. The Film Plot Summary clearly relates to the topic in a proper historical context.

B = 84–89   This grade is assigned when work is good. Most instructions for the activity have been followed and the student demonstrates understanding of the time period being studied. The Poster is neatly produced and in color. The Film Plot Summary clearly relates to the topic in a proper historical context.

C+ = 80–83   This grade is assigned when the work is just above average. Instructions for the activity have not been totally completed. The Poster and Film Plot Summary demonstrates a shallow interpretation of the time period. Parts of the product are missing.

C = 74–79   This grade is assigned when the work is average. Instructions for the activity have not been totally completed. The product demonstrates a weak interpretation of the time period. The Poster is in pencil. Little imagination is evident and the product represents a laissez-faire approach to the assignment.

D+ = 70–73   This grade is assigned when work is of poor or limited quality. Instructions have not been followed. The product demonstrates little interpretation of the time period. The Poster is sloppy or messy. The Film Plot Summary is insubstantial. Little effort or thought has been given to the activity.

D = 64–69   This grade is assigned when work is very poor. Instructions have not been followed. The product demonstrates little thought, reflection, or imagination. The Poster is sloppy and the Film Plot Summary is very limited or incomplete.

F = Do You Really Want To Know??

General References

Baron, Robert C. ed. 1994a. *Soul of America: Documenting Our Past—Volume I: 1492–1870.* Golden, CO: Fulcrum.

———. ed. 1994b. *Soul of America: Documenting Our Past—Volume II: 1858–1993.* Golden, CO: Fulcrum.

Bloom, Benjamin, ed. 1956. *Taxonomy of Educational Objectives: Classification of Educational Goals. Handbook 1: Cognitive Domain.* New York: Longman, Green.

Burgoyne, Robert. 1997. *Film Nation: Hollywood Looks at US History.* Minneapolis: University of Minnesota Press.

Carnes, Mark C., ed. 1996. *Past Imperfect: History According to the Movies.* New York: Henry Holt.

Carroll, Andrew, ed. 1997. *Letters of a Nation: A Collection of Extraordinary American Letters.* New York: Kodansha.

Colbert, David, ed. 1997. *Eyewitness to America.* New York: Pantheon.

Center for Learning. *U.S History.* Vols. 1–4. Rocky River, OH: The Center for Learning.

Davidson, James West, and Mark Hamilton Lytle. 2000. *After the Fact: The Art of Historical Detection, 4th edition.* New York: McGraw Hill Higher Education.

Foner, Eric. 1998. *The Story of American Freedom.* New York: Norton.

Foner, Eric, and John A. Garraty, eds. 1991. *The Reader's Companion to American History.* Boston: Houghton Mifflin.

Gagnon, Paul, ed. 1991. *Historical Literacy: The Case for History in American Education.* Boston: Houghton Mifflin.

Gardner, Howard. 1983. *Frames of Mind: The Theory of Multiple Intelligences.* New York: Basic Books.

———. 1993. *Multiple Intelligences: The Theory in Practice.* New York: Basic Books.

Johnson, Paul. 1998. *A History of the American People.* New York: HarperCollins.

Linenthal, Edward T. 1991. *Sacred Ground: Americans and Their Battlefields.* Urbana, IL: University of Illinois Press.

Loewen, James. 1995. *Lies My Teacher Told Me.* New York: New Press.

McDonald, Andrew. 1996. *Howard Fast: A Critical Companion.* Westport, CT: Greenwood Press.

Mansfield, Howard. 1993. *In the Memory House.* Golden, CO: Fulcrum.

Marzano, Robert J., Debra Pickering, and Jay McTighe. 1993. *Assessing Student*

Outcomes. Alexandria, VA: Association for Supervision and Curriculum Development.

Palmer, Parker J. 1993. *To Know As We Are Known.* San Francisco: Harper.

———. 1999. *The Courage to Teach.* San Francisco: Jossey-Bass.

Percoco, James A. 1998. *A Passion for the Past.* Portsmouth, NH: Heinemann.

Perret, Geoffrey. 1989. *A Country Made by War.* New York: Random House.

Primary Source Media. 1995–2000. *American Journey: History in Your Hands.* CD-ROM series. Farmington Hills, MI: Gale Group.

Roquemore, Joseph. 1999. *History Goes to the Movies.* New York: Main Street.

Rutherford, Paula. 1998. *Instruction for All Students.* Bloomington, IN: Just Ask Publications.

Teaching with Documents: Using Primary Sources from the National Archives, Volume 1. 1989. Washington, DC: National Archives Trust Fund Board.

Teaching with Documents: Using Primary Sources from the National Archives, Volume 2. 1998. Washington, DC: National Archives Trust Fund Board.

Trinkle, Dennis A., and Scott A. Merriman. 2000. *The History Highway 2000: A Guide to Internet Resources.* Armonk, NY: M. E. Sharpe.

Toplin, Robert Brent. 1996. *History by Hollywood: The Use and Abuse of the American Past.* Urbana, IL: University of Illinois Press.

Wiggins, Grant. 1998. *Educative Assessment.* San Francisco: Jossey-Bass.

Wiggins, Grant, and Jay McTighe. 1998. *Understanding by Design.* Alexandria, VA: Association for Supervision and Curriculum Development.

Zinn, Howard. 1995. *A People's History of the United States, 1492–Present.* New York: Harper Perennial.

———. 1997a. *A People's History of the United States: Teaching Edition.* New York: New Press.

———. 1997b. *The Zinn Reader: Writings on Disobedience and Democracy.* New York: Seven Story Press.